Commentaries on St. Paul's Epistles to
Timothy, Titus, and Philemon

Other Titles of Interest from St. Augustine's Press

Commentaries on St. Paul's Epistles to Timothy, Titus, and Philemon

Thomas Aquinas

Translated by Chrysostom Baer, O. Praem.
Preface by Most Rev. Joseph Perry

ST. AUGUSTINE'S PRESS
South Bend, Indiana
2007

Manufactured in the United States of America.

1 2 3 4 5   12 11 10 09 08 07

Library of Congress Cataloging in Publication Data
Thomas, Aquinas, Saint, 1225?–1274.
Commentaries on St. Paul's Epistles to Timothy, Titus, and Philemon /
Thomas Aquinas; translated and introduced by Chrysostom Baer;
preface by Joseph Perry.
p. cm
Includes bibliographical references and index.
ISBN-13: 978-1-58731-128-4 (hardcover: alk. paper)
ISBN-10: 1-58731-128-3 (hardcover: alk. paper)
ISBN-13: 978-1-58731-129-1 (paperbound: alk. paper)
ISBN-10: 1-58731-129-1 (paperbound: alk. paper)
1. Bible. N.T. Pastoral Epistles – Commentaries. 2. Bible. N.T. Philemon –
Commentaries. I. Title.
BS2735.53.T46 2007
227'.8307 – dc22   2007032327

∞ The paper used in this publication meets the minimum requirements of the American National Standard for Information Sciences – Permanence of Paper for Printed Materials, ANSI Z39.48-1984.

ST. AUGUSTINE'S PRESS
www.staugustine.net

Contents

Commentary on the Epistle to Philemon

Preface

Without doubt, Thomas Aquinas [1225–1274] ranks among the greatest, if not the first, of philosopher-theologians in service to holy church. A scriptural commentator, one might say by way of hobby only, but most especially, Aquinas laid the foundation for thought and theological discourse in the Catholic Church. A large man with a great mind fundamentally, Thomas squeezed holiness out of early Greek thought as a *ratio* for a philosophy centered in the Christian mysteries. Not just brilliant, Thomas also possessed innate spiritual qualities that rendered him a vowed religious in the Dominican style. As a friar he conjoined humility and a quiet demeanor uncharacteristic, perhaps, of those who tower intellectually over rank and file.

Under Thomas, theology became an astute science, henceforth to be known as "Thomism." So enlightening were his offerings and enduring his legacy that scholasticism in the Thomistic school, by decree of Pope Leo XIII (1878–1903), was universally enjoined upon the education of clerics in the church.

We have here in these lectures on the pastoral epistles of the New Testament samples of Thomas's pedagogy. The unfinished five-volumed *Summa Theologiae* ranking first among his opuses, biblical commentaries are also among the vast works of Aquinas. For in the course of his master studies as a young friar he was required to lecture on the Bible and other works.

These letters are called *pastoral*, for they express the concerns of the writer to those being addressed and because they demonstrate a concern for the orderly pastoral care of the Christian communities where these individuals are engaged, always arguing to the new Christian mindset incumbent upon all because of the Christ event, while urging a new order of relationships intra-church and a new courage in the midst of the onslaughts by the powers that be. The scripture scholar, Robert J. Wild, s.j., opines that, "although the word, *philosophia,* does not appear in the pastorals, the vocabulary manner of argumentation, parenetic thrust and general style of these letters situated them firmly within the general milieu of Greco-Roman philosophical discourse. The writers of the pastorals view Pauline Christianity as the only true philosophy or way of life. He or they call(s) church leaders, and by extension, all Christians to a renewed commitment and enthusiasm for this teaching. What Paul said and what Paul did are proposed as the exemplification of this way of life, the pastorals make no reference to the existence of any apostle except Paul."

The ordering called for in those neophyte Christian communities was none too different in respects than the ordering called for in the medieval church and its varied challenges, subjects treated by Thomas's pen.

Interest in the *Angelic Doctor* is unabated even in these times of modern philosophies and a certain anti-Aristotelianism, for which reasons we applaud the young cleric translators and their eagerness to engage Thomas in the Latin language from which he lectured. Indeed, these exercises afford them and the student-reader of this book a glimpse into Aquinas' classroom.

Most Reverend Joseph N. Perry
Titular Bishop of Lead
Auxiliary Bishop of Chicago

Translator's Introduction

Once the *Commentary on the Epistle to the Hebrews* had been translated, the immediate and logical conclusion was that the commentaries of St. Thomas on I and II Timothy, Titus, and Philemon must in due course be likewise presented to modern students in an English translation.

The Angelic Doctor laid out his schema for the Pauline epistles in the prologue to the lectures on Romans. Their principle of formal unity is found in the grace of Christ, which admits of a threefold division. First, in the Mystical Body, which can be considered in itself, and then we have the letter to the Romans; in the sacraments, I and II Corinthians and Galatians; then in its unifying power within the Church. This last can be divided according to the institution of ecclesial unity, as is found in Ephesians; the strengthening of that unity, in Philippians; and the defense of that unity, as in Colossians, I and II Thessalonians.

Second, grace in the Mystical Body may be considered in the principal members of this Body, first inasmuch as they are concerned with spiritual matters, and so we have I and II Timothy, and Titus. For three things are fitting to a prelate: ruling over the people, suffering for them, and defending them against evil. But the principal members of the Mystical Body are also concerned with temporal matters, and so we have Philemon, wherein the Apostle shows how masters ought to relate to their servants, and vice versa.

Third, this grace in the Mystical Body may be considered in the Head of the Mystical Body, i.e. Christ Himself; thus, the epistle to the Hebrews, the translation of whose commentary is already available by the same publisher.

The Blessed Apostle Paul saw the duties of a bishop, and by extension of every cleric, as threefold: to rule over the flock entrusted to him; to suffer for it, even unto death; and, to protect it from the attacks of evildoers. The first of these responsibilities forms the subject matter of the first epistle to Timothy: what his obligations are as bishop, how he ought to govern the church entrusted to him, and in particular how to deal with the various types of people in his care. The second office of a bishop, namely offering up one's life for the flock, is the topic of the second epistle to Timothy: what the dangers to the flock are, why Timothy is ready to resist them, and how he is, in fact, to do so. The necessity of protecting the Church from heretics constitutes the third of the pastoral epistles, this time to Titus: why it is necessary and how to resist evil teachers efficaciously.

This volume seemed incomplete, however, without including the commentary on the small epistle to Philemon, which certainly would not merit publication on its own otherwise. And although the treatment is directly about masters and slaves, which might seem not to have much practical application nowadays, yet is it an undeniable facet of human nature that some are in authority while others are subject. If there is to be peaceable concord between these two so often opposed parties, we must draw our paradigm of behavior from this epistle—a pattern of love, mutual respect, and subordination in all things to the mission of the Gospel.

Torrell hypothesizes that St. Thomas commented on the Pauline epistles in Rome some time between 1265 and 1268.[1] Its format is what is called a *reportatio,* "a more or less carefully corrected clean copy of a course of lectures heard by a student."[2] This accounts for the short, simple, and often choppy sentence structure, which has not been eliminated in the translation.

The Marietti edition has been used for the Latin original, as the critical Leonine is not yet available. Paragraph numbering provided by Marietti has been maintained for easy reference, but their sometimes frequent errors in Scriptural citations have been corrected without notice.

The more interested student will find in the endnotes references to parallel places (Loc. Parall.) where St. Thomas discusses the same topic in a different context. For Scriptural quotations, the Douay-Rheims version seemed best, as it is closer to the Latin St. Thomas used than other modern translations are. Personal pronouns referring to God have been freely capitalized the for the sake of clarity, but where St. Thomas' version differs from the Douay-Rheims, this has been so marked in an endnote. As an appendix there is also a list of the names of the books of the Bible in their modern version as well as that of the Douay.

In times past, such a translation as this would have been neither necessary nor desired; those who wanted to study St. Thomas would simply have read him in the original Latin. But now knowledge of Latin is unfortunately scarce, almost as much as the desire to read the works of the Common Doctor of the Church.

The hope on the horizon is the growth in the number of young men aspiring to serve as priests. Many of these look to the Church's traditional theology of the priesthood as the key to a renewal of the entire sacerdotal body. As a model they take the paragon of pastoral virtue found in Chaucer's Pastor:

This noble example to his sheep he gave.
First following the word before he taught it,
And it was from the gospel he had caught it.

This little proverb he would add thereto
That if gold rust, what then would iron do?
For if a priest be foul in whom we trust
No wonder that a common man should rust;
And shame it is to see – let priests take stock –
A soiled shepherd and a snowy flock.
The true example that a priest should give
Is one of cleanness, how the sheep should live.
       – *Canterbury Tales,* The Prologue, 506–16

To such young and aspiring clerics this volume is dedicated in the hope that with God's grace there may be fulfilled in them the words of David: "Let Thy priests be clothed with justice: and let Thy saints rejoice" (Ps. 131:9).

The Commentary of St. Thomas Aquinas on
The First Epistle of St. Paul to Timothy

The Pastoral Epistles

There are three epistles, according to the three things which befit a prelate: to rule the people, to suffer for his subjects, and to check evil men. The first is found in the first epistle to Timothy; the second, in the second, where he treats of martyrdom; and the third in the epistle to Titus, where he teaches how to avoid heretics.

Synoptical Outline of I Timothy

Prologue

The power of the earth is in the hand of God, and all the iniquity of the Gentiles is abominable,[1] *and in His time He will raise up a profitable ruler over it. — Eccles. 10:4*

1. These words befit the matter of this epistle. In earlier epistles he instructed the Church about those things which pertain to its unity, and here he treats of the rulers of the Church themselves, who are as it were its principal members. This instruction and its profit must be seen to regard this.

Instruction is in God since **in the hand of God,** etc., and this in three ways. First, it proceeds from Him. Rom. 13:1: *There is no power but from God.* Next, it ought to be regulated according to God. Prov. 8:15: *By me kings reign, and lawgivers decree just things.* Again, the power of rulers is established according to the arrangement of God. Dan. 2:21: *And He changeth times and ages: taketh away kingdoms and establisheth them.*

Likewise, their profit is shown since it is to restrain the evil of man, since **all the iniquity of the Gentiles is abominable.** Below 1:9: *The law is not made for the just man.* Rulers of the law ought to relate to evil in three ways. First, they should hate it wholeheartedly. II Mach. 3:1: *And the hatred his soul had of evil,* etc. Second, they ought to prohibit it lest it be done. Prov. 20:8: *The king, that sitteth on the throne of judgment, scattereth away all evil with his look.* Third, they must punish evil deeds. Rom. 13:4: *For he is God's minister: an avenger to execute wrath upon him that doth evil.*

The profit of them is seen again when it says, **profitable ruler,** etc. A ruler is profitable for three things, which are noted in Ecclus. 49:17: *Joseph, who was a man born prince of his brethren, the support of his family, the ruler of his brethren,* to preserve the nation through his power. Is. 19:4: *And a strong king shall rule over them,* etc. *Ruler of his brethren,* guiding by his wisdom. Is. 32:8: *But the prince will devise such things as are worthy of a prince,* etc. Ecclus.

10:24: *In the midst of the brethren their chief is honourable. The support of his family,* to keep them from unjust men through justice. Ps. 17:28: *Thou wilt save the humble people; but wilt bring down the eyes of the proud,* etc.

2. And thus the matter of these epistles is evident, for they are intended for the instruction of the rulers of the faithful people. Among these some are leaders in spiritual matters, such as the prelates of the churches, whom he instructs first; whereas, some are leaders in temporal matters, and these he admonishes second in the epistle to Philemon.

Regarding the first there are three epistles, according to the three things which befit a prelate: to rule the people, to suffer for his subjects, and to check evil men. The first is found in the first epistle to Timothy; the second, in the second, where he treats of martyrdom; and the third in the epistle to Titus, where he teaches how to avoid heretics. All this is also evident in the arguments of the epistles.

Chapter One

Lecture One

**1 [n. 3] Paul, an apostle of Jesus Christ, according to the command-
ment of God our Saviour, and of Christ Jesus our hope:**
**2 [n. 5] To Timothy, his beloved son in faith. Grace, mercy, and peace
from God the Father, and from Christ Jesus our Lord.**

3. This letter is divided into a greeting and the epistolary narrative, which begins when he says in verse three [n. 7], **As I desired thee**. Regarding the first he does three things: first, he gives the person greeting; second, the person greeted [n. 5]; and third, the good things he wished for him [n. 6].

4. He describes the person greeting, first by his name, **Paul,** which befits his authority in two ways, for in the apostolate there are two things. First, the height of power, to which the humble are exalted. I Kg. 15:17: *When thou wast a little one in thy own eyes, wast thou not made head of the tribes of Israel?* And Paul means *little*. Second, the glory of wisdom, and this the Lord grants to little ones. Mt. 11:25: *And hast revealed them to little ones,* etc.

Second, by his authority, since he is an **apostle,** that is, one who has been sent. Jn. 20:21: *As the Father hath sent Me, I also send you.* I Cor. 9:2: *For you are the seal of my apostleship in the Lord.*

Third, from the origin of this authority, whence he says, **Jesus Christ, according to the commandment of God,** etc. Acts 13:2: *Separate Me Paul and Barnabas, for the work whereunto I have taken them.* I Kg. 13:14: *The Lord hath sought Him a man after His own heart,* etc. From this it is clear that prelates are held by the necessity of precept to those things which are of their office. I Cor. 9:16: *Woe is unto me if I preach not the gospel.* **And of Christ Jesus our hope.** He is our hope, that we may come unto Him. Phil. 1:23: *Having a desire to be dissolved and to be with Christ,* etc. Or, **our hope,** since through Him we hope to acquire eternal goods. I Pet. 1:3: *Who according to His great mercy hath regenerated us unto a lively hope,* etc. Rom. 15:4: *That through patience and the comfort of the scriptures, we might have hope.*

5. He describes the person greeted in three ways. First, by name when he says **To Timothy,** about whom it is spoken in Acts 16. Second, by his affection when he calls him **beloved.** Phil. 2:20: *For I have no man so of the same mind.* Third, by filiation, saying **son in faith,** since he was converted by him. I Cor. 4:17: *For this cause I have sent to you Timothy, who is my dearest son and faithful in the Lord,* etc.

6. Then he first states the good things wished for him; second, whence they come.

But it must be known that in the other epistles two things are given, but here three, since prelates need more. And so he says, **Grace, mercy,** first to himself, then to others. And here mercy is taken for the remission of sins, since this is the mercy of God; and grace for the gift of graces needed by a prelate. Or grace, as in the other epistles, for justifying grace, but mercy for that divine gift exalting one by spiritual charisms. Wis. 4:15: *That the grace of God, and His mercy is with the saints, and that He hath respect to His chosen.* **And peace** be with you, and through you to others. Ps. 71:3: *Let the mountains receive peace.*

But from where? **From God** to give to the people. Jas. 1:17: *Every best gift, and every perfect gift, is from above, coming down from the Father of lights.* **And from Christ Jesus our Lord,** through Whom He has given us the greatest and most precious promises, as it says in II Pet. 1:2.

Lecture Two

3 [n. 7] As I desired thee to remain at Ephesus when I went to Macedonia, that thou mightest charge some not to teach otherwise,

4 [n. 10] Not to give heed to fables and endless genealogies: which furnish questions rather than the edification of God, which is in faith.

5 [n. 11] Now the end of the commandment is charity, from a pure heart, and a good conscience, and an unfeigned faith.

7. Here begins the epistolary narrative. And this epistle is as it were a pastoral rule which the Apostle handed on to Timothy, instructing him about all the things which pertain to the government of prelates and the disposition he ought to have.

First, then, he instructs him about the administration of spiritual matters; second, about temporal matters, when he says in chapter four [n. 136], **Now the Spirit manifestly saith.** Again, it pertains to the prelate first that he teach the faith lest the faith of his subjects be corrupted. Lk. 22:32: *But I have prayed for thee, that thy faith fail not: and thou, being once converted, confirm thy brethren.* Second, that he instruct them about those things which pertain to the worship of God, which cannot be if faith be not true. Therefore, first he instructs him about the faith; second, about the worship of God, when he says in chapter two [n. 55], **I desire therefore;** third, he treats the institution of offices, when he says in chapter three [n. 86], **A faithful saying.**

But it must be known that in the early Church there was a dangerous error of some teachers, that legal observances had to be kept along with the Gospel. This the Apostle rejects: first, by showing the condition of the Law; second, through his own experience, when he says in verse twelve [n. 31], **I give Him thanks.**

Regarding the first he does three things: first, he shows what from the Law is to be repudiated; second, what in it is to be accepted, when he says [n. 11], **Now the end of the commandment;** third, he makes a conclusion about the condition of the Law, when he says in verse eight [n. 20], **But we know.**

Now, what others wickedly added to the Law is to be repudiated, not what was given by God, unless it is already according to a carnal understanding. First, he teaches that false fables and traditions are to be rejected; second, he assigns the reason why, when he says [n. 10], **which furnish questions.**

8. He says, then: I say that you ought to do what I have asked you to, although I could command you. Ecclus. 32:1: *Have they made thee a ruler? be not lifted up: be among them as one of them.* **That thou mightest charge some.**

Or otherwise. Two things pertain to the prelate: first, that he might restrain those teaching falsities. And so he says, **that thou mightest charge some not to teach otherwise.** Gal. 1:9: *If any one preach to you a gospel, besides that which you have received, let him be anathema.* Deut. 4:2: *You shall not add to the word that I speak to you, neither shall you take away from it.* Second, if it happens that some men teach falsities, he must prohibit the people from listening to them; wherefore he says, **Not to give heed to fables and endless genealogies.**

9. Now, there were certain heretics who detested the Old Testament and explained that the Apostle repudiated it by deriding its histories, saying **fables and endless genealogies,** etc. Against this Augustine says that the Apostle uses the histories and genealogies of the Old Testament. Gal. 4:22: *For it is written that Abraham had two sons,* etc. If therefore he had reprobated them, he would not have used them.

He then says **fables,** not the law given in writings but by mouth, namely, the Talmud: not what Moses handed on orally, but what others added, stupid fables, for example, that Adam had another wife, from whom, they say, demons were born. Mt. 15:6: *And you have made void the commandment of God for your tradition.* II Tim. 4:4: *But will be turned into fables.*

10. The reason for this is that these **furnish questions,** that is, contentions. II Tim. 2:14: *Contend not in words.* Prov. 20:3: *It is an honour for a man to separate himself from contentions.*[2] **Rather than the edification of God, which is in faith,** when someone is strengthened in the truth of the faith, to which all doctrine ought to tend.

11. Then when he says, **Now the end,** he shows what from the Law ought to be retained. Regarding this he does two things: first, he shows this; second, what danger there is for those who do not retain it, when he says in verse six [n. 17], **From which things some going astray,** etc.

12. About the first it must be known that the Old Law is called a law of commandments since it was contained in commands and precepts. Eph. 2:15: *The law of commandments contained in decrees.* Above all things that to which all the commands are ordered is to be held, and this is charity. Mt. 22:37: *Thou shalt love the Lord thy God with thy whole heart,* etc. And a little later: *On these two commandments dependeth the whole law and the prophets.*

13. But how is charity the end of a precept?

To understand this, two things must be considered. First, that all the precepts of the Law regard acts of virtue, and through all the acts of virtue one man is ordered to another. Second, that the object of one virtue is the end of another, since whenever one power regards some end, all things which belong to the same end are ordered to that power as to an end. For example, the bridle-making ability is for the horse-riding ability, since its end is the service of the knight, and this ability in turn is ordered to the duke.

But the theological virtues have the last end for their object. The other virtues regard those things which are for the end. Therefore, all the virtues look to the theological virtues as their end. And among the theological virtues that one has more the notion of an end which relates more closely to the last end. Now, faith shows this end, and hope makes one tend to it, but charity unites to it. Therefore, all are ordered to charity, and thus charity is called the end of the precepts.

14. But since those things which are for the end dispose for that end, and the precepts are for charity, they dispose one for it. And so he says, **from a pure heart.** For the precepts of virtue are given for this, that a heart may be pure. Of those virtues whose matter is the passions, some are ordered to the mode of regulating these passions, just as it is temperance which orders concupiscence, meekness anger, fortitude fear and foolhardiness. Now, by these passions is purity of heart disturbed, and so these virtues make a heart pure.

15. But is this not required for charity?

I respond that yes, it is impossible that an impure heart be ready for charity, since for each man the delectable is that which is conformed to himself. The impure heart loves what befits it according to its passion. Therefore, it is necessary that it be freed from passions. Cant. 1:3: *The righteous love thee.*

16. Some virtues are what regulate a man regarding his neighbor, and from this it follows that he would have a good conscience, since he does not do to another what he does not want done to himself. Mt. 7:12: *All things therefore whatsoever you would that men should do to you, do you also to them.* And so, what is against one's neighbor is against one's conscience. Hence he says, **and a good conscience.** He who does not have a good conscience cannot love God purely, since he who does not have a good conscience fears punishment. Now there is no fear in charity; for fear flees God and is not united to Him. And therefore the precepts, which regulate the conscience, dispose well to charity.

Other virtues are for having the true faith, namely, the virtues by which we worship God, latria and the like. These are ordered to removing errors and strengthening the firmness of faith regarding God in men's hearts. For he who does not have the true faith cannot love God, since he who believes falsely about God already does not love Him. For he does not love who does not believe, since the affection is not attached except to that which the intellect proposes. And so, those things that make the true faith are ordered to charity. Thus he says, **from a pure heart,** for they make this. Mt. 5:8: *Blessed are the clean of heart: for they shall see God.* **And a good conscience.** II Cor. 1:12: *For our glory is this, the testimony of our conscience.* **And an unfeigned faith,** that is, a true one.

And so the virtues and precepts are ordered to the end of charity, which is taken according to these three things, etc.

Lecture Three

6 [n. 17] From which things some going astray, are turned aside unto vain babbling:

7 [n. 19] Desiring to be teachers of the law, understanding neither the things they say, nor whereof they affirm.

8 [n. 20] But we know that the law is good, if a man use it lawfully:

9 [n. 22] Knowing this, that the law is not made for the just man, but for the unjust and disobedient, for the ungodly, and for sinners, for the wicked and defiled, for murderers of fathers, and murderers of mothers, for manslayers,

10 [n. 28] For fornicators, for them who defile themselves with mankind,[3] for liars, for perjured persons, and whatever other thing is contrary to sound doctrine,

11 [n. 30] Which is according to the gospel of the glory of the blessed God, which hath been committed to my trust.

12 [n. 31] I give Him thanks Who hath strengthened me, even to Christ Jesus our Lord, for that He hath counted me faithful, putting me in the ministry;

13 [n. 33] Who before was a blasphemer, and a persecutor, and contumelious. But I obtained the mercy of God, because ignorant I did it in unbelief.[4]

14 [n. 36] Now the grace of our Lord hath abounded exceedingly with faith and love, which is in Christ Jesus.

17. Above the Apostle showed the dignity and profit of the virtues [n. 11]; here he declares their necessity, since whosoever departs from them falls into the danger of false doctrines. Regarding this he does two things: first, he posits the falsity of the doctrine into which they have fallen; second, the condition of teachers of such falsehoods, when he says [n. 19], **Desiring to be teachers**.

18. He says therefore: The end of the precept, etc., and these are the chief points of the Law from which certain men depart. Ps. 11:3: *They have spoken vain things.*

And note that having receded from charity is the cause of false doctrine, since those who do not love charity fall into lying. II Thess. 2:11: *Who have not believed the truth, but have consented to iniquity.* The same applies to those who lose purity of heart, for having a heart infected with passions they judge according to their affections and not according to God. I Cor. 2:14: *But the sensual man perceiveth not these things that are of the Spirit of God,* etc. Likewise, for those having an evil conscience, since they cannot rest in the truth. And hence they seek falsities so that they might rest in them. Below 1:19: *Having faith and a good conscience.* And again, for those who have a feigned confidence. Is. 21:2: *He that is unfaithful dealeth unfaithfully.*

19. Then when he says **Desiring,** etc., the condition of teachers of falsities is given: first, inordinate ambition; second, their defect.

Regarding the first he says, **Desiring to be,** etc. Mt. 23:6–7: *And they love the first places at feasts...and to be called by men, Rabbi.* Jas. 3:1: *Be ye not many masters,* etc. Regarding the second he says, **understanding neither.** Ps. 81:5: *They have not known nor understood: they walk on in darkness.* Wis. 5:6: *The light of justice hath not shined unto us.* **The things they say** by those in authority, which they do not understand, **nor whereof they affirm** by means of conclusion.

20. Then when he says, **But we know,** etc., he posits the condition of the Law regarding two things: first, the goodness of the Law; second, the end and intention of the lawgiver, when he says [n. 22], **Knowing this.**

21. He says then, **But we know** for certain **that the law is good,** not evil, as the heretics say. Ps. 18:8: *The law of the Lord is unspotted,* etc. Rom. 7:12: *Wherefore the law indeed is holy, and the commandment holy, and just, and good.* But it happens that a man might use a good thing amiss. Since, then, the Law is good, it is required that a man use it well. And so he says, **if a man use it lawfully.** Otherwise, he will die, as it says in Rom. 8.

Now, in the Law some things are moral, and others ceremonial. The ceremonies were given as figures of Christ and the Church, yet they need to be understood not only carnally but also spiritually; both as a figure of future things and so that you could know that they will not be kept forever, but will pass away with the coming of truth. Jer. 31:31–32: *And I will make a new covenant with the house of Israel, and with the house of Juda: not according to the covenant which I made with their fathers,* etc. And in this way does the Gloss explain it.

But the Apostle seems to be speaking of moral precepts, since he adds that the Law was given because of sin, and so there are the moral precepts. And it is a legitimate use of these that a man not attribute to them more than is contained in them. The Law was given so that sin might be known. Rom. 7:7: *For I had not known concupiscence, if the law did not say: Thou shalt not covet,* etc.; this is said in the Decalogue. Therefore, there is no hope of justification in them, but only in faith. Rom. 3:28: *For we account a man to be justified by faith, without the works of the law.*

22. Then when he says, **Knowing this,** he shows the condition of the Law regarding the intention of the lawgiver: first, he gives the supposed intention; second, the true intention, when he says [n. 24], **but for the unjust.**

23. He excludes the supposed intention when he says, **the law is not made for the just man,** etc.

Here there could be a twofold false understanding. One is that the just man does not keep the Law, which is false since unless he kept it regarding moral matters he would not be just. Hence even Christ was made under the Law. The other false understanding is that the just man is not obligated by the precepts of the Law, and he would not sin if he acted against them.[5]

But the true sense is the following: what is imposed on someone is imposed as a burden; for the Law was not imposed on the just as a burden, for their interior habits inclined them to that for which the Law was instituted, and so it is not a burden to them. Rom. 2:14: *These having not the law are a law unto themselves.*

Or otherwise. The Law is not given for the just but for the unjust, as if to say: If everyone were just, there would be no necessity for giving the Law, since every man would be a law unto himself. The intention of good men ought to be that they lead others to virtue. Now, some men by themselves are well disposed to virtue; others have a well-disposed mind, but through others, and for them a paternal and not forceful admonition suffices; and others are well disposed neither by themselves nor through others, and so for them a law is altogether necessary, as is clear in the *Ethics.*

24. Then when he says, **but for the unjust,** etc., he gives the true intention: first, he describes in general those for whom law is necessary; second, in particular, when he says [n. 26], **for murderers of fathers.**

25. Now, it must be known that, as it says in I Jn. 3:4, *sin is iniquity,* and therefore it is repugnant to any law. Since law is twofold, though, namely natural and positive, what is *per se* evil is repugnant to natural law, and what is evil because it is prohibited is repugnant to positive law.

Regarding the first he says, **but for the unjust,** who act contrary to natural law. Is. 24:5: *They have transgressed the laws, they have changed the ordinance, they have broken the everlasting covenant,* etc. Regarding the second he says, **and disobedient,** namely, to human precept. Rom. 1:30: *Disobedient to parents.* These two respect the notion of sin.

He gives other things which are taken from a comparison to that, and this is either against God, against neighbor, or in itself. Impiety is against God since piety implies the worship of God, and so he says, **for the ungodly.** For what is against one's neighbor, he says, **and for sinners.** Ps. 1:5: *Therefore the wicked shall not rise in judgment: nor sinners in the council of the just,* etc. Gal. 2:15: *We by nature are Jews, and not of the Gentiles sinners.*

But according to Augustine in *On Christian Doctrine,* sin is distinguished into two realms, namely, into spiritual matters, which are called transgressions, and carnal matters, which are called iniquities. And so he says, **for the wicked,** regarding spiritual things. Prov. 17:9: *He that concealeth a transgression,* etc. Regarding carnal things he says, **and defiled.** Mal. 2:11: *For Juda hath profaned the holiness of the Lord,* etc.

26. Then he enumerates the sins specifically. First, he names some

specifically; second, he gathers others together in general, when he says [n. 30], **and whatever other thing,** etc. First, he posits the sins of deed; second, of the mouth, when he says [n. 29], **for liars,** etc. Regarding the first, he first discusses transgressions; second, iniquities [n. 28].

27. Those are called transgressions which harm one's neighbor. And as much as the neighbor is closer, so much more grave is the sin, since we are bound to him the more. And so he speaks first about one's father, then one's mother. Ex. 20:12: *Honour thy father and thy mother,* etc., and afterwards in 21:15: *He that striketh his father or mother shall be put to death.* Then it continues with the other forms of homicide, saying in 21:14, *If a man kill his neighbor on set purpose,* etc.

28. Then he treats of iniquities, and first those which are according to nature when he says, **For fornicators.** Heb. 13:4: *For fornicators and adulterers God will judge.* Then he treats of iniquities contrary to nature, saying, **for them who defile themselves with mankind.** I Cor. 6:10: *Nor the effeminate...shall possess the kingdom of God.*

29. Then he gives the evils of the mouth, first regarding simple lying, and so he says, **for liars.** Eph. 4:25: *Wherefore putting away lying, speak ye the truth,* etc. Second, regarding swearing, saying, **for perjured persons.**

30. And then he gathers the others together in general, saying, **and whatever other thing is contrary to sound doctrine.** Job 6:30: *And you shall not find iniquity in my tongue, neither shall folly sound in my mouth.* Tit. 2:1: *But speak thou the things that become sound doctrine.*

Then when he says, **Which is according to the gospel,** he shows that the Gospel communicates sound doctrine. This he describes in three ways. First, by its end, when he says, **of the glory,** which it announces. Ps. 95:3: *Declare His glory among the Gentiles.* Second, by the author of glory when he says, **of the blessed God.** Below 6:15: *Which in His times He shall shew Who is the Blessed and only Mighty,* etc. Third, from his ministry when he says, **which hath been committed to my trust.** Gal. 2:7: *When they had seen that to me was committed the gospel of the uncircumcision.*

31. Then when he says, **I give Him thanks,** he proves through experience in himself what he was in the time of the Law and what he attained in the time of grace. First, he shows what happened to him in either time; second, he induces Timothy to imitate him, when he says in verse eighteen [n. 48], **This precept I commend.** Regarding the first he does two things: first, he shows what was given to him in the Law, and what was given to him in the Gospel; second, he gives the reason why, when he says in verse fifteen [n. 37], **A faithful saying.** Again, the first part is divided into three particulars: first, he gives the dignity attained in the Gospel; second, the sins to which he was subject under the Law, when he says [n. 33], **Who before was a blasphemer;** third, how he was liberated, when he says [n. 34], **But I obtained the mercy of God.**

32. But to be a minister of the Gospel, three things are required. First, that it be committed to him. Rom. 10:15: *And how shall they preach unless they be sent,* etc. Second, suitability, that is, that he be faithful. I Cor. 4:2: *Here now it is required among the dispensers, that a man be found faithful.* Likewise, that he be strong in perseverance.

And these three he places in a reverse order: first the third, saying, **Who hath strengthened me** for fulfilling the imposed duty. Ez. 3:14: *For the hand of the Lord was with me, strengthening me.* The second he posits when he says, **for that He hath counted me faithful.** Mt. 24:45: *Who, thinkest thou, is a faithful and wise servant, whom his Lord hath appointed over His family.* And this since he sought only what was of God. The first he shows when he says, **putting me in the ministry,** that is, committing to me this ministry. Acts 13:2: *Separate Me Paul and Barnabas, for the work whereunto I have taken them.* II Cor. 11:23: *They are the ministers of Christ...I am more.*

33. But of what sort was he in the state of the Law? A sinner. First, against God, and so he says, **Who before was a blasphemer,** namely, against the name of Christ. Lev. 24:14: *Bring forth the blasphemer without the camp, and let them that heard him, put their hands upon his head, and let all the people stone him.* For which reason this was fitting for him. Likewise, he sinned against his neighbor, and so he says, **and a persecutor**. I Cor. 15:9: *For I am the least of the apostles, who am not worthy to be called an apostle, because I persecuted the church of God.* **And contumelious,** in words and deeds. Jer. 20:10: *For I heard the contumely*[6] *of many,* etc.

34. Then when he says, **But I obtained the mercy of God,** he shows how he was liberated through Christ. Regarding this he does two things: first, he posits the liberating mercy; second, he shows that he was superabundantly filled with good things when he says [n. 36], **Now the grace.**

35. Regarding the first he says, **But I obtained the mercy of God.** Lam. 3:22: *The mercies of the Lord that we are not consumed.* Rom. 9:18: *He hath mercy on whom He will; and whom He will, He hardeneth.* But on my part there is some excuse for sin, **because ignorant I did it in unbelief.** Saying less, he signifies more, since it is one thing to act ignorantly, and another to act through ignorance. He does something ignorantly who does not know what he does; yet if he knew, he would still do it, just like a man believing himself to kill a wild animal but who actually slew his enemy, whom he would have killed just as willingly if he had known who it was. But he acts through ignorance who does something he would not have done had he known what he was doing, just like a man who kills his own father, thinking him to be an enemy, whom he would not have killed had he known who it was.

But Paul acted through ignorance, since if he had known that Christ was the Son of God, he would not have done this. But the Jews did not kill Christ through ignorance but ignorantly, since even if they had known He was the Christ, they would just as willingly have killed Him. Lk. 12:47: *And that servant who knew the will of his lord, and prepared not himself, and did not according to his will, shall be beaten with many stripes,* etc.

36. Regarding the second he says, **Now the grace,** etc. Rom. 5:20: *And where sin abounded, grace did more abound.* **With faith and love.** He made there the effect of faith through operating love, **which is in Christ Jesus.** Gal. 3:14: *That the blessing of Abraham might come on the Gentiles through Christ Jesus.*

Lecture Four

15 [n. 37] A faithful saying, and worthy of all acceptation, that Christ Jesus came into this world to save sinners, of whom I am the first.[7]

16 [n. 44] But for this cause I have obtained mercy: that in me first Christ Jesus might shew forth all patience, for the information of them that shall believe in Him unto life everlasting.

17 [n. 45] Now to the king of the ages, immortal, invisible, the only God, be honour and glory for ever and ever. Amen.

18 [n. 48] This precept I commend to thee, O son Timothy; according to the prophecies going before on thee, that thou war in them a good warfare,

19 [n. 51] Having faith and a good conscience, which some rejecting have made shipwreck concerning the faith.

20 Of whom is Hymeneus and Alexander, whom I have delivered up to Satan, that they may learn not to blaspheme.

37. Above the Apostle showed his own condition, both regarding his sins under the Law and regarding good things received in the time of grace [n. 31]; here he shows the reason for these benefits, which is taken from the divine mercy. First, he treats the divine mercy in general; second, he applies it to himself, when he says [n. 41], of whom I am the first; third, he offers thanks, when he says [n. 45], Now to the king of the ages. Regarding the first he does two things: first, he praises the truth about to be related; second, he treats the divine mercy, when he says [n. 39], that Christ Jesus.

38. Regarding the first he says, **A faithful saying,** etc. There are two things in a praiseworthy word, namely, that it be true and that it be acceptable. For sometimes a word is true and harsh, arousing hatred. Gal. 4:16: *Am I then become your enemy, because I tell you the truth?* But this word first has truth, and so he says, **A faithful saying.** Apoc. 22:6: *These words are most faithful and true.* Likewise, it is acceptable because it concerns our salvation, and so he says, **and worthy of all acceptation.** Zach. 1:13: *And the Lord answered the angel, that spoke in me, good words, comfortable words.* Another reading has it: *A human word,* that is, for the reception of men. Tit. 3:4: *But when the goodness and humanity*[8] *of God our Saviour appeared.*

39. And this word is such **that Christ Jesus came into this world.** That He came into the world expresses His two natures: His divinity, in which He was before He appeared in the world – Jn. 16:28: *I came forth from the Father, and am come into the world* – and His humanity, in which He appeared. And since He is God, He fills heaven and earth, as it says in Jer. 23:24, and so it does not befit

Him according to His divine nature to be in any place, though it does according to His human nature. Jn. 1:10–11: *He was in the world...He came unto His own, etc.*

But why did He come? **To save sinners,** that is, for the salvation of men. Jn. 3:17: *For God sent not His Son into the world, to judge the world, but that the world may be saved by Him.* Jn. 12:47: *For I came not to judge the world, but to save the world.*

40. But if no one had been a sinner, would He have become incarnate? It seems not, since He came to save sinners. Therefore, the incarnation would not have been necessary. The Gloss agrees: "Take away the wound and there is no need for medicine."

I respond that from the words of the saints this is clear enough. But this question is not of great authority because God ordained things to happen according as things were to be done. But we do not know what He would have ordained if He had not foreknown sin. Nevertheless, the authorities seem to signify expressly that He would not have become incarnate if man had not sinned, to which opinion I myself am more inclined.

41. Then when he says, **of whom I am the first,** he applies it to himself. First, he acknowledges himself to be a sinner; second, he says that he has been saved, when he says [n. 44], **But for this cause I have obtained mercy.**

42. He says, then, **of whom I am the first.** Here a heretic says that the soul of Adam was in Paul, and passed from body to body, as if he said: I am the first sinner since the soul of Adam is my soul. But this is contrary to the Apostle in Rom. 9:11: *For when the children were not yet born,* etc. Therefore, the soul does not exist before the body. **First,** then, not in time but in magnitude of sin. And he says this out of humility. Prov. 18:17: *The just is the first accuser of himself.* Prov. 30:2: *I am the most foolish of men.*

43. But was the Apostle the greatest sinner? It seems that Judas was greater.

But some say that the sin of Paul was more general, since it was against the whole Church. But this is nothing, for Paul persecuted in unbelief while many Jews acted out of malice.

It must be said then that he was first, not because he was the greatest of the sinners who then lived, but because he was the greatest of those who were saved, as if to say: He **came into this world to save sinners, of whom,** namely, of those sinners who were saved, **I am the first.** This is to be understood of those who had come before the Apostle, since many others had also persecuted the Church prior to him.

44. And he says this to show that everything God does, He does to show His goodness. Prov. 16:4: *The Lord hath made all things for Himself.* Ecclus. 42:16: *And full of the glory of the Lord is His work.* Also for profit, and so he says, **for this cause I have obtained mercy.** First, for the sake of His glory. Hence, **first** is explained as first in time, or as the chief.

That in me first Christ Jesus might shew forth all patience, that is, perfect patience, since having been provoked He did not punish but rather exalted His adversary, and this for our profit. And so he says, **for the information of them,** that is, for their instruction, as if to say: Lest sinners despair approaching Him. I. Pet. 5:3: *Being made a pattern of the flock from the heart.*

45. Then when he says, **Now to the king,** he gives thanks. And regarding this he does two things: first, he praises Him to Whom he gives thanks; second, he gives thanks, when he says [n. 47], **be honour and glory.**

46. He praises Him first for His power; second, from the peculiarity of His nature.

Regarding the first he says, **Now to the king of the ages.** His dominion is the greatest, since He alone rules and has free power, not according to a constitution like a politician. And so he says, **the only God.** Apoc. 19:16: *King of kings and Lord of lords.* Ps. 46:8: *For God is the king of all the earth.* Moreover, the power of most kings lasts not more than fifty years, but His is for all ages. Ps. 144:13: *Thy kingdom is a kingdom of all ages,* etc. Ecclus. 10:4: *The power of the earth is in the hand of God.* To Him the peculiarity of the divine nature is befitting.

Regarding the second it must be known that in natural things the first difference is between corruptible and incorruptible. Certain incorruptibles are visible and corporeal, such as the earthly bodies; certain are invisible and spiritual, such as the angels. According to the Platonists, these are divided into gods, who by nature are supreme, and intellects which are not gods but divine, and souls. But for us there is one God alone. Deut. 6:4: *Hear, O Israel, the Lord our God is one Lord.*

He therefore says first, **immortal,** to distinguish Him from corruptible things, **invisible,** to show that it pertains to Him to be invisible and to distinguish Him from visible things. He says, **the only God,** and not only immortal and invisible, since He alone is God by nature, although He could be said to be alone immortal and invisible, that is, in a special way more than others. Below 6:16: *Who only hath immortality.*

47. Then when he says, **be honour and glory,** he gives thanks, as if to say: Honor is to be shown to Him by the subjection of all creation, unto the manifestation of the excellence of His goodness, clarity, and glory. Apoc. 7:12: *Benediction, and glory, and wisdom, and thanksgiving, honour, and power, and strength to our God for ever and ever.* **For ever and ever,** since the age of others is but a very little time. Is. 40:6: *All flesh is grass, and all the glory thereof as the flower of the field.*

48. Then when he says, **This precept,** etc., he instructs Timothy to persevere in what he told him. First, he reminds him of what has been committed to him; second, he admonishes him in its appropriate use [n. 50]; third, he teaches the manner of using it [n. 51].

49. He says therefore, **This precept,** namely, that you keep the end of the

Law, that is, that you maintain charity always, and not the fables of the Jews, **I commend to thee,** as a faithful deposit, since for this reason it has been committed to you.

50. And how? **According to the prophecies,** etc., that is, because this Gospel is not discordant with the prophecies which he had learned before, since he was the son of a Jewish mother. II Pet. 1:19: *And we have the more firm prophetical word: whereunto you do well to attend, as to a light that shineth in a dark place, until the day dawn, and the day star arise in your hearts.* I Thess. 5:20: *Despise not prophecies.* Or, **according to the prophecies,** that is, according to which I and the other saints knew about you through the spirit of prophecy that it was to be handed over to you. **That thou war in them,** namely, in the prophecies, **a good warfare.**

Warfare is twofold: one is spiritual, and the other is carnal. II Cor. 10:4: *For the weapons of our warfare are not carnal, but mighty to God unto the pulling down of fortifications, destroying counsels,* etc. In a good warfare two things are required on the part of the soldier: that he do nothing contrary to military discipline and that he not faint in idleness. I Cor. 9:25: *And every one that striveth for the mastery, refraineth himself from all things,* etc. Likewise, on the part of the warfare two things are required: that it fight off those contrary to the republic and that it subject those who need to be subject. Thus also spiritual warfare is ordered to destroying everyone who extols himself and to subjecting every intelligence unto obedience to Christ, as it is said in II Cor. 10. And this is true warfare, about which he says, **that thou war in them.**

51. Here also he first posits the mode of using it; and then its necessity, when he says [n. 52], **which some rejecting.**

He says, therefore, **that thou war in them,** etc., as if to say: You can fight a good war first through the good **faith** which you have. I Jn. 5:4: *And this is the victory which overcometh the world, our faith.* And through **a good conscience,** since a man easily departs from what harms him; hence, remorse of conscience is as a certain stimulus which stings a man with a bad conscience, and so he quickly falls away from sin through a good conscience and right faith. Acts 23:1: *I have conversed with all good conscience before God until this present day.* II Cor. 1:12: *For our glory is this, the testimony of our conscience.*

52. The necessity of a good conscience is shown next when he says, **which some rejecting,** etc. First, he gives the fault; second, the punishment [n. 53]; third, the fruit of punishment [n. 54].

He gives the fault by saying, **which,** namely, a good conscience, **some rejecting have made shipwreck concerning the faith.** For he who wanders from the faith destroys everything he has. Heb. 11:6: *But without faith it is impossible to please God.* And he dies because, as it says in Hab. 2:4 and Heb. 10:38, *The just shall live in his faith.* **Of whom is Hymeneus and Alexander.** II Tim. 4:14: *Alexander the coppersmith hath shewn me much evil,* etc.

53. Then their punishment is given when he says, **whom I have delivered up,** since he excommunicated them, so that the faithful might avoid them lest they be contaminated by them. And the Apostle's excommunication was so powerful that the ones excommunicated were soon thereafter attacked by the devil and vexed corporally. I Cor. 5:4–5: *In the name of our Lord Jesus Christ, you being gathered together, and my spirit, with the power of our Lord Jesus; to deliver such a one to Satan for the destruction of the flesh, that the spirit may be saved in the day of our Lord Jesus Christ.*

Yet they are also handed over to be vexed spiritually, since they lose the suffrages of the Church, which aid greatly against the devil. And **I have delivered them up** just as *God delivered them up to a reprobate sense,* as it says in Rom. 1:28, as if taking away His assistance and the prayers and communion of the Church.

54. And this is not out of hatred, but from charity for their profit. I Cor. 5:5: *To deliver such a one to Satan for the destruction of the flesh, that the spirit may be saved in the day of our Lord Jesus Christ.* Hence he says, **that they may learn,** at least through punishment, **not to blaspheme.** Now a man learns to flee sin in three ways: sometimes from punishment, when the body is afflicted; sometimes from the shame of excommunication; and sometimes from this, that when the Church hands someone over to Satan he falls headlong into manifest sins, whence, being ashamed, he may be humbled, and withdraw himself from even secret sins which before he did not know he had.

Chapter Two

Lecture One

1 [n. 55] I desire therefore, first of all, that supplications, prayers, intercessions, and thanksgivings be made [n. 57] for all men:
2 For kings, and for all that are in high station: that we may lead a quiet and a peaceable life in all piety and chastity.
3 [n. 60] For this is good and acceptable in the sight of God our Saviour,
4 Who will have all men to be saved, and to come to the knowledge of the truth.
5 [n. 63] For there is one God, and one mediator of God and men, the man Christ Jesus:
6a Who gave Himself a redemption for all.

55. Above the Apostle taught Timothy how to lead the people to the form of the true faith, and here he treats of those things pertaining to worship, namely, prayers and supplications. First, he gives the doctrine on prayer in general; second, he descends to the particular conditions of men, when he says in verse eight [n. 70], I desire therefore. Again, he first distinguishes the diverse modes of prayer; second, he shows for whom one ought to pray when he says [n. 57], for all men; third, he gives the reason, when he says [n. 60], For this is good.

56. He says therefore: Since it is so that Christ came to save sinners, **I desire therefore,** etc. In this he openly shows that among all things necessary for the Christian life, the chief is prayer, which has power against the dangers of temptation and for progress in the good. Jas. 5:16: *For the continual prayer of a just man availeth much.*

He therefore distinguishes prayer into four types: **supplications, prayers, intercessions, and thanksgivings,** of which three pertain to good things to be sought and last to benefits received.

For benefits to be sought, three things are required: first, that the one asking ought to give a reason why it should be granted to him; second, he should show why it is reasonable; third, he should conclude his petition. And just as rhetoricians do, so also we ought to do in prayer: first, to think of a reason why it should be granted to us, which is not our merits but the divine mercy. Dan. 9:18: *It is not for our justifications that we present our prayers before Thy face, but for the multitude of Thy tender mercies.* And for this there is **supplications,** which are attestations through sacred things, such as: "Through Thy passion and cross, free us, O Lord."

This reason having been considered, we must reflect how this holy thing is the cause of our salvation. And so **prayers,** which are the ascent of the mind to God, are required. Ps. 68:14: *But as for me, my prayer is to thee, O Lord.* Now prayer[1] is as it were reason of the mouth.[2] For the persuasive arguments of the rhetoricians are called orations because they persuade; but in one way for them, and another for us, since we do not intend to change the mind of God, Who is always ready to do good, but rather to elevate our hearts to God in prayer.

Third, **intercessions.** Jas. 1:6: *But let him ask in faith, nothing wavering.*

Again, regarding gifts that have been received, there are thanksgivings. I Thess. 5:18: *In all things give thanks.* Phil. 4:6: *But in every thing, by prayer and supplication, with thanksgiving, let your petitions be made known to God.*

Hence this mode of prayer is found in the Church of God: *Almighty and eternal God...,* which is the ascent of the mind to God, *Who hast given to the Church such a benefit...,* thanksgiving, *grant, we beseech Thee...,* intercession, *through our Lord Jesus Christ...,* supplication.

Likewise in the Mass there is supplication until the Body and Blood of Christ, since in them there is the commemoration of holy things from which we gain confidence to ask for benefits. In the mystery of the consecration there is prayer since it is a meditation on those things that Christ did. Up to communion there is intercession for the living and the dead and for oneself. At the end there is thanksgiving.

Or, these four are referred to the four things we want to obtain in prayer, such that supplication is referred to the difficult things we ask for, such as the conversion of the wicked; prayer, when we ask for grace for those already converted, that they progress even more; intercession, so that rewards may be granted for merits; and thanksgiving for benefits already received.

57. Then when he says, **for all men,** he shows for whom one ought to pray. Regarding this he does two things: first, he shows that he must pray for all men; second, he assigns the fruit of prayer, when he says [n. 59], **that we may lead.**

58. Regarding the first he says then that one must pray **for all men.** The reason for this is that prayer is the interpreter of our desires, for by praying we ask for what we desire. And charity requires that we desire what is good for all men, to whom it extends itself. Jas. 5:16: *Pray one for another, that you may be saved.*

But for whom especially? **For kings,** etc. Bar. 1:11: *And pray ye for the life of Nabuchodonosor the king of Babylon, and for the life of Balthasar his son.* And the Apostle says in Rom. 13:1, *Let every soul be subject to higher powers.* I Pet. 2:13: *Be ye subject therefore to every human creature for God's sake: whether it be to the king as excelling.* Indeed, it befits subjects to be devoted to their lords in their duties.

59. The profit is that through this we can procure our good. For in their peace is our peace. Hence he says, **that we may lead,** etc. In these two things lies the peace of the world. In fact, the Church has its own peace, in which the world has no place, because there is no peace for the impious. But there is a certain peace for both, and the Church needs this. Jer. 29:7: *And seek the peace of the city, to which I have caused you to be carried away captives.*

Worldly peace is sometimes disturbed from within and sometimes from without. II Cor. 7:5: *Combats without, fears within.* Regarding the first he says **quiet;** regarding the second, he says, **and a peaceable life.**

And although earthly peace is common to the good and the wicked, yet each uses it in a different way. For the evil used it for two things: the worship of demons, since they attributed that prosperity to false gods, and lust, since carnal vices abounded in times of peace. Wis. 14:22: *Whereas they lived in a great war of ignorance, they call so many and so great evils peace.* But the saints used peace contrariwise, in the worship of the true God and in chastity. And so he says, **in all piety and chastity.** Tit. 2:12: *We should live soberly, and justly, and godly in this world.*

60. Then when he says, **For this is good,** the reason for prayer is given. Regarding this he does two things: first, he gives the reasons; second, he proves a certain argument, when he says [n. 63], **For there is one God.** Again, he first gives a reason on the part of the species of the work; second, on the part of God, when he says [n. 62], **acceptable in the sight of God.**

61. He gives the reason, then, on the part of the species of the work, since when something is good *per se,* we ought to do it; but to pray for others is of this kind, since it is an act of charity. And so he says, **For this is good.** Ps. 51:11: *For it is good in the sight of Thy saints.*

62. On the part of God, since it is **acceptable in the sight of God.** Ps. 50:20: *Then shalt Thou accept the sacrifice,* etc. And this does not happen unless there be charity in the oblation. And he says **Saviour** because only God saves. Is. 43:11: *There is no saviour besides Me.*

And he proves that it is accepted when he says, **Who will have all men to be saved,** etc. II Pet. 3:9: *Not willing that any should perish, but that all should return to penance.*

On the contrary, all things whatsoever He willed, He has done; therefore He saves all men. But if you say that He does not because man does not will it, then it seems unfitting that the Almighty would be impeded by the will of someone not almighty.

I respond that to will is given sometimes for the will of gracious purpose and sometimes for the will of a sign. For the will of a sign He wills to save all men, since He proposes to all the precepts, counsels, and remedies for salvation.

The will of gracious purpose can be explained in four ways. In one way, so that it is a causal speaking, as when God is said to do something when He makes others to do something, as it says in Rom. 8:26, *The Spirit Himself asketh for us,* that is, He makes us to ask. Therefore God wills, since He makes His saints to will that all men be saved. For to will this ought to be in the saints, since they do not know who is predestined and who is not.[3]

In another way, so that it is an accommodated distribution, that is, all who will be saved, since no one is saved except through His will, just as in one school the master teaches all the boys of that city, since no one is taught except by him.

In another way, so that it is a distribution of singulars for genera, not of genera for singulars, that is, no kind of man is excepted from salvation, since at one time it was given only to the Jews but now to all men. And this is more to the intention of the Apostle.

In the fourth way, according to the Damascene, so that it is understood to regard the antecedent will, not the consequent will. For in the will of God, although there is no prior and posterior, yet His will is called antecedent or consequent. Likewise, according to the order of things willed, according to which the will can be considered in two ways: in the universal or absolutely, and according to certain circumstances and in particular. And the absolute and universal consideration is prior to the particular consideration and the consideration compared to something else. Thus the absolute will is as it were antecedent, and the will of something in particular is as it were consequent. For example, a merchant wills to save all his goods absolutely, and this is antecedent will. But if he consider safety, he does not will to save all his goods in comparison to other things, such as when the sinking of the ship follows with safety. And this will is consequent. Thus in God the salvation of all men considered in itself has the notion that it is able to be willed. And the Apostle here speaks thus, and so His will is antecedent. But if the good of justice be considered, and that sin is to be punished, He does not will it. And this is His consequent will.

And he adds, **and to come to the knowledge of the truth,** since there is no salvation except through the knowledge of the truth. Jn. 8:32: *And you shall know the truth, and the truth shall make you free.*

63. Then when he says, **For there is one God,** he proves what he said by a reason, and there are three proofs. One is on the part of God, one on the part of the man Christ [n. 64], and another on the part of the witnesses to Christ [n. 65].

He says therefore that God wills all men, etc. It is clear that **there is one God** of all men, Who saves. Rom. 3:29: *Is He the God of the Jews only? Is He not also of the Gentiles? Yes, of the Gentiles also. For it is one God,* etc.

64. Then the reason is given on the part of the man Christ when he says, **and**

one mediator, etc. There he first proves his intention; then he brings in a sign when he says, **Who gave Himself.**

He says, then: The man Christ Jesus is the mediator of God and men, not merely of some, but between God and all men, and this He would not have been unless He willed to save all men. And it can be said that Christ the mediator is like unto either extreme, to God and man, inasmuch as He is God and inasmuch as He is man, since a mean ought to have something of the extremes. And these are man and God. But since the mean is distinct from either of the extremes and the Son is not another God from the Father, it is better said that He is the mediator according as He is man. For thus does He communicate with either extreme.

For in God there are two things, namely, justice and immortality; in man there is injustice and mortality. The means therefore are two: one in which there is justice and mortality, and another in which there is immortality and injustice. Both are means, but the first befits Christ, and the second the devil. Thus the devil is a separating mean, since through injustice he separates us from divine justice; but Christ is a conjoining mean, since He is just and mortal, and through His death He joins us to the justice of God. I Jn. 2:2: *And He is the propitiation for our sin,* for some efficaciously, but for all sufficiently, since the price of His blood is sufficient for the salvation of all. But it does not have efficacy except in the elect on account of an impediment.

Lecture Two

6b [n. 65] Whose testimony in due times has been confirmed.[4]

7 [n. 67] Whereunto I am appointed a preacher and an apostle, (I say the truth, I lie not,) a doctor of the Gentiles in faith and truth.

8 [n. 70] I will therefore that men pray in every place, lifting up pure hands, without anger and contention.

9 [n. 74] In like manner women also in decent apparel: adorning themselves with modesty and sobriety, not with plaited hair, or gold, or pearls, or costly attire,

10 [n. 77] But as it becometh women professing godliness, with good works.

65. Above the Apostle said that God wills all men to be saved, and he proved it on the part of God, Who is the one God of all men, and on the part of Christ, Who is the one mediator of all; here he proves the same on the part of testimony. First, he brings in some witnesses; second, his own testimony, when he says [n. 67], Whereunto I am appointed.

66. He says therefore: But surely it did not suddenly enter the mind of God to save the whole world, Who before had chosen to save the Jews alone? Excluding this he says, **Whose testimony in due times;** as if to say: This law is not rash, but from ancient times was confirmed through the Law and the prophets. Is. 44:8: *You are My witnesses.* Acts 10:43: *To Him all the prophets give testimony,* etc. **Has been confirmed,** by the fulfillment and manifestation of signs, and the preaching of the Apostles. **In due times,** namely, those in which it was predetermined that it would come about. Eccles. 3:1: *All things have their season.* Or the testimony of the Apostles has been confirmed in determined times. Acts 1:8: *But you shall receive the power of the Holy Ghost coming upon you, and you shall be witnesses unto Me in Jerusalem, and in all Judea, and Samaria, and even to the uttermost part of the earth,* etc.

67. Then when he says, **Whereunto I am appointed,** he gives his testimony. First, he shows his office; second, the use of his office, when he says [n. 69], **I say the truth.**

68. He says therefore, **Whereunto,** namely, the office of testifying, **I am appointed** by God. Jn. 15:16: *I have chosen you; and have appointed you, that you should go, and should bring forth fruit; and your fruit should remain.* **A preacher,** since He appointed me to preach. Mk. 16:15: *Go ye into the whole world, and preach the gospel to every creature.* In any craft there are two things: those working as servants and those who organize them, namely, the architects. But in the office of the Church those who organize are the Apostles, and so he says, **and an apostle,** as it were with authority. I Cor. 9:2: *For you are the seal of my apostleship in the Lord.*

69. The service of this office is to preach the truth, and this is the duty of preachers, that they preach the truth. Prov. 8:7: *My mouth shall meditate truth.* Eph. 4:25: *Speak ye the truth every man with his neighbour.* But there is not any doctrine which does not have some truth; yet in this is a doctrine condemned, that it mixes falsity with truth. And so he says, **I say the truth, I lie not.** Prov. 8:8: *All my words are just.* Job 6:30: *Neither shall folly sound in my mouth.* And this is the service of this office, to preach the truth without lying; this befits my office, who am **a doctor of the Gentiles.** A doctor, or teacher, begets science in the soul of the student. But science is not about something false; hence, he who teaches what is false is not a doctor.

But on the contrary, it says in Mt. 23:8, *But be not you called Rabbi.*

I respond that this does not prohibit the ministry of teaching but the ambition for the office of teacher. Acts 9:15: *This man is to Me a vessel of election, to carry My name before the Gentiles,* etc. Is. 49:6: *I have given thee to be the light of the Gentiles.*

And I ought to teach them **in faith and truth,** since I must teach them the faith and right morals. And he says **in faith,** that is, about those things that pertain to the present state, in which we live according to faith, **and truth,** regarding the state of glory.

70. Then when he says, **I will therefore,** he descends to the specific grades of men. Regarding this he does two things: first, he admonishes men about prayer; second, women, when he says [n. 74], **In like manner women.**

71. He says therefore, **I will,** etc. He demands three things from men in prayer: first, that their prayer be assiduous; second, pure [n. 72]; third, peaceful [n. 73].

Assiduous, as in every time and in every place. And he says **I will,** since it is good that a man pray, and I the doctor **will that men pray in every place,** not in Jerusalem only, as the Jews, nor in Mount Garizim, like the Samaritans, as it says in Jn. 4:21. A man can pray spiritually and mentally in every place. Soph. 2:11: *And they shall adore Him every man from his own place, all the islands of the Gentiles.*

But then how does the Lord reprehend the Pharisees for standing in street corners, as it says in Mt. 6:5? I respond that mental prayer can be done everywhere, but the exterior sign of prayer ought not to happen in every place since a man ought not to appear singular in exterior manners, because for this reason vainglory can arise.

But then why are churches made now? Not because a place is necessary for prayer, but for praying well since prayer requires solitude and quiet.

72. Likewise, pure. And so he says, **lifting up pure hands.** Augustine: What we do exteriorly by praying makes our interior affection to be aroused. For genuflections and the such are not *per se* acceptable to God, but through them as signs

of humility a man is interiorly humbled, just as the lifting up of hands signifies the lifting up of the heart. Lam. 3:41: *Let us lift up our hearts with our hands to the Lord in the heavens.* **Lifting up,** etc., that is, praying with devotion of the heart. Job 8:5–6: *Yet if thou wilt arise early to God, and wilt beseech the Almighty: If thou wilt walk clean and upright, He will presently awake onto thee, and will make the dwelling of thy justice peaceable.*

73. Likewise, peaceful. And so he says, **without anger and contention.**

And he posits two things: first, that the mind be without anger, which disturbs the soul to inflict harm on one's neighbor, from which the mind of one who prays ought to be free. Ecclus. 28:3: *Man to man reserveth anger, and doth he seek remedy of God?* Second, a man ought to be free from debate, which can be understood in two ways. In one way, according to the Gloss, that we, as if not believing His words, do not argue against God by murmuring against His decrees. Rom. 9:20: *O man, who art thou that repliest against God?* Also, against one's neighbor, lest we break peace with him, which happens through arguing. For peace is necessary for one who prays. Mt. 18:19: *Again I say to you, that if two of you shall consent upon earth, concerning any thing whatsoever they shall ask, it shall be done to them by My Father Who is in heaven.*

74. Then when he says, **In like manner women,** he commands women: first, regarding prayer; second, regarding teaching, when he says in verse eleven [n. 78], **Let women learn in silence.** Again, first he shows what is required from a woman in prayer; second, he explains what he had said, when he says [n. 76], **not with plaited hair.**

75. Regarding the first it must be known that all things required for a man in prayer are required also for a woman; and so he says, **In like manner women also,** as if to say: Let them observe all that has been said. But he adds two things: ornament and modesty, saying, **in decent apparel: adorning themselves with modesty.** The reason for which is that just as women are of softer bodies than men, so are they of weaker reason. Now, it is of reason to order acts and the effects of each thing. Now, ornament consists of due order and disposition. So in interior glory, unless all things be ordered in their disposition by reason, they do not have spiritual beauty. And therefore, since women are deficient in reason, he requires of them adornment.

Likewise, modesty regards shameful deeds, and so it is laudable in those who are accustomed to fall into shamefulness, such being youth and women. And so this is praised in them, but not in the perfect and in old men. Ecclus. 26:19: *A holy and shamefaced woman is grace upon grace.*

Likewise, he requires sobriety; hence it follows, **and sobriety.** For since reason is weak in women, and sobriety preserves the power of reason, so inebriation is most reprehended in women. Wherefore, in ancient times among the Romans, wine was not given to women.

76. **Not with plaited hair, or gold,** etc. He explains what he had said, and first regarding apparel, then about modesty when he says, **But as it becometh women.** Regarding the first, he first excludes bodily apparel; then he gives spiritual apparel when he says, **But as it becometh women.**

Regarding the first he says: What I said about apparel I do not understand to regard the externals, since **not with plaited hair,** that is, not with an elegant head or even the whole body. But chiefly women adorn their heads, something natural to women, as is said in I Cor. 11:15. And so they have adornments of the head.

But there is a twofold veil for the head. One is natural, namely, hair, as is said in I Cor. 11:5; the other is artificial, and in both of these do they adorn themselves since they braid their hair. Hence he says, **not with plaited hair,** that is, in curls. Is. 3:24: *Instead of curled hair, baldness.* Likewise, he prohibits artificial things when he says, **or gold, or pearls.** I Pet. 3:3: *Whose adorning let it not be the outward plaiting of the hair, or the wearing of gold, or the putting on of apparel.* Or, **not with plaited hair, or gold,** that is, not having hair plaited with gold or pearls.

But regarding the whole body he says, **or costly attire,** for here the Apostle condemns this, as it is in Is. 3:17.

77. But is this a sin?

I respond that according to Augustine two things are to be considered in the adornment of women: simple adornment and cosmetics. Simple adornment, for example in clothing and gold and suchlike, can be with sin in three ways. First, from an evil intention, as from the desire to arouse concupiscence, from ostentation, or from vainglory. Prov. 7:10: *And behold a woman meeteth him in harlot's attire prepared to deceive souls.* Second, if it deviate from the custom of the country, which happens in diverse ways. For what exceeds the accustomed manner of the country is from frivolity. Third, if it exceed the condition of one's status. But, given a right intention, the custom of the country, and the condition of one's station, it is not a sin. But cosmetics are always a sin. For women are not allowed to be adorned except for their husbands, and men do not want to be deceived, as cosmetics would appear to them.

Therefore, let there be no such adornment, **But as it becometh women professing godliness.** For the exterior works of man are as a certain profession of the interior man, just as religious have a habit for this, and clerics likewise. Hence, unless the interior man is in accordance with the exterior, it is pretence. So likewise regarding other interior works. For we ought to cherish godliness interiorly, that is, have the worship of God, and exteriorly profess and show through good works what is concordant with godliness, and likewise to be interiorly what we show exteriorly.

Or, I say that they ought to adorn themselves not exteriorly but according to what befits those **professing,** that is, those things which they ought to profess, **godliness** through good works. Ecclus 19:27: *The attire of the body, and the laughter of the teeth, and the gait of the man, shew what he is.*

Lecture Three

11 [n. 78] Let women learn in silence, with all subjection.
12 [n. 80] But I suffer not a woman to teach in the churches,[5] nor to use authority over the man: but to be in silence.
13 [n. 81] For Adam was first formed; then Eve.
14 [n. 83] And Adam was not seduced; but the woman being seduced, was in the transgression.
15 [n. 85] Yet she shall be saved through childbearing; if she continue in faith, and love, and sanctification, with sobriety.

78. Above the Apostle made arrangements for women regarding prayer; here, regarding teaching: first, he posits his own ordinance regarding the teaching of women; second, he gives the reason why, when he says [n. 81], For Adam was first; third, he responds to a tacit question, when he says [n. 85], Yet she shall be saved. First he shows what befits women; second, what is not befitting them, when he says [n. 80], But I suffer not.

79. Regarding the first he posits three things that befit them: silence, learning, and subjection, which three proceed from one reason, namely, the defect of reason in them upon whom he first imposes silence, saying, **Let women learn in silence,** etc. Jas. 3:2: *If any man offend not in word, the same is a perfect man.* I Cor. 14:34: *Let women keep silence in the churches: for it is not permitted them to speak,* etc. For the words of a woman are inflammatory. Ecclus. 9:11: *For her conversation burneth as fire.*

Second, that they learn, since to learn is proper to those who are deficient in reason. I Cor. 14:35: *But if they would learn any thing, let them ask their husbands at home.* But to men it is given to teach.

Third, he imposes subjection, since it is natural that the soul rule the body, and reason the lower powers. And so, as the Philosopher teaches, whenever two things relate to each other thus, as soul to the body, and reason to the sensuality, natural lordship is for the one who has greater reason, and that one holds superiority, while the one deficient in reason is subject. Gen. 3:16: *Thou shalt be under thy husband's power, and he shall have dominion over thee.*

80. Likewise, he excludes from women those things not befitting them, saying, **But I suffer not a woman to teach,** etc. And there are two things: first, that they do not teach.

But on the contrary, it says in Prov. 31:1, *The vision wherewith his mother instructed him.*

I respond that one type of teaching is public, and this does not befit a woman, and so he says **in the churches;** the other type is private, and in this way a mother teaches her son.

But on the contrary it says in Judg. 5 (Title): *Debbora taught the people of Israel.*

I respond that that teaching is through the spirit of prophecy, and the grace of the Holy Spirit does not discern between man and woman. Yet she did not teach publicly, but by the instinct of the Holy Spirit she gave her counsel.

Second, lordship over a man is forbidden them. Ecclus. 25:30: *A woman, if she have superiority, is contrary to her husband.* And the Philosopher says that the lordship of women is the corruption of the family, as a tyrant is in a kingdom.

And thus he prohibits two things against two things which befit them; but the first he repeats, saying, **but to be in silence.**

81. Then when he says, **For Adam,** he assigns the reason for what he had said: first, from the order of creation; second, from the order of fault, when he says [n. 83], **And Adam was not seduced.**

82. Regarding the first it must be known that in the order of things, what is perfect and what is imperfect are ordered in diverse ways, since in one and the same thing the imperfect precedes the perfect in time, and the perfect precedes the imperfect by nature. But in diverse things the perfect is prior both in time and by nature since nature always begins from perfect things. And he treats this order here, since the man is perfect in human nature, and woman is a misbegotten male. Hence Adam was formed first. Gen. 2:7: *And the Lord God formed man of the slime of the earth.* Then the woman was formed, as something imperfect originating from something perfect, namely, his rib. I Cor. 11:8: *The man is not of the woman, but the woman of the man.* And so it is that man is not said to be made on account of the woman, but to the likeness of God. Gen. 1:26: *Let Us make man to Our image and likeness.* But the woman was made for the sake of man; therefore the man ought to rule.

83. Likewise on the part of fault. For the order of generation and corruption is contrary, since what is first in generation is last in corruption. Now, sin is the corruption of nature, and so generation begins first from Adam, but corruption from the woman. Hence he says, **And Adam was not seduced,** that is, first, since he was stronger, but the tempter began with the weaker so as to seduce the stronger more easily. He alludes here to the words of Adam in Gen. 3:12. For since the Lord rebuked Adam, he said, *The woman, whom Thou gavest me to be my companion, gave me of the tree,* etc. And so he says, **And Adam was not seduced; but the woman.**

Now, seduction is twofold: in general and in a particular thing worthy of choice, which is ignorance of choice. Therefore, whosoever sins is seduced by the ignorance of choice in a particular eligible thing. **But the woman** was **seduced,** ignorant in general, when she believed what the serpent said; the man did not believe this, but was deceived in the particular, namely, that he ought to humor his wife and eat with her, and, inexperienced in divine severity, he believed it would be forgiven him easily.

84. But on the contrary, ignorance is the punishment for sin; therefore, punishment preceded fault.

I respond that it did not precede since she was immediately elated at the words of the serpent, at the fact that another should be solicitous about her, and from that elation was she seduced; hence elation preceded ignorance.

85. Then when he says, **Yet she shall be saved,** he responds to a tacit question. For someone would say that if the woman is not for the sake of the man and the beginning of sin is from her, then she is harmful to the man; but if something is not for the sake of something else yet is harmful to that thing, it ought to be taken away; therefore, woman ought not to be saved.

It must be said, therefore, that salvation is twofold: one is temporal, and this is common with the brutes; the other is eternal, and this is proper to man. Is. 51:8: *But My salvation shall be for ever.* But the woman did not lose either salvation: neither temporal since the female sex is not immediately deprived on account of their generation of children, nor eternal since according to her soul she is capable of grace and glory. And so regarding the first he says, **she shall be saved,** that is, she shall not be eradicated, and this **through childbearing,** to which she has been ordained by God. Regarding the second he says, **if she continue.**

But since *if* signifies a cause, will not she who has not continued not be saved, when the Apostle says that a woman does better if she marries not?

I respond that in one way this saying can be figurative, and thus by man the superior reason is understood, the lower reason is the woman, good works are the children of the lower reason, and charity is what she conceives through a man, and through these charitable works shall she be saved. Another understanding is literal, so that *through* does not bespeak a cause but repugnance. And this is the sense: Woman shall be saved, even if she approaches salvation through generation, that is, if she marries and does not remain a virgin. And then the "through" speaks the augmentation of salvation, as if through the generation of sons for the worship of God she shall be saved the more. Ecclus. 7:25: *Hast thou children? instruct them, and bow down their neck from their childhood.*

Regarding the attainment of eternal salvation he posits three things. First, something regarding the intellect; second, the affections; third, the exterior act.

In the intellect is faith, through which the intellect is subjected to Christ; hence he says, **in faith.** Heb. 11:6: *But without faith it is impossible to please God.* And since faith avails nothing without love, regarding the affections he immediately adds, **and love.** I Cor. 13:2: *And if I should have all faith, so that I could remove mountains, and have not charity, I am nothing.* For external actions he posits two things against lewdness, which consists in two things: lust, regarding which he says, **and sanctification,** that is, in chastity. I Thess. 4:3: *For this is the will of God, your sanctification; that you should abstain from fornication.* Likewise intemperance, against which he says, **with sobriety.** Tit. 2:12: *We should live soberly, and justly, and godly in this world.*

Chapter Three

Lecture One

1 [n. 86] **A faithful saying: if a man desire the office of a bishop, he desireth a good work.**
2 [n. 91] **It behooveth therefore a bishop to be blameless, the husband of one wife, sober, prudent, of good behaviour, chaste, given to hospitality, a teacher,**
3 [n. 102] **Not given to wine, no striker, but modest, not quarrelsome, not covetous.**

86. Above the Apostle instructed Timothy about those things which pertain to the right faith and worship of God [n. 7]; here he instructs him about ecclesiastical duties. First, he gives the instruction; second, the occasion or necessity of this instruction, when he says in verse fourteen [n. 123], These things I write. Again, first he instructs him regarding those things which pertain to a bishop; second, those that pertain to a deacon, when he says in verse eight [n. 109], Deacons in like manner.

87. But since according to Dionysius there are three orders – bishops, who rule; presbyters, who illuminate; and deacons, who purify – why does he not make mention of presbyters?

I respond that the presbyters are understood to be together with the bishops: not that there is a lack of distinction between them according to the thing, but according to their names, since a presbyter is the same as an elder, while a bishop is an overseer.

Regarding this he first treats the desire of becoming a bishop; second, he describes the condition of a bishop, when he says [n. 91], **It behooveth therefore.**

88. He puts forward the assertion of this institution, saying, **A faithful saying,** namely, the one I will say or have said. Apoc. 22:6: *These words are most*

faithful and true. **If a man desire the office of a bishop,** etc. And from this some have taken occasion for the ambition of becoming a bishop or prelate, but they do not rightly understand what is said here. For the Apostle wants to show what pertains to the episcopacy. For bishop (*episcopos*) is a Greek word: *scopos* being the same as *looking,* and *epi* being *above.* The bishop is, therefore, as it were an overseer.

Two things, then, are to be considered in a bishop: his superior grade and profitable action for his people. For some cast an eye at what surrounds him, namely, that he who rules is honored and that he has power. Those who for these reasons desire to be a bishop do not know what a bishop is. Therefore, the Apostle says what a bishop is, and that he who desires to be one desires **a good work.** He does not say that he has a good desire, but **a good work,** namely, one profitable for the people.

89. But is it not lawful to desire it? Augustine says no. The Gloss: "The superior place, without which the people cannot be ruled, even if it be held and administrated decently, yet is desired but indecently." And he says the same in Book XIX of *On the City of God.* The reason for which is that no one ought to desire something beyond his powers and not proportioned to himself; otherwise he would be stupid. Horace: "Let him who knows not how to play in the fields withhold himself from war."

Therefore, he could well desire the episcopacy whose ability is proportioned to it. But for this no one is suitable because according to his standing and conduct he ought to surpass all other men in manners and contemplation, so that in respect to himself others may be his flock. Now, to presume this suitability about oneself is the greatest pride. Thus, he either desires the accoutrements of being a bishop, and then he does not really know what it is he wants, since this is not the episcopacy; or, he wants its work, and this is pride. And so it is not to be accepted unless it be imposed.

90. The Gloss: "If you say that the state of a bishop is more perfect than the state of religious, which it is licit to desire, then it is licit to desire the episcopacy."

I respond that perfection relates differently to each, since the state of a bishop presumes perfection, and so no one may desire it unless he already be perfect; but the state of religious is the way to perfection, and so perfection already acquired is not required for it, but a man would be held to acquire it if he were not already perfect. And this is clear from Jn. 21:17, where the Lord says to Simon, *If thou wilt be perfect,*[1] *feed My sheep,* and to the young man in Mt. 19:21, *If thou wilt be perfect, go sell what thou hast.*

Thus, therefore, by the name of the episcopacy a good work is to be understood. I Pet. 5:3: *Neither as lording it over the clergy, but being made a pattern of the flock from the heart.* As if to say: If you desire the episcopacy, this is what you desire: a good work.

91. But what kind of man the bishop ought to be he shows when he says, **It**

behooveth therefore a bishop, etc. First, he instructs him in general; second, specifically, when he says [n. 93], **the husband of one wife.**

92. He says therefore: I say that he desires a good work, but not everyone is suitable for this; he ought to be such: first, **blameless.** Hence it is said of Zachary in Lk. 1:6 that he walked in all the commands and justifications without blame. Lev. 21:17–18: *Whosoever of thy seed throughout their families, hath a blemish, he shall not offer bread to his God. Neither shall he approach to minister to Him.*

It is not to be understood that he must be entirely without sin, since it says in I Jn. 1:8, *If we say that we have no sin, we deceive ourselves,* etc. Nor is to be said, as some say, that whosoever sins mortally after baptism is not suitable, for such are few, but **blameless,** that is, not subject to any sin for which he might be blamed by others, since it is indecent if the one who corrects is himself blameworthy. Mt. 7:5: *Thou hypocrite, cast out first the beam in thy own eye, and then shalt thou see to cast out the mote out of thy brother's eye.*

93. Then when he says, **the husband of one wife,** etc., he instructs him in particular: first, regarding the bishop himself; second, regarding the multitude, when he says in verse four [n. 103], **One that ruleth well.** Again, the first is in two parts: first, he shows with what virtues he should be adorned; second, from what his mind ought to be immune, when he says [n. 102], **Not given to wine.**

94. Now every moral virtue first regards the passions; and there are two which make for sanctity, namely, chastity and sobriety, since through delectation or delectable things of the flesh the soul is most disturbed. And so first he posits what pertains to chastity, saying, **the husband of one wife.** Likewise Tit. 1:6.

Now, in this there seems to be discord between Augustine and Jerome. For Jerome says that this is understood to be after baptism, since if before baptism he had two wives, or one first and then another, he is not impeded from ordination, since through baptism all things are wiped away. Augustine and Ambrose say the contrary, since whether before or after, if he had two wives, he is not ordained.

95. But does not baptism wipe all things away?

I respond that it does as regards sins but not irregularities, which are incurred occasionally even without sin solely by ecclesiastical institution; but matrimony is not a sin even in pagans.

96. But what is the cause of this institution? Is he not more impeded who has many concubines?

I respond that this happens not only on account of incontinence, but on account of the manifestation of the sacrament, since Christ is the spouse of the Church, and the Church is one. Cant. 6:8: *One is my dove.*

97. Second, he treats sobriety, saying **sober.** Tit. 2:12: *We should live soberly, and justly, and godly in this world,* etc. For here he teaches a bishop, who is an overseer, to be vigilant. Lk. 2:8: *And there were in the same country shepherds watching,* etc. And drunkenness is an obstacle to vigils. I Pet. 5:8: *Be sober and watch,* etc.

98. Third, he ordains the reason why, saying **prudent,** since this is the ruler

of all the virtues, and the bishop is chosen to rule others. Mt. 10:16: *Be ye therefore wise.* Mt. 24:45: *Who, thinkest thou, is a faithful and wise servant,* etc.

99. Next he posits the virtues which order exterior actions: first, regarding the bishop himself; second, regarding others [n. 101].

100. Regarding the first he says, **of good behaviour, chaste.** A man is adorned when he is well composed in his deeds and words. For adornment signifies a beauty which consists in proportion; hence is he adorned when he acts and speaks as he ought. Ecclus. 44:6: *Rich men in virtue, studying beautifulness.*

This is required in a bishop since through exterior actions we judge about the interior ones. Ecclus.19:27: *The attire of the body, and the laughter of the teeth, and the gait of the man, shew what he is.* Since a prelate is placed in the sight of men, he ought to be so adorned. Hence it is said about Ambrose that he refused to ordain certain men because they carried themselves negligently. Likewise, it sometimes happens that vile things occur to someone through the deeds or words of others, and for this he ought to be chaste so that he may be ashamed if he see or hear it. Augustine says in his *Rule,* "The impure eye is the messenger of the impure heart." Ecclus. 7:21: *The grace of her modesty is above gold.*

101. Then when he says, **given to hospitality,** he treats the bishop in relation to others. Now, it is imposed upon a bishop that he tend the sheep, as it says in Jn. 21:15 and I Pet. 5:2. Almsgiving is twofold: corporal and spiritual; therefore, he must tend them in both.

Regarding the first he says **given to hospitality,** namely, of strangers and friends. Rom. 12:13: *Pursuing hospitality.* Heb. 13:2: *And hospitality do not forget.* Job 31:32: *The stranger did not stay without, my door was open to the traveller.* Regarding the second he says, **a teacher.** Eph. 4:11: *And He gave some apostles, and some prophets, and other some evangelists, and other some pastors and doctors.* And this is the office proper to prelates. Jer. 3:15: *And I will give you pastors according to My own heart, and they shall feed you with knowledge and doctrine.*

102. Then when he says, **Not given to wine,** etc., he removes the opposing vices. Now, he removes three: one which pertains to the concupiscence of the flesh, another to anger, and the third to cupidity.

Regarding the first he says, **Not given to wine.** He says less, but signifies more. Eph. 5:18: *And be not drunk with wine, wherein is luxury.* It is as if to say: not gluttonous, not excessive.

Regarding anger he posits two things: first, regarding the act he says, **no striker.** He rightly prohibits this after wine since the drunk are easily given to striking. **But modest,** that is, patient. Phil. 4:5: *Let your modesty be known to all men.* Ps. 91:15: *They...shall be very patient,[2] that they may shew, that the Lord our God is righteous, and there is no iniquity in Him.* Christ having suffered did not strike back. Then regarding words when he says, **not quarrelsome.** II Tim. 2:24: *But the servant of the Lord must not wrangle.* I Cor. 11:16: *But if any man* *seem to be contentious, we have no such custom, nor the church of God.* And this because bishops are the successors of the Apostles, whom Christ instructed to announce peace. Likewise, in Christ's passion He said, *Peace I leave with you, My peace I give unto you.*

Regarding temporal things he says, **not covetous,** since he is placed as judge and regulator of the Church. If he were covetous, he would easily fall from justice. Ex. 23:8: *Neither shalt thou take bribes, which even blind the wise, and pervert the words of the just.* But alas! Jer. 6:13: *For from the least of them even to the greatest, all are given to covetousness.*

Lecture Two

4 [n. 103] One that ruleth well his own house, having his children in subjection with all chastity.

5 [n. 106] But if a man know not how to rule his own house, how shall he take care of the church of God?

6 [n. 107] Not a neophyte: lest being puffed up with pride, he fall into the judgment of the devil.

7 [n. 108] Moreover he must have a good testimony of them who are without: lest he fall into reproach and the snare of the devil.

8 [n. 109] Deacons in like manner chaste, not double tongued, not given to much wine, not greedy of filthy lucre:

9 [n. 113] Holding the mystery of faith in a pure conscience.

10 [n. 114] And let these also first be proved: and so let them minister, having no crime.

11 [n. 115] The women in like manner chaste, not slanderers, but sober, faithful in all things.

103. Above the Apostle showed what kind of man a bishop ought to be in himself [n. 93]; here he shows what sort of man he should be in comparison with the multitude: first, with regard to the multitude of the domestic family; second, to the multitude of the Church, when he says [n. 107], Not a neophyte; third, to the multitude of infidels, when he says [n. 108], Moreover he must have. Again, he first shows that from a bishop is required due rule of his family; second, the good instruction of his children, when he says [n. 105], having his children.

104. He says therefore: A bishop ought to be the head of his house, that is, his family, so as to rule it well. For good governance is not just the acquisition of riches, since these are not the goal of a household but the means; its goal is an upright life. Ecclus. 44:6: *Living at peace in their houses.*

105. Now, in a domestic family, the children are especially chief. And so he says about them, **having his children in subjection,** that is, ruling his own children not weakly from some tenderness of love which sometimes extends itself to children.

Among other things which are required in the children of a bishop, which he had before he became a bishop, it is required that they be chaste. And so he adds, **with all chastity,** since their evil lives would be a testimony against their parent and prelate. Ecclus. 10:2: *As the judge of the people is himself, so also are his ministers: and what manner of man the ruler of a city is, such also are they that dwell therein.* Wis. 4:6: *For the children that are born of unlawful beds, are witnesses of wickedness against their parents in their trial.* The second reason is that, since the people gather at the house of the bishop, it befits the children to be chaste. This is against I Kg. 2:22, where the sons of Heli, who were not chaste, seduced women coming to the tabernacle. Hence Heli also was punished by the Lord.

106. Then when he says, **But if a man,** he gives the reason for his command.

It could also be said: What is it to a bishop that he rule his family well, upon whom the care for the community is imposed? And so he says, **But if a man know not how to rule his own house,** etc., that is, his own family. Lk. 16:10: *He that is faithful in that which is least, is faithful also in that which is greater.*

Yet it frequently happens that some are not good rulers in small homes who nevertheless rule well over greater groups. But when he says, **know not,** this refers to negligence. For he who neglects little things easily neglects great things, although he who does not have care of small things sometimes carries himself well in greater things.

107. Next he shows how he ought to relate to the multitude of the Church, in which he ought not be a novice in the faith, but experienced. Hence he says, **Not a neophyte,** that is, one newly having the faith. Acts 1:21: *Wherefore of these men who have companied with us all the time,* etc. Likewise Num. 11:16: *And the Lord said to Moses: Gather unto Me seventy men of the ancients of Israel, whom thou knowest to be ancients and masters of the people,* etc. But, as it says in Wis. 4:8: *For venerable old age is not that of long time, nor counted by the number of years.*

For it sometimes happens that in some neophytes grace abounds, and they have together with youthful years the maturity of age; these are promoted by way of exception, as was Ambrose, by divine dispensation. Hence, what he says here pertains not only to those who are neophytes in age but also in perfection. And the reason for this is **lest being puffed up with pride,** etc. For when someone newly come to the faith is promoted to some position, he thinks himself better than others and very necessary, as if unless he were there, they would have no means of providing for the Church.

And he says, **of the devil,** since he was condemned on account of the sin of his pride.

108. Then when he says, **Moreover he must have,** etc., he shows how he ought to relate to the multitude of infidels, and he gives instructions.

First, that he be of good fame. Col. 4:5: *Walk with wisdom towards them that are without, redeeming the time.* I Pet. 2:12: *Having your conversation good among the Gentiles.* And this is necessary for a prelate since the behavior of the whole congregation is judged by the prelate.

On the contrary, II Cor. 6:8: *By evil report and good report.*

I respond that infamy sometimes arises by the fault of the one who is defamed, and he prohibits this; sometimes from the malice of detractors, and in this he ought to have patience, and about this does the Apostle speak in that place. But here he speaks of someone assuming the episcopacy, who if he be good and defamed falsely ought to bear it patiently.

Then he gives the reason; hence he adds, **lest he fall into reproach,** etc. Here he touches upon a twofold danger: first, lest he become a source of shame and through this his authority be lessened and his courage to correct be taken away as a consequence. Mt. 7:5: *Cast out first the beam in thy own eye,* etc. Second, **lest he fall into…the snare of the devil,** namely, by enduring impatiently, through which he would be aroused by infamies to hatred, despair, and the suchlike. And it happens that a prelate would be odious to the laity if he neglected the worship of divine praise. Mal. 2:8–9: *You have made void the covenant of Levi, saith the Lord of hosts. Therefore have I also made you contemptible, and base before all people.*

109. Then when he says, **Deacons in like manner,** he shows those things which pertain to deacons, which in Greek is the same as ministers. For in the primitive Church there were only three orders, as Dionysius says, namely, bishops, presbyters, and ministers; they were not divided into diverse grades but were all in one order on account of the lack of ministers and the newness of the Church.

First, then, he shows of what kind they ought to be in themselves; second, regarding others, when he says [n. 115], **The women.** Again, first he shows of what kind they ought to be; second, how they are to be examined, when he says [n. 114], **And let these also.** Likewise, he shows of what kind they are to be regarding their own bodies; second, regarding exterior matters, when he says [n. 112], **not greedy;** third, regarding other things, when he says [n. 113], **Holding the mystery.** Again, regarding the body, he first shows how they ought to be regarding the qualities of the whole body; second, regarding the restraint of the mouth [n. 111].

110. He says therefore: I say that bishops are to be modest; deacons are to be as well. For he who acts contrary to purity is incapable of spiritual things, since he refuses to give his mind, which is necessary for such men to keep elevated, to spiritual things. Is. 52:11: *Be ye clean, you that carry the vessels of the Lord.* Lk. 12:35: *Let your loins be girt.*

111. Then he shows how they are to act with their mouths. The mouth serves for speaking and eating. Regarding the first he says, **not double tongued.** Ecclus. 28:16: *The tongue of a third person hath disquieted many, and scattered them from nation to nation.* Such deacons will not be ministers of peace.

Regarding the second he says, **not given to much wine.** Prov. 23:29–30: *Who hath woe? whose father hath woe? who hath contentions? who falls into pits? who hath wounds without cause? who hath redness of eyes? Surely they that pass their time in wine, and study to drink of their cups.* Is. 5:22: *Woe to you that are mighty to drink wine, and stout men at drunkenness.*

112. Then when he says, **not greedy of filthy lucre,** he shows how they ought to relate to exterior things. For on account of greed for gain they are diverted not only from justice but also from the truth, saying what they ought not. And so he prohibits them temporal gain, by which is to be understood every dishonest gain.

113. But regarding the affections he says, **Holding the mystery,** etc., and he instructs them: first, regarding the faith; second, regarding a pure conscience.

Hence he says, **the mystery of faith,** that is, not just simple faith but the understanding of it which is hidden in faith. For a mystery is the same thing as something hidden, since ministers ought to know not only those things about the faith which the people also know, but also the mysteries, for they must instruct others. I Pet. 3:15: *Being ready always to satisfy every one that asketh you a reason of that hope which is in you,* etc.

Likewise, a pure conscience since an impure one makes a man err in the faith. Above 1:5: *Now the end of the commandment is charity, from a pure heart, and a good conscience, and an unfeigned faith.*

114. Then when he says, **And let these also first be proved,** etc., he shows how they should be examined.

For someone could say: I think all men to be good. For this ought to be your supposition, but in regard to their promotion all are to be examined. Hence these also are examined, and he says, **And let these also first be proved.**

Having no crime, that is, no mortal sin; he does not intend to speak of venial sin, since it says in I Jn. 1:8, *If we say that we have no sin, we deceive ourselves, and the truth is not in us.* Nor does he say, "had," but **having,** that is, who are well known and have the crime of infamy. Otherwise this would derogate from the keys of the Church.

115. Then when he says, **The women,** etc., he shows how they ought to relate to others. And first he gives his instruction; second, the reason why, when he says in verse thirteen [n. 122], **For they that have ministered well.** Regarding the first, he does two things: first, he shows how they should relate to their wives, which they had in the primitive Church, and he speaks about their state; second, how they should relate to the children, when he says in verse twelve [n. 121], **who rule well their children.** Again, the first is in two parts: first, he shows how their wives ought to be; second, in what way they ought to carry themselves with others, when he says in verse twelve [n. 119], **Let deacons be.**

116. He requires four things from their wives: chastity, modesty, sobriety, and faithfulness.

He says therefore: Just as I said about deacons, so I say about their wives, that they ought to be **chaste.** Ecclus. 26:19: *A holy and shamefaced woman is grace upon grace.* Again, modest in their speech, **not slanderers.** Eccles. 10:11: *If a serpent bite in silence, he is nothing better that backbiteth secretly.* And **sober,** which is the greatest adornment of women. Above 2:9: *In like manner women also in decent apparel: adorning themselves with modesty and sobriety.* And **faithful,** whether to God regarding the true faith or to their husbands.

117. But what fault is it of a deacon, if his wife is evil?

I respond that someone is barred from the ministry not only because of fault, but also because of some impediment to the ministry. And so if, without their fault, their wives should be evil, yet there is a twofold impediment: first, since they are evil, they need greater care, and for this reason their husbands are less available for ecclesiastical ministries; second, men are corrupted by their wives. Likewise, it would be dangerous, for many frequent the houses of the ministers of the Church.

118. But the Cathaphrygians said that because women are treated amid the treatment of deacons, then women can be ordained to sacred orders.

But it must be known that in the law some women are sometimes called deaconesses, not because they have such an order, but because of some ministry for the Church, just as in the Greek a deacon is a minister.

Lecture Three

12 [n. 119] **Let deacons be the husbands of one wife: who rule well their children, and their own houses.**

13 [n. 122] **For they that have ministered well, shall purchase to themselves a good degree, and much confidence in the faith which is in Christ Jesus.**

14 [n. 123] **These things I write to thee, hoping that I shall come to thee shortly.**

15 [n. 125] **But if I tarry long, that thou mayest know how thou oughtest to behave thyself in the house of God, which is the church of the living God, the pillar and ground of the truth.**

16 [n. 129] **And evidently great is the mystery of godliness, which was manifested in the flesh, was justified in the spirit, appeared unto angels, hath been preached unto the Gentiles, is believed in the world, is taken up in glory.**

119. Above the Apostle showed of what sort deacons and their wives ought to be [n. 115]; here he shows how deacons should relate to their wives, children, and family. First, he gives an instruction; second, the reason for it, when he says [n. 122], For they that have ministered well.

120. He says therefore: I said that wives of deacons should be chaste. Although there must be chastity in their wives on their account, it is more necessary in them themselves so that they can be altogether immune from contact with women. But since in that case few would be ministers, he allows that they should be husbands of one wife, since to have had more is a sign of incontinence and against the significance of the sacrament. And hence it is that the Lord instituted matrimony of one with one other. Hence also the first wife is blessed, and not the second.

121. Then he admonishes them about how to relate to their children, saying, **who rule well their children,** by teaching them in good discipline and a good life. Ecclus. 7:25: *Hast thou children? instruct them,* etc.

122. Next he exhorts them to rule well the whole house, that is, the whole family, with meekness. Ecclus. 4:35: *Be not as a lion in thy house,* etc.

And he gives the reason for this, saying, **For they that have ministered well,** etc., as if to say: What you require of a bishop is reasonable since he is a prelate. But why is this required of a deacon, who is a minister? He responds, saying, **For they that have ministered well.** He first shows that the good use of this ministry is the way to a higher dignity, then that it is also the way to eternal life. Regarding the first he says, **For they that have ministered well** by exercising the office of deacon (for what in Greek is called a deacon in Latin is called a minister), **shall**

purchase to themselves a good degree, that is, they merit to be promoted to a higher grade. Mt. 25:21: *Because thou hast been faithful over a few things, I will place thee over many things.* And he says **good** since he said above in verse one: *If a man desire the office of a bishop, he desireth a good work.* Yet their goal is not in this, but with this ministry they have remuneration from God. Jn. 12:26: *Where I am, there also shall My minister be.* And so he says **much confidence,** namely, in the assistance of grace now and glory in the future; and this **in the faith,** that is, through faith in Christ. II Cor. 3:4: *And such confidence we have, through Christ, towards God.* Is. 12:2: *I will deal confidently, and will not fear.*

123. Then when he says, **These things I write to thee,** he gives the reason for the aforementioned admonitions [n. 86]. And first, he excludes a supposed cause; second, he provides the true cause, when he says [n. 125], **But if I tarry long;** third, he assigns a reason, when he says [n. 126], **which is the church.**

124. Regarding the first it must be known that Timothy could believe that from what the Apostle wrote he would not see him again; otherwise it would be superfluous to admonish him in a letter. And so he says, **These things I write to thee,** my son. And he calls him his son because he was so very dear to him. I Cor. 4:17: *For this cause have I sent to you Timothy, who is my dearest son and faithful in the Lord.* And he says **hoping,** as if not certain. II Jn. 1:12: *Having more things to write unto you, I would not by paper and ink: for I hope that I shall be with you, and speak face to face.* I write therefore, although I have hope, since hope can be prolonged for a long time. Prov. 16:1: *It is the part of man to prepare the soul: and of the Lord to govern the tongue.*

125. And so he says, **But if I tarry long,** etc. I Thess. 2:18: *Satan hath hindered us.* I therefore write **if I tarry long, that thou mayest know how thou oughtest to behave thyself in the house of God.** Ps. 67:7: *God who maketh men of one manner to dwell in a house,* etc.

126. Then when he says, **which is the church,** he gives the reason why he ought to behave in such a manner in it. And he assigns a reason for this cause, which is twofold: first, by recommending the Church itself; second, the unity of the Church, when he says [n. 129], **And evidently great.** Regarding the first, he does two things: first, he recommends the Church on the part of Him Whose Church it is; second, from the truth of that Church, when he says [n. 128], **the pillar.**

127. On the part of Him Whose Church it is, since that is **the living God.** The Church is as it were a gathering, for in the Church is the gathering of the faithful. Rom. 8:30: *And whom He called,* etc. And they are gathered in God. Jn. 17:21: *That they also may be one in Us,* etc. And so he says, **which is the church of the living God.** And he adds **living** to distinguish Him from other gods to whom the Gentiles were gathered. For they are dead, just as the God of the Church is alive. Jn. 5:26: *For as the Father hath life in Himself,* etc. He therefore ought to behave

in it thus so that we may live spiritually. Ps. 92:5: *Holiness becometh Thy house, O Lord, unto length of days.*

128. The second reason is from the truth of the Church. For it is natural for man to desire the knowledge of the truth. Hence, Augustine says that beatitude is the end of man since it is nothing other than rejoicing in the truth. This became known to the philosophers through creatures, as it says in Rom. 1:19. But in this they wavered, since they did not have certitude of the truth: at some times because they were corrupted with errors, at other times because it was scarcely found among them that they would agree in the truth. But in the Church is firm knowledge and the truth. Hence he says **pillar.** Ecclus. 24:7: *My throne is in a pillar of a cloud.* Ecclus. 26:23: *As golden pillars upon bases of silver,* etc. And it is called golden because it is holy in itself. **And ground,** regarding others, because they cannot be grounded in the truth except through the sacraments of the Church. Lk. 22:32: *And thou, being once converted, confirm thy brethren,* etc. Ps. 74:4: *I have established the pillars thereof.* Since the Church gathers in God and gives knowledge of the truth, we must be in it.

129. Then when he says, **And evidently great,** he commends the truth of the Church: first, Christ, for the manifestation of Whom it has appeared; second, he treats of its exaltation, when he says [n. 135], **is taken up.** Now, he commends Christ in two ways: first, regarding His divine nature; second, regarding His human nature, when he says [n. 131], **which was manifested.**

130. He says, then, **And evidently great is the mystery**[3] **of godliness,** since a sacrament is the same thing as a holy secret.[4] Now, nothing is so secret as what we carry in our hearts. Much more, therefore, is what is in the heart of God holy and secret. I Cor. 2:11: *So the things also that are of God no man knoweth, but the Spirit of God.* Is. 24:16: *My secret to myself, my secret to myself.* Is. 45:15: *Verily Thou art a hidden God.* And this is the Word of God in the heart of the Father. Ps. 44:2: *My heart hath uttered a good word.* Indeed, this secret is the sacrament **of godliness.** But the secret of man is ever vain. Ps. 93:11: *The Lord knoweth the thoughts of men, that they are vain.* Inasmuch as it is restorative for the world, it is **of godliness.** Likewise, **great** for He is true God, of Whose greatness there is no end.

131. Therefore, this secret which lies in the heart of the Father has been made man. And so he describes Him next according to His human nature: first, regarding His flesh; second, His soul.

Regarding the first he says, **which was manifested in the flesh.** Just as a word which lies in the heart is manifested in a sensible word, so the Word of God was hidden in the heart of God, but was manifested in the flesh. Jn. 1:14: *And the Word was made flesh,* etc.

Regarding the second he says, **was justified in the spirit.** This can be explained in two ways. First, lest it be believed that flesh was conceived before, he says, **in the spirit,** that is, He was conceived through the Holy Spirit. Mt. 1:20: *That which is conceived in her, is of the Holy Ghost.* Lk. 1:35: *And therefore also the Holy which shall be born of thee shall be called the Son of God.* And this because *the Holy Ghost shall come upon thee,* etc. Second, in a holy human spirit, about which it speaks in Jn. 19:30: *He gave up the ghost.* And thus what was manifested in the flesh was yet with a spirit. And I say a justified spirit because He was just, without any sin.

132. Then when he says, **appeared,** he shows His manifestation: first, to the angels; second, to men, when he says [n. 134], **hath been preached.**

133. He says, then, that this sacrament appeared to the angels and exceeded even the knowledge of the angels. That is said to appear which has it in its power to be seen and not to be seen, and is not under the power of the one seeing. Hence it is not said: A stone appears to me, but I see a stone. If, then, an angel had it in his own power to see the Word, it would not be said that the Word appeared to him, but that he saw when he wanted. And so the Apostle says, **appeared unto angels,** since they did not see Him in their own natures. And it is true that from the beginning He appeared to angels, when from their conversion to Him He built them up; but when He was incarnate, many mysteries were made known to the angels which before they had not known. And so Bede says that in the nativity glory appeared to the angels which had not been seen among men in truth before.

134. And this in two ways: first, regarding the ministry of the Apostles; second, regarding the knowledge of the people to whom it was made manifest.

Indeed, once it was made manifest only to the Jews, but now to the Gentiles. And so he says, **hath been preached unto the Gentiles.** Mt. 28:19: *Going therefore, teach ye all nations,* etc. Ps. 95:3: *Declare His glory among the Gentiles.* And this efficaciously because it **is believed in the world.** And this is what the Lord prayed in Jn. 17:18. And it is most amazing that through simple, poor and powerless men the whole world has been converted. I Cor. 1:26: *Not many mighty, not many noble,* and this *that no flesh should glory in His sight.*

135. Second, he makes it clear that only the truth of God does this, since it, namely, Christ, **is taken up in glory,** since, being manifested, He was taken up into heaven. Mk. 16:19: *And the Lord Jesus, after He had spoken to them, was taken up into heaven.* Phil. 2:11: *And that every tongue should confess that the Lord Jesus Christ is in the glory of God the Father.*

Chapter Four

Lecture One

1 [n. 136] Now the Spirit manifestly saith, that in the last times some shall depart from the faith, giving heed to spirits of error, and doctrines of devils,
2 [n. 140] Speaking lies in hypocrisy, and having their conscience seared,
3 [n. 141] Forbidding to marry, to abstain from meats, which God hath created to be received with thanksgiving by the faithful, and by them that have known the truth.
4 For every creature of God is good, [n. 145] and nothing to be rejected that is received with thanksgiving:
5 [n. 148] For it is sanctified by the word of God and prayer.

136. Above the Apostle instructed Timothy about those things which pertain to the arrangement of the Church in spiritual matters: regarding instruction of the faith, the worship of God, and the disposition of ministers [n. 7]; here he instructs him about the arrangement of the Church regarding exterior things. First, regarding food; second, regarding the states of men and riches, when he says in chapter six, verse one [n. 232], Whosoever are servants under the yoke. Likewise, first, he treats of the use of foods; second, the dispensation of foods, when he says in chapter five, verse three [n. 180], Honour widows. Again, first he excludes superstitious abstinence; second, he prefers godliness to licit abstinence, when he says in verse seven [n. 153], exercise thyself. Again, first he foretells the false doctrine of illicit abstinence; second, he instructs him to propose this to the brethren, when he says in verse six [n. 149], These things proposing to the brethren. Again, he first manifests an error; second, he excludes it, when he says [n. 141], which God hath created. Again, he first foretells a future error on the part of those deceived;

second, on the part of the deceivers, when he says [n. 140], Speaking lies in hypocrisy. Again, he first posits the agent of the denunciation; second, the defection from the faith, when he says [n. 138], that in the last times; third, the cause of this defection, when he says [n. 139], giving heed.

137. He says therefore: Great is the mystery of godliness that was justified in the spirit, but beyond this mystery the Holy Spirit foretells something in the future. For to Him it pertains to reveal mysteries. II Cor. 14:2 and Jn. 16:13: *And the things that are to come, He shall shew you.* Therefore, the Spirit foretells future secrets in the heart of the Father. But at one time He spoke in likenesses. Num. 12:6: *If there be among you a prophet of the Lord, I will appear to him in a vision, or I will speak to him in a dream.* Os. 12:10: *And I have spoken by the prophets, and I have multiplied visions.* But in the New Testament **the Spirit manifestly saith.** Jn. 16:25: *But will shew you plainly of the Father.*

138. And he foretells the future defection from the faith; hence he says, **in the last times,** etc. The last times are called the ultimate age because we are the ones upon whom the end of the ages has come. Yet this time is more fully last as much as it is closer to the last day. And just as faith was more fervent in the primitive Church on account of its nearness to Christ and the recently instituted sacraments, so in the last times, compared to the times of the Apostles, **some shall depart from the faith,** since they will be carnal, and errors will abound the more in the end. Gen. 49:1: *Gather yourselves together that I may tell you the things that shall befall you in the last days.*

139. The cause of the defection is twofold: one is on the part of the devil who seduces. II Cor. 11:3: *But I fear lest, as the serpent seduced Eve by his subtilty,* etc. And so he says, **giving heed to spirits of error,** namely demons, whose office it is to drive men into error. Jn. 8:44: *He is a liar, and the father thereof.* I Kg. 22:22: *I will go forth, and be a lying spirit,* etc. And he says **spirits** because a greater demon has many ministers.

But how will they attend to them? Surely they will not see them? No, but they will speak in them. And so he adds a second cause: false doctrine. And according to the Gloss he here calls false teachers demons not unjustly. For just as good men are now and then called angels, so are these, because of their eminent malice, called demons. Jn. 6:71: *Have not I chosen you twelve; and one of you is a devil?*

140. On the part of those deceiving there is a twofold cause: one, their falsity; the other, the perversity of their conscience.

Regarding the first he says, **of devils,** that is, of men possessed by demons, and of these I say that they are **Speaking lies.** Jer. 23:26: *How long shall this be in the heart of the prophets that prophesy lies, and that prophesy the delusions of their own heart?*

And notice that by a simple lie without the cloak of appearance no one could deceive anyone. And so these can deceive no one unless they feign some cloak either of a good intention, or pretense, or false authority. I Cor. 3:18: *Let no man deceive himself,* etc. II Tim. 3:5: *Having an appearance indeed of godliness,* that is, feigned godliness.

And of demons, I say, **having their conscience seared.** Searing is a corruption of the flesh with fire, from which rottenness continually flows forth. So from the fire of a perverse will, anger, hatred, and concupiscence, a conscience is ulcerated and the false doctrines of demons flows forth. Tit. 1:15: *Both their mind and their conscience are defiled.*

141. Then he shows what this false doctrine is, and he touches the heresy of the Manichaeans who condemned marriage, contrary to Mt. 19:6: *What therefore God hath joined together, let no man put asunder;* I Cor. 7:36: *A woman[1] sinneth not, if she marry.* Likewise, the Manichaeans prohibit the use of foods, that is, they command abstinence from foods.

Now, someone can licitly abstain from foods with the intention of ruling his flesh, as Timothy abstained from wine, or because of scandal, as the Apostle says in I Cor. 8:13, *Wherefore, if meat scandalize my brother, I will never eat flesh, lest I should scandalize my brother.* He can also do so illicitly: in one way, because of a precept of the Law, as if the legal statutes were still to be observed, against what he says in Gal. 2. In another way, according to the heresy of the Manichaeans, not because it is prohibited in the Law (which they condemn), but because they say that in meat, sheep, wine, and suchlike, that is, in any particles of these, the divine nature is mixed, which is not able to be thought about God. Now, it does not seem that he says this about legal observances about food, since he says **in the last times,** but about the food prohibited by the Manichaeans.

And he calls these Manichaeans demons because of all the heresies they give most honor to the devil since they make him a principle equal to the good God, establishing him as a principle of visible things.

The Apostle disproved this erroneous doctrine in two ways: first, from the intention of the God Who creates food; second, from the condition of the creature, when he says [n. 143], **For every creature.**

142. He says, then, that they prohibit abstinence, and this contrary to the intention of God, Who **hath created** them **to be received.** Gen. 9:3: *Even as the green herbs have I delivered them all to you.*

But you say: Were not the plants made for the animals, and the animals for man?

I respond that yes, even according to the Philosopher in Book I of the *Politics,* for the imperfect is ordered to the more perfect. And so, just as in generation there is a manifold perfection – first plants, then animals, and finally man – so also in the use of things.

And this likewise for their reception, but **with thanksgiving.** I Thess. 5:18: *In all things give thanks,* for they have been granted to you by God. Ps. 21:27: *The poor shall eat and shall be filled,* etc.

And he adds **by the faithful,** since those who receive with thanksgiving are faithful. For no one can give thanks to God for what is illicit. Indeed, he is stupid who gives thanks to God for fornication because God is not the agent of evil. Therefore, he gives thanks who understands that the use of food is licit. And this becomes known by faith alone; for this reason he says **by the faithful.**

143. Then when he says, **and by them that have known the truth. For every creature,** etc., he disproves the error from the condition of the creature: first, he proposes that creation is good in itself; second, he gives its use [n. 145].

144. He says, then, **For every creature of God is good,** namely, in its nature. Gen. 1:31: *And God saw all the things that He had made, and they were very good.* And from a good agent there is nothing but good.

145. But since there are many things good in themselves, yet whose use is not good, therefore he proves that every creature is good not only in itself but also regarding its use. And first he posits his argument; second, he proves it, when he says [n. 148], **For it is sanctified.**

146. He says, therefore, **and nothing** is **to be rejected** due to the divine law, although it may be for other reasons. For example, to eat poison, inasmuch as it is food, is not a sin, but it is to be rejected inasmuch as it is deadly. Likewise other foods, inasmuch as they are such, are not to be rejected, but inasmuch as they excite lust. Therefore, according to the discernment of reason and the regulation of charity, they are not to be rejected. Mt. 15:11: *Not that which goeth into the mouth defileth a man: but what cometh out of the mouth, this defileth a man.*

147. Why, then, were some foods in the Old Law prohibited? Augustine gives the reason in *Against Faustus* that in that state, not only words but also actions prefigured Christ. And so in food, vestments, and sacrifices, there were prefigurements of the future state. Thus, they are not prohibited in themselves but because they are figures of what is unclean, as pork was a sign of an unclean life. And so the prohibition of its flesh is a sign that in the law of Christ all uncleanness is prohibited. This is the example of Augustine. The word *foolish* can be considered inasmuch as it is a sound composed of letters, and thus it is good, or inasmuch as it is a sign and significative of such a thing, and thus it is evil and prohibited. Therefore, the use of every creature is good in itself.

148. The reason for which is that, if it were evil, this could not be except inasmuch as the devil, after the sin of man, had received power over them: because man sinned, he received power over man and those things which are his. But this power was taken away by Christ, and this is called sanctification. Hence, whatsoever thing we bless is exorcized first, and there is a prayer expelling the devil. And so he says, **For it is sanctified by the word of God,** that is, by Christ Who sanctifies all, as it says Jn. 17:9, **and prayer** of the faithful. Jas. 5:16: *For the continual prayer of a just man availeth much.*

Lecture Two

6 [n. 149] These things proposing to the brethren, thou shalt be a
good minister of Christ Jesus, nourished up in the words of faith,
and of the good doctrine which thou hast attained unto.

7 [n. 152] But avoid foolish and old wives' fables: and exercise thyself unto godliness.

8 [n. 155] For bodily exercise is profitable to little: but godliness is
profitable to all things, having promise of the life that now is, and
of that which is to come.

9 [n. 164] A faithful saying and worthy of all acceptation.

10 For therefore in this[2] we labour and are reviled, because we hope
in the living God, Who is the Saviour of all men, especially of the
faithful.

149. Above the Apostle reproved the superstitious abstinence from foods [n.
136]; here he commands Timothy to propose the foregoing teaching to the faithful. First, he shows what he ought to propose; second, what he ought to avoid,
when he says [n. 152], **But avoid.** He therefore gives two reasons why he ought
to propose the aforementioned: one from the office committed to him, and the
other from his education [n. 151].

150. He says therefore **These things,** which I said above, namely, that every
creature is good and nothing is to be rejected, etc., **proposing,** etc. For Timothy
was established in the office of the ministry of Christ, since all who have the duty
of preaching and ruling are established as ministers of Christ. I Cor. 4:1: *Let a
man so account of us as of the ministers of Christ,* etc. Now, he is a good minister who follows the intention of his lord. And thus Christ taught in Mt. 15:11: *Not
that which goeth into the mouth defileth a man;* and so this office requires him to
teach this.

151. Likewise his very education requires this. Prov. 22:6: *A young man
according to his way, even when he is old he will not depart from it.* And so it is
unfitting that those nourished on the truth of doctrine should depart from it.
Hence the man departing from the doctrine, by which the Church instructs her
children, is not a good minister of Christ. And so he says, **nourished up in the
words of faith.** For the word of God is spiritual nourishment by which the soul is
sustained, as the body is by food. Mt. 4:4: *Not in bread alone doth man live, but
in every word that proceedeth from the mouth of God.*

This word of faith teaches first regarding what is to be believed, and so he
says, **nourished up in the words of faith;** second, regarding what is to be done,
and so he adds, **and of the good doctrine.** Or, the word of faith, which even the
simple have, and of good doctrine, which is had by spiritual masters.

152. Then when he says, **But avoid,** he shows what is to be avoided, **foolish and old wives' fables.**

For according to the Philosopher a fable is composed of wonders, and they were invented in the beginning (as the Philosopher says in the *Poetics*) with the intention of leading men to virtue and away from vice. Now, the simple are led better by representations than by reason. Hence delight is found in a wonderful representation, since reason delights in comparison. And just as a representation in deeds is delightful, so is a representation in words: and this is a fable, words representing something, and, by so representing, moving to something. For the ancients had fables accommodated to anything true, and they hid the truth in fables. Therefore, there are two things in fables: that it contain a true understanding and represent something useful, and that it befit that truth. If, then, a fable which is unable to show any truth is proposed, it is inane. But it is a foolish fable which does not properly represent, as are the fables of the Talmud.

153. Then when he says, **and exercise thyself,** with superstitious abstinence having been already excluded, he here compares virtuous abstinence to other virtues.

And it must be known that Timothy was a very abstinent man. Hence it says below in chapter five, verse twenty-three, that he should take a little wine, and perchance also be solicitous about those things which pertain to mercy, since those who do not spare themselves frequently do not spare others either. And so he leads him to prefer godliness to abstinence. And first he brings forth a reason for godliness; second, he prefers it to abstinence, when he says [n. 155], **For bodily exercise;** third, he confirms a certain dictum, when he says [n. 158], **having promise;** fourth, he gives the form of teaching godliness, when he says in verse eleven [n. 165], **These things command.**

154. He says therefore, **exercise thyself unto godliness.** It is piety, or godliness, through which we pay our duty of benevolence to parents and fatherland, just as it is religion through which we show due worship to God. For piety signifies a certain affection for one's own beginning. Now, the beginning of generation is father and fatherland, and so a man must be of good will to them. And the father of all is God. Mal. 1:6: *If then I be a father, where is My honour?* Thus the word *piety* is taken for the worship of God, as Augustine says in Book IV of *On the City of God.* Hence, *eusebia* is the same as piety. Job 28:28: *Behold godliness, that is wisdom,* according to another translation, where ours has it thus: *Behold the fear of the Lord, that is wisdom.* Tit. 1:1: *Acknowledging of the truth, which is according to godliness.* But regarding earthly godliness, it befits piety that a man be benevolent to his compatriots. Regarding Christian piety it is required that a man be benevolent to all men, since we are all of the same fatherland. And so godliness is taken for mercy.

Therefore, since he says, **exercise thyself unto godliness,** this can be taken to pertain to the worship of God and to showing works of mercy. The Gloss: "Unto godliness, that is, to the worship of almighty God and works of mercy." And he says "exercise" and not "do" since exercise bespeaks promptness; thus, the one who is exercised does this more easily, enjoyably, and steadfastly. Prov. 24:27: *Diligently till thy ground.*

155. Then when he says, **For bodily exercise is profitable to little,** he prefers piety to abstinence: first, what bodily exercise avails; second, what piety does, when he says [n. 157], **but godliness is profitable.**

156. The bodily exercise of fasting and the such are not good in their own nature but penal, and if man had not sinned, there would be none of them; they are medicinal goods. For just as rhubarb is good inasmuch as it relieves cholera, so also do these crush concupiscence. Therefore, for this are they somewhat profitable. I Cor. 9:27: *But I chastise my body, and bring it into subjection,* etc. Col. 3:5: *Mortify therefore your members which are upon the earth.* And so, if a man were in a state in which he could not sin, he would not need fasting and the like. Hence Chrysostom, commenting on Mt. 16: *And Jesus came into the quarters of Caesarea Philippi,* etc., says, "John the pure man needed the medicine of fasting. Christ was God and not a pure man, and so needed not such." Therefore, it is profitable for little, namely, only for the illness of carnal sin, and not spiritual sin, since sometimes on account of abstinence a man falls into anger, vainglory, and the like.

157. Then when he says, **but godliness is profitable,** he prefers godliness to abstinence; here it is taken in either way, namely, for the worship of God and for mercy. And it **is profitable to all things,** since it wipes away all sins. Ecclus. 3:33: *Water quencheth a flaming fire, and alms resisteth sins.* Likewise, it promotes the good. Ecclus. 17:18: *The alms of a man is as a signet with him, and shall preserve the grace of a man as the apple of the eye.* Again, it deserves the special mercy of God. Mt. 5:7: *Blessed are the merciful: for they shall obtain mercy.* And so, to show this, the Lord in Mt. 25:34 especially mentions works of mercy.

158. This he proves, adding, **having promise.** For in the precepts of the Decalogue one alone is found which pertains to godliness, namely, to honor father and mother, and under this all the precepts are contained, unto whatever benefice there is to be granted to one's neighbor; and among those precepts which regard one's neighbor, this is the only precept having a promise, namely, that you live a long life, as it says in Ex. 20:12. And the Apostle here interprets long life according to the present and future life; hence he says, **of the life that now is, and of that which is to come.** Prov. 3:16: *Length of days is in her right hand.*

159. But then there is the question, that sometimes someone is found following godliness who yet has not longevity.

I respond that, as the Philosopher says, these temporal goods are good inasmuch as they are useful for happiness. Hence, if someone were to have so much of temporal goods that on account of them he would be impeded from the good of virtue and happiness, this would not be for his good fortune but for evil, as it is said in Book X of the *Ethics*. And length of life is one of these temporal goods, and is good to the degree that it aids in virtue. Now, sometimes it is the occasion for sinning, and so God on occasion takes it away from man, not because He fails in His promise, but because He gives what is better. Wis. 4:11: *He was taken away lest wickedness should alter his understanding.*

160. There is another question, that the Apostle prefers godliness to bodily exercise since it has the hope of the present and the future life. But does not bodily exercise have hope? Otherwise the one fasting would not merit eternal life.

I respond that when there are two virtues and one contains the other, that which is of the superior virtue *per se* befits the inferior one *per accidens*. Now, the virtue to which it is befitting *per se* to merit eternal life is charity, whose proper and immediate effect is godliness. And so according to its proper notion it reaches to the merit of eternal life. But abstinence does not, except inasmuch as it is ordered to charity and godliness, since if the one fasting does not refer this to the love of God, he would not merit eternal life.

161. The third question is that Ambrose says here in a gloss, "Every height of Christian teaching is in mercy and godliness. If a man, following mercy and godliness, suffers the dangers of the flesh, he will without doubt be beaten, yet he will not perish."

There is here a doubt about the first part, that mercy and godliness are immediately ordered to charity, in which is the height of the Christian religion.

I respond that it was the opinion of some, as Augustine says in Book X of *On the City of God,* that those doing works of godliness, however much they sin corporally, do not in the end perish eternally. And this authority concurs. Likewise we read in Mt. 25:41 that Christ only upbraids those to be damned for a lack of mercy; therefore eternal punishment is due only to the unmerciful.

But Augustine says to the contrary that the Apostle says in Gal. 5:21, *They who do such things shall not obtain the kingdom of God.* For however much someone exercises works of mercy, if he dies in mortal sin, he will not enter the kingdom.

To the other side it is to be said that the one who is not merciful will not receive mercy, according to Ecclus. 30:24: *Have pity on thy own soul, pleasing God.* And this happens if a man be joined to God through love; otherwise he is not merciful.

To what it says in the Gospel, Augustine responds that whoever sins is not thrust immediately into hell, since a place of penance remains for him; but he is thrust there who finally dies in sin, and penitence pertains to mercy.

162. But what of: "If a man, following mercy and godliness, suffers the dangers of the flesh, etc."?

I respond that he speaks of mortal danger. And when he says, "Yet he will not perish," although this is not the case from worthiness, yet it is from congruence, inasmuch as the mind is disposed to good; hence the Lord revives a man after a fall. And this chiefly seems to be in godliness, since a man, by bestowing good to others, leads them to pray for himself. And the Lord sometimes grants pardon to sinners by the prayers of the saints, inasmuch as pardon for sins and the gift of grace is obtained for them, since man can merit first grace for another congruently; otherwise it would be for nothing that the Church prays for sinners.

163. Then when he says, **A faithful saying,** he shows that the future life is promised to us: first he shows this from the labor of the saints; second, from their hope, when he says, **because we hope;** third, from the goodness of God, when he says, **Who is the Saviour.**

164. Therefore he says that this **saying,** namely, that godliness has a promise, is **faithful.** This was explained above.

And why? **For therefore in this,** that is, because of this, that we might attain eternal life, **we labour.** II Tim. 2:6: *The husbandman, that laboureth, must first partake of the fruits.* Likewise that we might do good, although we endure evils; hence he says, **and are reviled.** Jas. 1:4: *And patience hath a perfect work.* Rom. 5:3–4: *Knowing that tribulation worketh patience; and patience trial,* etc.

And we endure because of the hope of life, **because we hope in the living God,** Who is the savior of the present and future life.

Again, from the duty of God, which is to save. Is. 43:11: *I am, I am the Lord: and there is no saviour besides Me.* And so God was made incarnate and called Jesus. Mt. 1:21: *He shall save His people from their sins.* And Jesus is the same as savior because He saves all with bodily salvation – so he says, **of all men** – and the good with spiritual salvation – and so he says, **especially of the faithful.**

Lecture Three

11 [n. 165] These things command and teach.

12 [n. 167] Let no man despise thy youth: but be thou an example of the faithful in word, in conversation, in charity, in faith, in chastity.

13 [n. 170] Till I come, attend unto reading, to exhortation, and to doctrine.

14 [n. 172] Neglect not the grace that is in thee, which was given thee by prophecy, with imposition of the hand of the priest.³

15 [n. 175] Meditate upon these things, be wholly in these things: that thy profiting may be manifest to all.

16 [n. 176] Take heed to thyself and to doctrine: be earnest in them. For in doing this thou shalt both save thyself and them that hear thee.

Chapter 5

1 [n. 177] An ancient man rebuke not, but entreat him as a father: young men, as brethren:

2 [n. 179] Old women, as mothers: young women, as sisters, in all chastity.

165. Above the Apostle exhorted Timothy to godliness [n. 153]; here he gives him the form of teaching piety. First, he enjoins him to teach godliness; second, how to be suitable to teach godliness, when he says [n. 167], **Let no man despise;** third, how to teach diverse people in diverse ways, when he says [n. 177], An ancient man.

166. The teaching of godliness consists in two things: what is to be done and what is to be believed. Those who have authority must not only teach what is to be done but also command it. And so he says, **These things command.** Tit. 2:15: *Rebuke with all authority.* Regarding what is to be believed he says, **and teach.** Mt. 28:19: *Teach ye all nations.* Job 4:3: *Behold thou hast taught many.*

167. Then when he says, **Let no man,** etc., he shows how he should be fit for the aforementioned point: first, for commanding; second, for teaching, when he says [n. 170], **Till I come.** He does two things regarding the first: first, he teaches how he should exclude contempt; second, he makes this clear through what it is to be excluded, when he says [n. 169], **but be thou an example.**

168. A precept does not have efficacy except through the authority of the one commanding, and so when an authority is despised, commands are in vain, which happens most in adolescence, for such are not believed to be prudent. Hence, according to the Philosopher, no one elects youths as leaders. And so he says, **Let no man,** etc., as if to say: Although you are young, yet let your manners exhibit

maturity. Tob. 1:4: *And when he was younger than any of the tribe of Nephtali, yet did he no childish thing in his work.*

169. Then he shows how contempt is excluded, saying, **but be thou,** etc., so that you may show yourself to be such as an example of doing what you teach with words.

And it is to be noticed that there is a manifold difference among those things in which the prelate is the example. For certain things are ordered to one's neighbor, some to God, and some to oneself. Regarding one's neighbor he says, **be thou an example of the faithful,** so that what you command with words you should fulfill in deeds. I Pet. 5:3: *Being made a pattern of the flock from the heart.* And this likewise in speaking; hence he says **in word,** that is, a word well pondered, ordered, and circumspect. Col. 4:6: *Let your speech be always in grace seasoned with salt.* I Pet. 4:11: *If any man speak, let him speak, as the words of God.* Likewise **in** exterior **conversation,** so that as he excels in place and dignity, so should he in honest conversation. I Pet. 2:12: *Having your conversation good among the Gentiles.* Mt. 5:16: *That they may see your good works, and glorify your Father Who is in heaven.*

Man is ordered to God by charity, which perfects the affections; hence he says, **in charity.** I Cor. 13:1: *If I speak with the tongues of men,* etc. Col. 3:14: *But above all these things have charity.* Likewise through faith, which illumines the intellect; hence he says **in faith.** Heb. 11:6: *But without faith it is impossible to please God.* This especially befits prelates, who are guardians of the faith. For this reason in Lk. 22:32 the Lord prays especially for the faith of Peter: *But I have prayed for thee, that thy faith fail not.*

Regarding himself, chastity orders life and mind since it is extremely indecent that the lives of ministers be discordant with the life of the Lord. Ecclus. 10:2: *As the judge of the people is himself, so also are his ministers.* Now, Christ so loved chastity that He willed to be born from a virgin, and He Himself kept it; hence it follows: **in chastity.**

170. Then when he says, **Till I come,** etc., he shows how he should be fit for teaching: first, he does this; second, he gives a reason for the foregoing admonitions when he says [n. 172], **Neglect not the grace.**

171. A man is suitable to teach by two things: reading, by which he acquires knowledge, and practice, by which he is made ready. And so he says, **Till I come, attend unto reading** of holy books. I Mach. 12:9: *Having for our comfort the holy books that are in our hands.* Jn. 5:39: *Search the scriptures.* And this is signified in Ex. 25:12–15, where it is said that in the ark there always had to be poles in the rings, and rings on the corners, as it were always ready to be carried.

For practice it is necessary to have exhortation regarding things to be done, and teaching regarding what is to be known. And so he adds, **to exhortation, and to doctrine.** Jer. 3:15: *And I will give you pastors according to my own heart, and they shall feed you with knowledge and doctrine.*

172. Then when he says, **Neglect not,** he gives the reason for the foregoing admonition: first, he gives the cause from the gift received; second, the cause from the reward expected, when he says [n. 176], **Take heed.** Again, first he gives the reason; second, he shows how what is contained in the reason is able to be fulfilled, when he says [n. 175], **Meditate upon these things.**

173. He says therefore, **Neglect not,** as if to say: Indeed, see that he who receives grace ought not to be negligent in it but make it fruitful. The servant hiding his money in the ground is punished for his negligence, as it says in Mt. 25:24–30. **Neglect not the grace that is in thee.** By this understand either the episcopal dignity, or the gift of knowledge or of prophecy or of miracles, in which nothing is to be neglected. II Cor. 6:1: *Receive not the grace of God in vain.*

Grace, I say, **which was given thee by prophecy,** that is, through divine inspiration. For in the primitive Church, when elections took place innocently and for the sake of God, no one was assumed to the episcopacy except through divine election, as were Ambrose and Nicholas. And here he calls this inspiration prophecy. Hence, the Gloss says this was through the election of the saints, for the saints did not choose a man they did not know to be chosen by God. Likewise, the Apostle foresaw this to be profitable to the people. Prov. 29:18: *When prophecy shall fail,* that is, such a mode of election, *the people shall be scattered abroad.*

And how? **With imposition of the hand of the priest.** Another text has *hands of the priest.* As was said above [n. 109], the names of presbyters and bishops are used indiscriminately, since they were priests and presbyters, that is, bishops, who were received with the imposition of hands. Num. 27:18: *Take Josue the son of Nun, a man in whom is the Spirit, and put thy hand upon him.* The Lord also imposed hands on children, as it says in Mt. 19:15. Likewise, the Apostles imposed hands on the seven deacons, as is related in Acts 6:6. And so hands are imposed on those ordained to the episcopacy.

174. But there is the question why priest is said in the singular when a bishop must be ordained by three?

I respond that he says this because, even if many are fitting, yet one of them is principal and the others are assistants. Nevertheless, it can be said that then this practice did not yet exist and then there were few bishops, who could not be gathered together.

Another text has *of the priesthood,* that is, of those who imposed hands on him not inasmuch as they were men, but inasmuch as they were priests. And this imposition signifies a gathering of grace, not that the ministers give grace, but that they signify the grace given by Christ. Hence, it belongs to them alone who are ministers of Christ. And so he says *of the priesthood* or *of the priest* since there is one imposition of hands which happens by deacons and one by priests.

175. Then when he says, **Meditate upon these things,** he shows how what was said is to be fulfilled, namely, by continually meditating on those things

which respect his office. Heb. 13:17: *For they watch as being to render an account of your souls.* **Meditate,** that is, think frequently of those things which pertain to the care of your flock. **Be wholly in these things,** that is, let all your powers be for these things. And why? **That thy profiting may be manifest to all.** Mt. 5:15: *Neither do men light a candle and put it under a bushel,* etc. Phil. 4:5: *Let your modesty be known to all men.*

176. And he ought to keep these things on account of the promised reward, and so he adds, **Take heed to thyself and to doctrine.** Some so attend to doctrine that they neglect care of themselves, but the Apostle says that he should attend first to himself and afterwards to doctrine. Ecclus. 30:24: *Have pity on thy own soul, pleasing God.* For which reason Jesus began to do and to teach. **Be earnest in them,** that is, do them often. II Tim. 4:2: *Be instant in season.* And the fruit of this will be copious since **in doing this thou shalt both save thyself and them that hear thee,** which is indeed great. Jas. 5:20: *He must know that he who causeth a sinner to be converted from the error of his way, shall save his soul from death, and shall cover a multitude of sins.* Dan. 12:3: *They that instruct many to justice, as stars for all eternity.* For this reason the reward of an aureole is due to doctors.

177. Then when he says, **An ancient man,** etc., he shows how he ought to hand on his doctrine to different men in different ways. And he gives two diversities: one according to age; the other according to sex. According to age: first, regarding men; second, regarding women, when he says [n. 179], **Old women.**

178. He says, then, **An ancient man rebuke not, but entreat him as a father.** Lev. 19:32: *Honour the person of the aged man.* And so they are not to be rebuked sharply but entreated. I Pet. 5:1: *The ancients therefore that are among you, I beseech, who am myself also an ancient.* And if an aged Peter did this, how much more should a young man?

On the contrary, it says in Is. 65:20, *The child shall die a hundred years old, and the sinner being a hundred years old shall be accursed.*

I respond that an old man loses the honor of old age because of his excessive malice, and then he is to be rebuked.

Young men, as brethren. Mt. 23:8: *All you are brethren.* Ez. 34:4: *You ruled over them with rigour.*

179. On the part of women there is the difference of age: **Old women, as mothers.** This is especially the case with those who are not young. Below 5:3: *Honour widows.* **Young women, as sisters,** with the love of charity. And this **in all chastity.** For spiritual love for women, unless it be cautious, degenerates to carnal love; thus, in those things which pertain to young women chastity is to be used, and so the Apostle adds this. Wherefore, the Pope writing to them says, "My beloved in Christ," but to men he says simply, "Beloved sons."

Chapter Five

Lecture One

3 [n. 180] **Honour widows, that are widows indeed.**
4 [n. 182] **But if any widow have children, or grandchildren, let her learn first to govern her own house, and to make a return of duty to her parents: for this is acceptable before God.**
5 [n. 185] **But she that is a widow indeed, and desolate, let her trust in God, and continue in supplications and prayers night and day.**
6 [n. 189] **For she that liveth in pleasures, is dead while she is living.**
7 [n. 190] **And this give in charge, that they may be blameless.**
8 [n. 191] **But if anyone have not care of her own, and especially of those of her house, she[1] hath denied the faith, and is worse than an infidel.**

180. Above the Apostle instructed Timothy about the use of foods and about abstinence [n.136]; here he instructs him about the dispensation of foods for spiritual persons, namely, those foods that were dispensed to widows and teachers. First, therefore, he instructs him about widows; second, about teachers, when he says in verse seventeen [n. 211], **Let the priests that rule well.**

Concerning the first he first shows how foods must be administered to widows and teachers through the Church; second, he manifests what he said, when he says [n.182], **But if any widow;** third, he shows the reason for what was said, when he says [n.191], **But if anyone.**

181. Therefore he says, **Honour widows,** not only by showing reverence, but by giving necessities. For by *honor* these two things are understood. Whence in the precept of honoring one's parents even giving assistance is understood; as if

he said: Provide in necessities. And this began from the beginning of the Church. Acts 6:1: *There arose a murmuring of the Greeks against the Hebrews, for that their widows were neglected in the daily ministration.* II Mach. 3:10: *These were sums deposited, and provisions for the subsistence of the widows and the fatherless.*

But to which widows? **That are widows indeed.** Widow is said as one parted[2] from her husband, that is, separated. For she is truly a widow who does not have other persons by which she may be sustained, and to her necessities are given from the alms of the faithful.

182. Then when he says, **But if any widow,** he shows who are true widows; first, he shows who are not true widows; second, who truly are when he says [n. 185], **But she.** Concerning the first, he first treats the arrangement of those who are indeed widows; second, he assigns a reason when he says [n. 184], **for this.**

183. Therefore, he instructs that such should **learn to govern** their **own house.** Tob. 10:13: *They taught their daughter to take care of the family.*[3] And he says **first** since a widow who is assumed to the care of the Church ought to be vigilant with respectability. And so he says, **let her learn.** Likewise, she ought to serve her parents, and thus he says, **a return,** etc., as if he said: As her parents nourished her, so she must nourish them if she has them.

184. And the reason for this is assigned when he adds, **for this is acceptable,** etc., since these returns are made not only to men, but also to God. And this is clear since the Lord gave a particular command about this in Ex. 20:12. Thus, the Lord Jesus also did not wish it omitted in the Gospel. Likewise, nature teaches this, that a man should repay benefits to those who gave them. But no one has given as much as parents.

185. Then when he says, **But she that is a widow indeed,** he treats about true widows: first, he shows which are true widows; second, how they must be instructed, when he says [n. 187], **let her trust in God.**

186. Therefore, he says, **But she that is a widow indeed, and desolate,** that is, who does not have human consolation, namely, sons or parents, and such a one who does not have other shelter, **let her trust in God,** for regarding temporal aids she is aided through the Church.

187. And she ought to be instructed: first, that she may be trained in good; second, that she may beware of evil, when he says [n. 190], **And this give in charge.** Regarding the first he does two things: first, he shows with what this widow ought to be occupied; second, he assigns a reason when he says [n. 189], **For she.**

188. Therefore he says, **let her trust in God,** and let her exercise the suitable act of hope, since it is done through prayer and supplication, through which what is hoped for is obtained. For prayer is the elevation of the mind to God;

supplication is the asking through something sacred. And therefore he adds, **and continue in supplications and prayers.** And he says, **night and day,** since it is impossible that the soul of man be without some care. And therefore, a widow who has nothing else in which she is occupied ought to be devoted always to God. Lk. 2:37: *Anna departed not from the temple,* etc. Judith 8:5: *And she made herself a private chamber in the upper part of her house for praying.*[4]

189. Then when he says, **For she,** he gives the reason why she ought to be devoted always to prayer, namely, that it is impossible that a soul not be occupied with some delight. And when an idle soul is not occupied with useful things, it is necessary that it be occupied with carnal things. And therefore he says that a widow so desolate should be devoted to prayer, since if she does not have this occupation, she gives herself to pleasures, and thus she dies the death of sin. Apoc. 3:1: *Thou hast the name of being alive: and thou art dead.* Is. 38:19: *The living,* namely interiorly, *the living,* namely exteriorly, *he shall give praise to Thee.*

And although pleasures be an occasion of death to all men, yet they are especially to women, since by their nature they have softness of mind. Therefore, since pleasures soften the mind, it necessarily follows that women be softened all the more. Jer. 31:22: *How long wilt thou be dissolute in pleasures,*[5] *O wandering daughter?* Apoc. 18:7: *As much as she hath glorified herself, and lived in pleasures,*[6] *so much torment and sorrow give ye to her; because she saith in her heart: I sit a queen, and am no widow; and sorrow I shall not see.*

190. Then when he says, **And this give in charge,** he shows that they must be instructed to guard themselves from evil. And therefore he says that they should forbid this, commanding that the women who are sustained by the Church **may be blameless.** Ps. 92:7: *Holiness becometh Thy house, O Lord.*

191. Then when he says, **But if anyone,** he assigns a reason for this since he said, **let her learn first,** etc., saying that it is fitting that a widow be instructed concerning this, since this is from necessity. And therefore he says, **of her own,** namely, of those whose care rests upon her, and **especially of those of her house.** Cant. 2:4: *He set in order charity in me.*

And as Augustine said, we can will good to all, but those who are close to us are esteemed as a certain share, and therefore must be more loved. Ambrose says in his book *On Duties* that the reason for this is that perhaps for those for whom it is not shameful to receive from one's own, for them it would be shameful to receive from others. **She hath denied the faith** through works, since if she does not preserve the faith in those whom nature joined to her, it follows that neither does she in others. Tit. 1:16: *They profess that they know God: but in their works they deny Him.*

192. But is this true? **And is worse than an infidel.** The contrary of which

is seen through Augustine. Jn. 15: 22: *If I had not come,* etc. He says about this text that here He speaks about the sin of infidelity, which is graver than other sins, since sins against God are graver than those against a neighbor.

I respond that the state of the faithful from the unfaithful can be considered in two ways. First, regarding the state of sin, and thus the unfaithful are in the state of sin, since they do nothing acceptable to God. Second, regarding one sin, and then the contrary; for if both the faithful and the unfaithful commit adultery, the faithful sins more, since he does an injury to the faith. And thus he says that if a faithful disdains the care of his parents, he sins more gravely than if an unfaithful had done this. II Pet. 2:21: *For it had been better for them not to have known the way of justice, than after they have known it, to turn back.*

Lecture Two

9 [n. 193] **Let a widow be chosen of no less than threescore years of age, who hath been the wife of one husband.**

10 [n. 196] **Having testimony for her good works, if she have brought up children, if she have received to harbour, if she have washed the saints' feet, if she have ministered to them that suffer tribulation, if she have diligently followed every good work.**

11 [n. 200] **But the younger widows avoid. For when they have grown wanton in Christ, they will marry:**

12 [n. 204] **Having damnation, because they have made void their first faith.**

13 [n. 205] **And withal being idle they learn to go about from house to house: and are not only idle, but tattlers also, and busybodies, speaking things which they ought not.**

14 [n. 206] **I will therefore that the younger should marry, bear children, be mistresses of families, give no occasion to the adversary to speak evil.**

15 [n. 209] **For some are already turned aside after Satan.**

16 [n. 210] **If any of the faithful have widows, let him minister to them, and let not the church be charged: that there may be sufficient for them that are widows indeed.**

193. Above the Apostle showed that widows must be sustained by the Church [n.180]; here he shows which are to be sustained: first, he shows which must be chosen; second, which must be avoided, when he says [n. 200], **younger widows.** Concerning the first he does three things: first, he shows that she must be chosen on account of age; second, on account of chastity; third, on account of the exercise of good works [n.196].

194. On account of age, since she must be **threescore years of age.**

But of which choosing does he treat? To this it can be responded in two ways.

In the first manner, he speaks of an election in which one is chosen to direct the governing of the other widows who are nourished by the Church, and thus an old woman is preferred, that nothing may be suspected about her continence. Num. 4:3: *From thirty years old and upward, to fifty years old.*

But on the contrary, it seems that the Church does otherwise, since younger women are made abbesses.

I respond that it is disordered that excessively young women are made abbesses, but nonetheless the concern of the Church is not as great for those who are cloistered, as for those who are free.

In another manner, he speaks of an election in which one is chosen to be sustained by the stipends of the Church, and of such, one not less than sixty years of age is chosen, since young women can labor with their hands, as did the Apostle, who could have lived from the Gospel yet nonetheless labored, but old women should rest.

195. A widow must be chosen by her chastity. Therefore he says, **who hath been the wife of one husband.** As it is required in a bishop that he be the husband of one wife, so in an old woman that she be the wife of one man.

The Gloss: "He says this on account of the aforementioned sacrament." This Gloss is only an authority and profits little. For the reason does not seem to be taken from any sacrament, since the women did not receive any sacraments to be administered. But this is said for the sake of firmness, that they may have the continued intention of sustaining widowhood.

But Jerome, in a letter to Geruntia and in another case to Esicia, assigns another reason, namely, that there was a custom among the Gentiles that in sacrifices to gods no woman presided who had two husbands. And therefore the Apostle wished that those who were nourished by the foods of the Church be no less chaste. Judith 15:11: *Because thou hast loved chastity, and after thy husband hast not known any other,* etc. Lk. 2:36: *She had lived with her husband seven years from her virginity.* And therefore it is as a laudable sign of chastity, that she was the wife of one husband.

196. Then when he says, **for her good works,** etc., he shows that the widow must be chosen on account of the exercise of good works: first, in general; second, in particular, when he says [n. 198], **if she have brought up children;** third, he gives him to understand the same about all good works, when he says [n. 199], **if she have diligently followed every good work.**

197. Regarding the first he says, **for her goods works.** Prov. 31:31: *Let her works praise her in the gates.* And he says, **Having testimony.** Jn. 5:36: *The works which the Father hath given Me to perfect; the works themselves, which I do, give testimony of Me.* For exterior works show interior faith. Jas. 2:18: *Shew me thy faith without works; and I will shew thee, by works, my faith.*

198. But which works? First toward her own, then toward others. Toward her own he says, **if she have brought up children,** namely, in the fear of God and in chastity. Ecclus. 7:25: *Hast thou children? instruct them.*

Regarding others, he treats three works of piety. First mercy, since women, having soft hearts, are naturally merciful. Therefore, he first teaches hospitality when he says, **if she have received to harbour.** Rom. 7:13: *Pursuing hospitality.* Second, with this he likewise posits humility, saying, **if she have washed the saints' feet;** for thus must saints be received and honorably treated. Lk. 10:40: *But Martha was busy about much serving.* So did Christ, Jn. 8:14: *If then I being* *your Lord and Master, have washed your feet; you also ought to wash one another's feet.* The Gloss of Augustine, *The Tractates on John:* "The brothers do this themselves for one another even in the visible work itself, and what they do not do with their hands, they do not do with their heart. However it is much better that it also be done with the hands, lest the Christian disdain to do what Christ did. For in him who is humbled to the feet of his brother, humility is stirred up in the heart, or if it already existed, the effect of humility is strengthened."

Third, fortitude and constancy, namely, that she may assist the troubled; whence he says, **if she have ministered to them that suffer tribulation.** Heb. 10:34: *You had compassion on them that were in bands.*

199. Then when he says, **if she have diligently followed,** he concludes in what things she ought to be good, saying, **if she have diligently followed every good work,** that is, if she have pursued such works. Gal. 6:10: *Therefore, whilst we have time, let us work good to all men.*

200. Then when he says, **younger widows,** etc., he shows which widows must be avoided: first, he shows which; second, he assigns a reason when he says [n. 202], **For when they have grown wanton.**

201. Therefore he says: Widows of such an age shall be chosen, but avoid the younger widows, that is, you should not indiscriminately take widows into dependence on the Church, especially the infamous and the profligate. Or **avoid them**, regarding fellowship and familiarity. Ecclus. 42:14: *For better is the iniquity of a man,* that is, more secure for dwelling, *than a woman doing a good turn;* whence it is added: *and a woman bringing shame and reproach.* The first explanation is literal.

202. Then when he says, **For when they have grown wanton,** etc., a twofold reason is assigned from the twofold danger [nn. 203 and 205] which is imminent.

Concerning the first he does two things: first, he proposes the first danger; second, he responds to the question when he says [n. 204], **Having damnation.**

For if young women are assumed to dependence upon the Church, there are two consequences: that they should have satiety, and that they should not be forced to work with their hands. From both, however, danger is imminent.

203. From the first is the danger to chastity [n. 205], whence he says, **when they have grown wanton.** Sometimes wantonness is taken to mean superfluity of the venereal act, and thus it is one of the seven capital vices. Indeed, other times it is taken to mean every superfluity of corporal things, and thus it is taken here; as if he said: When they will have had a superabundance **in Christ,** that is, through the support of Christ, then **they will marry.** Ex. 32:6: *The people sat down to eat, and drink, and they rose up to play.* Valerius says, that the place of Ceres, that is, food, and of father Bacchus is near Venus. Os. 4:10: *And they shall eat and shall not be filled: they have committed fornication, and have not ceased.*

204. Then when he says, **Having,** etc., he responds to the tacit question.

For someone can say: What evil is there if they marry? For you say, along with I Cor. 7:28, *And if a woman[7] marry, she hath not sinned.* Therefore he says: **Having damnation, because they have made void their first faith,** etc., namely, of chastity, to which they have vowed themselves. For otherwise they would not have been taken for nourishment. Whence Augustine says here that from intention alone one incurs damnation. This is true if it be for a determinate man and with consent. Eccles. 5:3: *If thou hast vowed any thing to God, defer not to pay it.* Lk. 9:62: *No man putting his hand to the plough, and looking back, is fit for the kingdom of God.*

205. From the second, namely, that they do not work, three evils are incurred. The first evil is idleness. Ecclus. 33:29: *For idleness hath taught much evil.* Ez. 16:49: *Behold this was the iniquity of Sodom thy sister, pride, fulness of bread, and abundance, and idleness.* Prov. 12:11: *He that pursueth idleness is very foolish.*

From idleness follow these evils. The heart of a woman is not as strong as that of a man, and on account of this it is moved to diverse things. If therefore one is not bound to work, his heart is necessarily carried to diverse things. And therefore it is a danger that women be idle; whence the ancients kept them occupied.

Likewise, they are made unstable regarding place, since they are accustomed to go around to houses. Prov. 7:12: *Now abroad, now in the streets, now lying in wait near the corners.* Jer. 14:10: *[They] have loved to move their feet, and have not rested, and have not pleased the Lord.*

Regarding words he says, **tattlers.** For if they are not occupied, they devote much to idle talk. Prov. 7:10: *Talkative and wandering, not bearing to be quiet.*

Regarding the heart he says, **busybodies,** because if they are not occupied against this, they meddle in the affairs of others and thus speak **things which they ought not,** since they judge the things done by all. Ecclus. 9:11: *Her conversation burneth as fire.*

206. Then when he says, **I will therefore,** etc., he shows to which work they must be devoted, namely, that they should marry: first, he proposes the teaching; second, he assigns a reason when he says [n. 209], **For some are already.**

207. Therefore he says, **I will the younger** women, that is, widows, **to marry.** On the contrary, I Cor. 7:8: *It is good for them if they so continue;* therefore he ought to say: I will them to be continent.

I respond: Jerome says that he willed that, I Cor. 7:7, as his chief intention, but each one has his own gift from God. Therefore he adds in verse nine: *It is better to marry than to be burnt.* Therefore, it must be seen of which situation he is speaking, lest in that situation they should make void their first faith. Therefore, it is understood that he says here **I will,** not as his chief intention.

208. **Bear children,** and not kill them secretly through abortion. Above 2:15:

Yet she shall be saved through childbearing; if she continue in faith. **Be mistresses of families,** namely, that they be occupied, and not be tattlers wandering through houses. And likewise I wish this, that they **give no occasion to the adversary,** that is, either a devil, or a pagan, **to speak evil,** that is, that they be able to speak evil of the churches of God. On this he concludes the life of the widow, that she may live thus and not provoke others to lustfulness. I Pet. 2:15: *So is the will of God, that by doing well you may put to silence the ignorance of foolish men.*

209. And the reason for this is that certain ones vowing chastity **are already turned aside,** voiding the vow. And such follow **after Satan** through imitation, since he apostatized from the communion of angels.

210. Then when he says, **If any,** he shows which widows must be nourished by private persons: first, he shows the teaching; second, he assigns a reason when he says, **and not let the church be charged.**

Therefore, he says that she who is indeed a widow should hope in God, but if she have brothers or parents she should be sustained by them. And therefore he says, **If any of the faithful,** etc., since this is a work of piety.

And this is done **that the church not be charged,** etc. And this was necessary since then the Church did not have possessions, though now it has possessions reserved for this. I Thess. 2:9: *Working night and day, lest we should be chargeable to any of you.*

Lecture Three

17 [n. 211] Let the priests that rule well, be esteemed worthy of double honour: especially they who labour in the word and doctrine.

18 [n. 214] For the scripture saith: *Thou shalt not muzzle the ox that treadeth out the corn*: **and,** *The labourer is worthy of his reward.*

19 [n. 218] Against a priest receive not an accusation, but under two or three witnesses.

20 [n. 220] Them that sin reprove before all: that the rest also may have fear.

21 [n. 223] I charge thee before God, and Christ Jesus, and the elect angels, that thou observe these things without prejudice, doing nothing by declining to either side.

22 [n. 225] Impose not hands lightly upon any man, neither be partaker of other men's sins. Keep thyself chaste.

23 [n. 228] Do not still drink water, but use a little wine for thy stomach's sake, and thy frequent infirmities.

24 [n. 229] Some men's sins are manifest, going before to judgment: and some men they follow after.

25 [n. 231] In like manner also good deeds are manifest: and they that are otherwise, cannot be hid.

211. Above the Apostle taught about honoring the widows who are sustained by stipends of the Church [n.180]; here he teaches about the honor of priests: first, he establishes how Timothy should relate to them; second, he shows how certain sayings are to be understood, when he says [n.229], **Some men's sins.** Likewise, he shows first that priests are to be honored; second, he confirms this through an authority, when he says [n.214], **For the scripture saith.** Regarding the first he does two things: first, he shows that they are to be honored; second, he shows for what reason they are to be honored when he says [n.213], **especially they who labour.**

212. Therefore he says, **Let the priests that rule well.** A priest is the same thing as an elder, and in the same way that the old are accustomed to have prudence. Job 12:12: *In length of days prudence.* And so whoever is selected to rule the Church ought to be prudent, as it says in Lk. 12:42, *The faithful and wise steward,* etc. And so, the prelates of the church, namely, bishops and priests, are called presbyters. And therefore he says **that rule,** etc. Not only this, but they should rule well, for the glory of God and not for their own advantage. Ez. 34:2: *Woe to the shepherds of Israel, that fed themselves.* Similarly he should be prudent, to give to each in his own time. I Cor. 4:2: *Here now it is required among the dispensers, that a man be found faithful.*

Such **be esteemed worthy of double honour,** one of which is in the administration of necessities. Tob. 1:16: *And had ten talents of silver of that with which he had been honoured by the king,* etc. Prov. 3:9: *Honour the Lord with thy substance.* The other is in the showing of reverence. Ecclus. 4:7: *And humble thy soul to the ancient.* Heb. 13:17: *Obey your prelates.* Prov. 21:21: *For all her domestics are clothed with double garments.* Is. 61:7: *Therefore shall they receive double in their land.*

213. But here **especially** honor is particularly shown to them who deserve it by their own labor, indeed **who labour in the word** of preaching. Phil. 2:15: *Among whom you shine as lights in the world, holding forth the word of life.* Col. 3:16: *Let the word of Christ dwell in you abundantly, teaching in all wisdom.* Likewise **in doctrine,** that is, in teaching. Jer. 3:15: *And I will give you pastors according to My own heart, and they shall feed you with knowledge and doctrine.* Also Eph. 4:11 joins pastors and teachers because that is the office of a bishop.

214. Then when he says, **For the scripture saith,** he proves this through a twofold authority, and the first he introduces following the mystical sense, the other following the literal sense, when he says [n. 216], *The labourer is worthy.*

215. Therefore he says, **For the scripture saith,** from Deut. 25:4: *Thou shalt not muzzle the ox that treadeth out the corn.* In I Cor. 9:8 the Apostle proves this is to be understood about teachers because God has no care for bulls, not that they should be without divine providence, but because God does not care in what manner men handle bulls, who are able to make use of them as they wish. Whence that law is not about bulls, but it is said through a likeness. It is as if he had said: You should not hinder men laboring in the office of preaching and ruling so that they cannot live by that office. For by bulls teachers are understood. Prov. 14:4: *But where there is much corn, there the strength of the ox is manifest.* By crops the faithful are understood. Mt. 9:37: *The harvest indeed is great,* etc. Therefore, preachers and teachers are not to be prohibited from having expenses.

216. The other authority is *The labourer is worthy of his reward,* Mt. 10:10. Or better, it is in the Old Testament, although it is not so written. Neither was the Apostle accustomed to bring authority from the Gospel, except with the express of the speaker; but this is taken from Lev. 19:3: *The wages of him that hath been hired by thee shall not abide with thee until the morning.*

217. But are not expenses rewards? Augustine in the Gloss says yes: "Yet the Gospel is not for sale, such that it is preached for the sake of reward." For what is given to a man for a final recompense is sometimes called a reward, and in this case far be it from preachers to have such expenses be their reward. Sometimes that alone is a reward by which someone is made worthy by his laboring, and this is called a reward taken broadly. And so Augustine says: "Therefore let them take," etc.

218. Then when he says, **Against a priest,** he treats the correction of priests,

saying that priests who rule well are to be honored with a twofold honor, but evil ones are to be corrected. Regarding this he does three things: first, he says that an accusation against them is not to be admitted easily; second, that those at fault are to be corrected publicly, when he says [n. 220], **Them that sin;** third, that they should not be condemned rashly, when he says [n. 224], **that thou observe these things.**

219. He says therefore: You the greater elder, **Against a priest receive not an accusation,** etc. Two witnesses suffice if they be good men. The reason for this is in the Gloss, that a person of so high an order, who stands in place of Christ, is not to be accused lightly.

But it does not seem to suffice that the accusation of some is not admitted except under the testimony of two or three. Deut. 17:6: *By the mouth of two or three witnesses shall he die that is to be slain.* Hence, it is to be noted that it is one thing to accept an accusation and another to condemn the accused. The latter a judge ought not to do unless the accused will have been convicted with witnesses, and this is common among men. But he ought not even receive one against a priest unless it is evident.

220. Then when he says, **Them that sin,** etc., he shows how he should be punished if he be found guilty: first, he shows how to correct him publicly; second, he adjures him to observe these things when he says [n. 223], **I charge thee before God.**

221. He says therefore, **Them that sin,** priests or whomever, **reprove before all.** And why? **That the rest also may have fear.**

Yet fraternal correction proceeds in one way and judiciary correction in another since the judge is a public person, and so he seeks the common good, which is injured by public sin because many are scandalized. Thus an ecclesiastical judge ought to punish publicly so that others may be edified. Eccles. 8:11: *For because sentence is not speedily pronounced against the evil, the children of men commit evils without any fear.* Prov. 19:25: *The wicked man being scourged, the fool shall be wiser.*

222. Notice that he says, **before all.** On the contrary, it says in Mt. 18:15, *But if thy brother shall offend against thee, go, and rebuke him between thee and him alone.*

Augustine responds in the Gloss that there is a distinction between times and sin, for one sin is hidden and another is public. The first needs a hidden remedy, that is, the sinner is to be corrected secretly, and the Lord is speaking about this. Hence He says, *against thee,* that is, alone and as it were secretly. But the Apostle is speaking about public sin, which needs a public punishment. And this is signified in the deaths of those whom the Lord raised. In Mt. 9:25 He raised a girl inside the house, by which a hidden sin is to be understood, for which reason He also sent the crowd out. But in Lk. 7:12 He raised the son of the widow outside the gate, before everyone, by which it is shown that a public sin is to be punished publicly.

223. Then he says, **I charge thee,** etc., since an ecclesiastical judge most assumes the person of God in judging, and so he is most confirmed by God because he judges justly.

For he ought so to argue before men that they not contemn the judgment of God. Here he shows three things. First is the divine authority, since God the Father judges with authority, and so he says, **before God.** Gen. 18:25: *Thou Who judgest all the earth.* Likewise, Christ the man, Who is evident in judgment. Jn. 5:27: *And He hath given Him power to do judgment, because He is the Son of man.* And so he says, **and Christ Jesus.** And again, the angels, as ministers. Mt. 25:31: *And when the Son of man shall come in His majesty, and all the angels with Him, then shall He sit upon the seat of His majesty.* Thus he adds, **and the elect angels.** Job 10:17: *Thou renewest Thy witnesses against me.*

224. Then when he says, **without prejudice,** he removes rash judgment, saying, **without prejudice,** so that you may not proceed rashly but with deliberation, **doing nothing by declining to either side.**

Or, **without prejudice,** that is, without previous examination. Ecclus. 33:30: *Do no grievous thing without judgment.* Job 29:16: *And the cause which I knew not, I searched out most diligently, otherwise thou wast not an intermediary between sides.*[8] Ex. 23:6: *Thou shalt not go aside in the poor man's judgment.*

225. Then when he says, **Impose not hands lightly,** he treats promotion, and this seems to be the reason for the first. For just as he ought not to punish swiftly, so he ought neither to promote unduly, that is, easily ordain men to sacred orders. Above 3:10: *And let these also first be proved,* etc. Num. 11:16: *Gather unto Me seventy men of the ancients of Israel, whom thou knowest to be ancients and masters of the people,* as if to say: those whom you find suitable.

And why? **Neither be partaker of other men's sins,** since if you promote them unduly, and consequently sin comes upon them or the people, this will be imputed to you. Or, he is a partaker **of other men's sins** because he does not correct when he can. Rom. 1:32: *They who do such things, are worthy of death; and not only they that do them, but they also that consent to them that do them.* Is. 52:11: *Touch no unclean thing.*

226. Then when he says, **Keep thyself chaste,** he shows him how he ought to comport himself. And this is reasonable enough since it happens that someone is so concerned with others that he neglects himself. Hence, first he exhorts him to chastity; second, from this he checks the immoderate use of abstinence, when he says [n. 228], **Do not still drink water.**

227. He says therefore: You, who ought to correct others, **Keep thyself**

chaste. I Cor. 9:27: *But I chastise my body, and bring it into subjection: lest perhaps, when I have preached to others, I myself should become a castaway.* Indeed, Timothy was a man of great abstinence, and he wore down his body to avoid sins of the flesh. Eccles. 2:3: *I thought in my heart, to withdraw my flesh from wine.*

228. And since on this account he was completely weak, he says, **Do not still,** that is, after you are so weak, **drink water.** And why? Because, as it says in Lev. 2:13, *Whatsoever sacrifice thou offerest, thou shalt season it with salt,* that is, the salt of discretion. Rom. 12:1: *Your reasonable service.* And so he says, **but use a little wine,** that is, not unto drunkenness. Ecclus. 31:36: *Wine drunken with moderation is the joy of the soul and the heart.* **For thy stomach's sake, and thy frequent infirmities** which have come upon you because of your abstinence. The Gloss: "Take pains so that, if possible, a duty begun may be gradually increased rather than lessened through thoughtlessness."

But it is to be noticed that Paul healed the sick and raised the dead, and yet counseled Timothy with medicine. By this we are to understand that he did not use miracles for all, but only when it was expedient on account of faith.

229. Then when he says, **Some men's sins,** etc., he shows how two things he said are to be understood, namely, **without prejudice** do nothing in condemnations; likewise, **Impose not hands,** etc. First, the first; second, the second [n. 231].

230. Regarding the first he says, **Some men's sins,** etc., as if to say: Above I said to condemn without prejudice but to show judgment, since some sins are notorious, and these do not need examination; others are secret and so need scrutiny. Hence, being without prejudice is understood for the former and not the latter, since **Some men's sins are manifest, going before to judgment: and some men they follow after.** Prov. 27:19: *As the faces of them that look therein, shine in the water, so the hearts of men are laid open to the wise.*

231. In the second place he says, **Impose not hands,** which is to be understood of those not manifestly good, since **In like manner also** their **good deeds are manifest.** Mt. 5:16: *So let your light shine before men, that they may see your good works, and glorify your Father Who is in heaven.* Jn. 3:21: *But he that doth truth, cometh to the light, that his works may be made manifest, because they are done in God.* **And they that are otherwise,** that is, which are not manifest, **cannot be hid,** since, as it says in Mt. 10:26, *Nothing is covered that shall not be revealed: nor hid, that shall not be known,* since either in the future or even now every iniquity will be made manifest. And there is no easy imposition of hands upon these.

Chapter Six

Lecture One

1 [n. 232] **Whosoever are servants under the yoke, let them count their masters worthy of all honour; lest the name of the Lord and His doctrine be blasphemed.**
2 [n. 234] **But they that have believing masters, let them not despise them, because they are brethren; but serve them the rather, because they are faithful and beloved, who are partakers of the benefit. These things teach and exhort.**
3 [n. 236] **If any man teach otherwise, and consent not to the sound words of our Lord Jesus Christ, and to that doctrine which is according to godliness,**
4 [n. 238] **He is proud, knowing nothing, but sick about questions and strifes of words; from which arise envies, contentions, blasphemies, evil suspicions,**
5 [n. 241] **Conflicts of men corrupted in mind, and who are destitute of the truth, supposing gain to be godliness.**
6 [n. 242] **But godliness with contentment is great gain.**
7 [n. 244] **For we brought nothing into this world: and certainly we can carry nothing out.**
8 [n. 246] **But having food, and wherewith to be covered, with these we are content.**

232. Above the Apostle instructed Timothy about the use of food and about the persons to whom the Church ministered food [n. 136]; here he treats other persons pertaining to the people of the Church: first, persons of lower status; second, persons of greater status, when he says in verse seventeen [n. 272], **Charge the rich**. Regarding the first he does three things: first, he gives instruction about

servants; second, he argues the contrary assertion when he says [n. 236], **If any man teach otherwise;** third, he admonishes that he should avoid the contrary and preserve the aforementioned teachings, when he says in verse eleven [n. 253], **But thou.** Again, the first is in two parts: first, he shows what ought to be grasped; second, he teaches that this must be taught when he says [n. 235], **These things teach.** Likewise, first he shows how servants should conduct themselves toward unbelieving masters; second, how they should conduct themselves toward faithful ones, when he says [n. 234], **But they.**

233. Therefore he says, **Whosoever are servants under the yoke,** namely, on account of the servile condition, which is said to be like a yoke, since just as bulls are kept under a yoke, lest they go where they wish, so servants are under a master that they may not be allowed to do what they wish to do. Gal. 5:1: *Be not held again under the yoke of bondage.* **Of all honour,** that is, of due reverence. Eph. 6:5: *Servants, be obedient to them that are your lords according to the flesh, with fear and trembling, in the simplicity of your heart, as to Christ.*

The reason for this is **lest the name of the Lord and His doctrine be blasphemed.** For if the unbelieving masters should feel their servants rebelling by reason of faith, they may condemn the name of Christ and blaspheme our doctrine. Rom. 2:24: *The name of God through you is blasphemed.* Therefore, those who have unbelieving masters should obey them, **lest the name of the Lord,** etc.

234. But how should they act toward faithful masters? **But they that have believing masters, let them not despise them,** since as it often happens, when familiarity is shown to lessers, they may be raised to pride. Prov. 30:21: *By three things the earth is disturbed, and the fourth it cannot bear: By a slave when he reigneth.*

And the reason for this is, according to the Philosopher, that men rationalize in such things; because if they see themselves equal in one thing, they believe that they are equal in all things and do not wish for themselves to be subject in anything, as in civil wars, since the people which is not subject believes itself wholly equal to nobles. And so it is able to happen that servants see themselves equal to their master in something, namely faith, and may consider themselves simply as equals. And therefore he says, **let them despise not.**

And he posits three things. The first is the gift of faith. Whence he says, **because they are faithful,** and this is exceedingly great, since the just man lives through faith. Likewise, the world is conquered through it. The second is the dignity of divine love; therefore he says, **beloved,** namely, more excellent than other creatures, since they are adopted into the sons of God. I Jn. 3:1: *Behold what manner of charity the Father hath bestowed upon us, that we should be called, and should be the sons of God.* The third is the benefit of grace; therefore he says, **who are partakers of the benefit,** namely, regarding the sacrament of the Lord.

I Cor. 10:16: *The bread, which we break, is it not the partaking of the body of the Lord?* Ps. 118:63: *I am a partaker with all them that fear Thee.*

235. **These things teach** the ignorant, **and exhort,** that knowing they may put them into practice. Tit. 2:15: *These things speak,* etc.

236. Then when he says, **If any man,** he excludes the contrary assertion: first, the mode of false teaching; second, its root, when he says [n. 238], **proud;** third, its effects, when he says [n. 239], **from which.**

237. If you wish to know whether a doctrine be erroneous, he shows this by three things. First, if it be against ecclesiastical doctrine. And therefore he says, **If any man teach otherwise,** namely, than I or the other Apostles. Gal. 1:9: *If any one preach to you a gospel, besides that which you have received, let him be anathema.* For the doctrine of the Apostles and prophets is called canonical, since it is like a rule for our intellect. And therefore no one ought to teach otherwise. Deut. 4:2: *You shall not add to the word that I speak to you, neither shall you take away from it.* Apoc. 22:18: *If any man shall add to these things, God shall add unto him the plagues written in this book.*

Regarding the second he says, **and consent not,** etc. For the Lord Jesus came to give testimony to the truth. Jn. 18:37: *For this was I born, and for this came I into the world; that I should give testimony to the truth.* And therefore He was sent by the Father as a doctor and teacher. I Mach. 2:65: *Give ear to him always, and he shall be a father to you,* etc. And therefore whatever does not conform to their words is erroneous. I Kg. 15:23: *It is like the sin of witchcraft, to rebel: and like the crime of idolatry, to refuse to obey.* And he says, **sound,** because in the words of Christ nothing is corrupt, nothing false, or perverse, since they are words of divine wisdom. Prov. 8:8: *All my words are just, there is nothing wicked nor perverse in them. They are right to them that understand, and just to them that find knowledge.*

Regarding the third, it says in Prov. 6:20, *My son, keep the commandments of thy father, and forsake not the law of thy mother.* Whence he says, **and to that doctrine which is according to godliness,** namely, ecclesiastical doctrine. This godliness is through the worship of God. Tit. 1:1: *According to...the acknowledging of the truth, which is according to godliness.*

238. The root of error, however, is twofold: the affection of pride and the defect of the intellect.

Regarding the first he says, **proud.** However, pride is called the root of error in two ways. First, the proud wish themselves to enter into those things to which they do not attain, and therefore it is unavoidable that they err and fail. Is. 16:6: *His pride and his arrogancy, and his indignation is more than his strength,* etc. Likewise, they do not wish to subject the intellect to another, but rely on their own prudence, and therefore are not obedient to Sacred Scripture. Contrary to this it is said in Prov. 3:5, *And lean not upon thy own prudence.* Prov. 11:2: *Where humility, there wisdom.*

Likewise, the defect of the intellect. It must be known that, as in the body, health is a certain equality of humors, so in the intellect, truth is a certain equality, since truth is the equaling of a thing and the intellect. Hence, as a sick man, when he does not have the equality of the humors, is wounded unto moderate contrary accidents, so in the intellect, when a man is not founded on truth nor has the virtue through which he is able to judge the truth, he falls into error by any difficult question. Whence he says, **sick about questions,** etc. Wis. 9:5: *A weak man, and of short time, and falling short of the understanding of judgment and laws.*

As Boëthius says, as a circle to its center, so the intellect relates to reason. For reason discourses by considering acts and defects and the relation of one thing to another. And unless it resolves unto the understanding of truth, reason is vain. Whence, when it accepts the truth of a thing, it has it as it were a center. However, certain men discourse yet do not attain a center. II Tim. 3:7: *Ever learning, and never attaining to the knowledge of the truth.* And therefore he says, **about questions,** that is, not attaining to that center.

And he says, **questions,** etc., because in some a doubt arose on the part of the reality, in others on the part of words and names. And therefore he says, **questions,** regarding the first, namely, about the reality. Above 1:4: *Which furnish questions rather than the edification of God, which is in faith.* Regarding the second he says, **strife of words,** which is understood to be when there is dissension arising only from words. Since the Lord says in Jn. 8:36, *If the Son shall make you free, you shall be free indeed,* and Mt. 17:25, *Then the children are free,* if from this anyone wished to infer that all Catholics, as they are sons of God, so are certainly free, there would be a strife of words since the Lord speaks there of spiritual freedom, not carnal.

239. Then when he says, **from which,** etc., he posits the effect of error: first, he posits the effect itself; second, he manifests certain things which he had said, when he says [n. 242], **But godliness.** Again, first he shows what evils would follow from false doctrine; second, in whom, when he says [n. 241], **men corrupted in mind.**

240. Among the evils which he posits, certain ones are within the heart, others are exterior.

Interiorly there are inordinate motions in regard to good or in regard to evil. In regard to good is envy, which is a sadness at the good of another; whence he says, **envies,** since it is able to be understood, either in the matter at hand or universally, since when anyone labors not toward truth, but only toward words, he does not see it with equanimity if someone else prevails. Job 5:2: *Envy slayeth the little one.* Likewise, in the case in question, because if servants are held to be free and not subject, the masters envy and grieve that the servants are made equal to them. From envy a man rises up against the neighbor whom he envies. And this is **contentions.** Prov. 20:3: *It is an honour for a man to separate himself from contentions.*[1] Or he rises up against God, and this is **blasphemies.** II Pet. 2:12: *Blaspheming those things which they know not,* etc.

In regard to evil is suspicion; whence he says, **evil suspicions,** namely, of the masters against Christians, as if we had imagined liberty for our profit, or that the whole Christian doctrine had been invented solely so that slaves would be free. Ecclus. 3:26: *And the suspicion of them hath deceived many, and hath detained their minds in vanity.* And from these follow **conflicts** against the faithful. Gen. 8:7: *There arose a strife between the herdsmen of Abram and of Lot.*

241. But this is not in the hearts of all, but of certain ones. And he posits three conditions of them, of which the first pertains to a defect of natural light, the second to a defect of knowledge, the third to the vice of inordinate affections.

Regarding the first he says, **men corrupted in mind,** that is, in natural reason, who pervert judgment. Ps. 13:1: *They are corrupt, and are become abominable.* Regarding the second he says, **are destitute of the truth,** namely, of their knowledge. Os. 4:1: *There is no truth, and there is no mercy, and there is no knowledge of God in the land.* Regarding the third he says, **supposing gain to be godliness,** that is, that the worship of God is ordered to the gain and acquisition of riches. Wis. 15:12: *They have counted our life a pastime, and the business of life to be gain, and that we must be getting every way, even out of evil.* Therefore, men of this kind, who believe this, easily despise and fall into the aforementioned evils.

242. Then when he says, **But godliness with contentment,** he declares what was said last, that the gain is godliness: first, he shows how godliness relates to gain; second, he shows that it does not consist in the gain of exterior riches when he says in verse nine [n. 247], **For they that will become rich.** Likewise, first he shows the first; second, he assigns a reason when he says [n. 244], **For we brought nothing.**

243. Therefore he says: They say that gain is godliness, but I say that **godliness is gain,** and so he adds **with contentment,** but of those riches which give contentment. And this consists in two things. The first is godliness, which orders other things to God and neighbor, and these are the virtues and gifts of grace. Wis. 7:14: *For she is an infinite treasure to men! which they that use, become the friends of God.* The second is the sustaining of life, that is, those things which are necessary for life. Mt. 6:33: *Seek ye therefore first the kingdom of God, and His justice,* etc. Above 4:8: *Godliness is profitable to all things.*

244. Then he says, **For we brought nothing,** etc., he assigns the reason for this: first, from the human condition; second, from its necessity, when he says [n. 246], **having.**

245. However, he posits the condition regarding two things, namely, its

beginning, since **we brought nothing,** etc. It is as if he said: What is necessity suffices, and the superfluous is not expedient, since **we brought nothing into this world.** Job 1:21: *Naked came I out of my mother's womb.* Likewise, regarding the end, since **we can carry nothing out.** Ps. 75:5: *They have slept their sleep; and all the men of riches have found nothing in their hands.* Job 27:19: *The rich man when he shall sleep shall take away nothing with him: he shall open his eyes and find nothing.* Eccles. 5:15: *As he came, so shall he return.*

246. Regarding necessity he says, **But having food, and wherewith to be covered,** since good things are on account of necessity. One good thing a man needs is against interior consumption, and this is food; or against exterior corruption, and so man needs coverings of clothes and a home. Heb. 13:5: *Let your manners be without covetousness, contented with such things as you have.* Ecclus. 29:28: *The chief thing for man's life is water and bread, and clothing, and a house to cover shame.*

Lecture Two

9 [n. 247] **For they that will become rich, fall into temptation, and into the snare of the devil, and into many unprofitable and hurtful desires, which drown men into destruction and perdition.**

10 [n. 250] **For cupidity[2] is the root of all evils; which some coveting have erred from the faith, and have entangled themselves in many sorrows.**

11 [n. 253] **But thou, O man of God, fly these things: and pursue justice, godliness, faith, charity, patience, mildness.**

12 [n. 257] **Fight the good fight of faith: lay hold on eternal life, whereunto thou art called, and hast confessed a good confession before many witnesses.**

13 [n. 260] **I charge thee before God, Who quickeneth all things, and before Christ Jesus, Who gave testimony under Pontius Pilate, a good confession,**

14 **That thou keep the commandment without spot, blameless, unto the coming of our Lord Jesus Christ,**

247. Above the Apostle showed what is the gain expedient to Christians, namely, godliness with contentment [n. 242]; here he shows that they incur great losses when seeking superfluous gain of riches: first, he shows the evils which follow from an inordinate desire for riches; second, he assigns a reason when he says [n. 250], **For cupidity.**

However, the evils which follow are twofold. For some originate from an exterior enemy; still others from an interior concupiscence, when he says [n. 249], **desires.**

248. Therefore he says: We are content with foods, etc., **For they that will become rich,** not to necessity but to an abundance of riches, **fall.** Ecclus. 10:10: *There is not a more wicked thing than to love money.* Eccles. 5:9: *He that loveth riches shall reap no fruit from them.* And he posits two things: **temptation** and **snare,** since first they tempt, insofar as riches allure and lead to other sins. I Thess. 3:5: *Lest perhaps he that tempteth should have tempted you,* etc. I Cor. 10:13: *Let no temptation take hold on you, but such as is human.* And they envelop in a snare, since riches are a temptation for those who do not have them, but a snare for those who do, since they do not willingly return that which they have taken. Prov. 21:6: *He that gathereth treasures by a lying tongue, is vain and foolish.*

249. From the interior concupiscence he posits three evils. First, that he fall **into many...desires.** For the perfection of man is that his heart be gathered into one, since as much as anything is one, so much is it similar to God, Who truly is one. Ps. 26:4: *One thing I have asked of the Lord,* etc. But on the contrary he who

seeks riches suffers, since his heart is dragged into diverse things. Os. 10:2: *Their heart is divided: now they shall perish.* And this since it says in Mt. 6:21, *For where thy treasure is,* etc.

Likewise, the desires of this kind are in many ways **unprofitable.** First, because they are spiritually unprofitable, since riches do not lead to beatitude. Wis. 5:8: *What hath pride profited us? or what advantage hath the boasting of riches brought us?* etc. Eccles. 5:9: *He that loveth riches shall reap no fruit from them.* Likewise, they are temporally unprofitable because they do not give what they promise. Eccles. 6:1–2: *There is also another evil, which I have seen under the sun, and that frequent among men: A man to whom God hath given riches, and substance, and honour, and his soul wanteth nothing of all that he desireth: yet God doth not give him power to eat thereof, but a stranger shall eat it up.*

Third, they are **hurtful.** Eccles. 5:12: *Riches kept to the hurt of the owner.* And he shows how they are hurtful, since they **drown men into destruction,** namely, in the present. On account of riches many have died. Likewise in the future; whence he says, **and perdition.** Acts 8:20: *Keep thy money to thyself, to perish with thee.* Or they refer to both spiritual losses. **Destruction,** that is, eternal death. Rom. 9:22: *Endured with much patience vessels of wrath, fitted for destruction,* etc. **And perdition,** that is, eternal punishment, which is called perdition on account of the punishment of loss, since they are as if having been condemned as lost, while they are unable to return into their homes, namely, the homes of eternity. Job 21:30: *The wicked man is reserved to the day of destruction, and he shall be brought to the day of wrath.*

250. Then when he says, **For cupidity**, etc., the reason for this is shown from two things: first, from the nature of desire, and then from experience when he says [n. 252], **which some,** etc.

251. He says therefore: They fall into temptation, etc. Why? Because **cupidity is the root of all evils.** It must be noted that according to some cupidity is taken in three ways. Sometimes for covetousness, according to which it is a particular sin, namely, the inordinate love of having riches. Sometimes as the genus of all sins, according to which it introduces an inordinate appetite for a temporal thing, and this is included in every sin since sin is a turning toward mutable good. But thus it is not the root, but the genus of all. In the third way it is a certain disorder of the soul for seeking temporal goods inordinately, and this is habitual of so many sins, though not in act; yet it is a certain root of all sins.

And cupidity is called the *root*, and pride the *beginning*. Ecclus. 10:15: *Pride is the beginning of all sin,* since pride bespeaks the corruption of the soul for departing from God. Now, the tree has nourishment from the root, and thus sin takes up nourishment from cupidity by a turning toward a mutable good.

But I believe that he speaks of cupidity according as it is a particular sin, when he says, **they that will become rich,** etc. And this is an inordinate love of money. And therefore I say that covetousness is the root of all evils. For all sins stand in the desire, and therefore the origin of sin is according to the origin of desirable things. For the origin of the desirable things proceeds from the end. And therefore to the greater measure that any sin has a more desirable end, so much more is it worse.

The end of any sin, however, is desirable on account of two things. First, on account of itself, and this is excellence, since for this man wishes that good, that he may excel. And this is pride, and therefore pride is the beginning of all sins. Likewise, on account of another, and this is what can do all things, and of this kind are riches, since through them man believes that he has all things. From this part covetousness is the root of all evils.

252. Then when he says, **which some,** he shows the same through experience. And he says, **coveting,** since to the greater degree that riches are had, so much more are they desired. Eccles. 5:9: *A covetous man shall not be satisfied with money.*

And first they fall into spiritual loss. Whence he says, **have erred from the faith.** The reason of which is that through the sound doctrine of faith many illicit gains are prohibited, from which they do not wish to desist, and they find another doctrine for themselves, wherein they have the hope of salvation. And usurers especially do this. Second, they **have entangled themselves in many sorrows,** even in the present, since there is anxiety in acquiring, fear in possessing, and pain in giving up. Job 20:22: *When he shall be filled, he shall be straitened, he shall burn, and every sorrow shall fall upon him.* And they shall suffer more in the future.

253. Then [n. 232] when he says, **But thou,** he admonishes the following of sound doctrine and the avoidance of evil doctrine: first, he shows the way he must follow; second, he binds him by the introduction of a precept, when he says [n. 260], **I charge.** Likewise, first he exhorts him to avoid the aforementioned sins; second, he shows what he should do when he says [n. 255], **pursue.**

254. And since a servant ought to imitate his master, as it is said Eccl. 10:2, *As the judge of the people is himself, so also are his ministers,* therefore he says, **O man of God;** as if he said: You are devoted to the service of God. Ps. 115:7: *I am thy servant.* I Jn. 2:6: *He that saith he abideth in Him, ought himself also to walk, even as He walked.* If therefore you are a man of God, you ought to do as Christ did, Who, as it says in Jn. 6:15, fled when they wished to make Him king. Heb. 12:2: *Who having joy set before Him, endured the cross, despising the shame.* And therefore **fly these things.** Ps. 54:8: *I have gone far off flying away; and I abode in the wilderness.*

255. What therefore should he do? He exhorts him to two things: first, to pursue spiritual arms; second, to fight with them, when he says [n. 257], **Fight the good fight.**

256. Now, spiritual arms are either for doing good or enduring evil.

The first is in comparison to a neighbor, to which we are ordered through two things, namely, justice and godliness, or mercy; the first without the second is severity, and the second without the first is laxity. Regarding the first he says, **pursue justice,** which is befitting prelates. Wis. 1:1: *Love justice, you that are the judges of the earth.* Regarding the second he says, **godliness,** that is, mercy. Prov. 20:28: *Mercy and truth preserve the king, and his throne is strengthened by clemency.*

However, in comparison to God, the first is that which perfects the intellect, **faith.** Heb. 11:6: *But without faith it is impossible to please God,* etc. The second is that which perfects the affections, **charity.** I Jn. 4:16: *He that abideth in charity, abideth in God, and God in him.*

For restraining evil there are two virtues, namely, **patience** and **mildness,** since man in evil incurs two inordinate passions, namely, inordinate sadness and the anger which comes from it. And therefore patience is against immoderate sadness. Lk. 21:19: *In your patience you shall possess your souls.* And mildness is against anger.

257. Then he induces him to an obligatory fight: first, he shows how he should fight; second, he brings in a reason [n. 259].

258. Therefore he says, **Fight the good fight,** by the example of soldiers who fight in two ways, sometimes by defending what they have and sometimes by acquiring what is not had; and this is incumbent upon the saints.

First, they must defend what they have, namely, faith and virtues; and therefore he says **of faith,** that is, for defending the faith. Ecclus. 4:33: *Even unto death fight for justice,* etc. Or **of faith,** that through faith you may avoid sins. I Jn. 5:4: *This is the victory which overcometh the world, our faith.* Or **of faith,** that is, that you may convert others to it. And he says, **good,** that is, a legitimate fight. I Cor. 9:25: *And every one that striveth for the mastery, refraineth himself from all things.* Then is it good when he refrains himself from all impediments. II Tim. 4:7: *I have fought a good fight.*

Second, they fight for acquiring what they do not have. And this is eternal life, which is acquired through battle. Mt. 11:12: *The kingdom of heaven suffereth violence, and the violent bear it away.* And therefore he says, **lay hold on eternal life,** that is, as it were holding on, may you conquer by your fight.

Or, you fight the fight of faith. And for what reward? That you may attain eternal life. I Cor. 9:25: *But we an incorruptible one.*

259. Then when he says, **whereunto thou art called,** he posits the reason for what was said, namely, **lay hold,** etc. First he responds to the objection, as if he says: You say that I ought to lay hold; indeed I have desired but am unable. Yes, you are able, since it is owed to you by right, since **thou art called** to it by God

and by the King of that kingdom. And therefore you ought to endeavor above all. I Pet. 2:9: *Who hath called you out of darkness into His marvellous light.*

Second, he posits the obligation; as if he says: Fight the good fight since you gave an oath about doing this, and therefore you are not allowed to resist. Whence he says, **and hast confessed a good confession before many witnesses,** that is, you acknowledged the good fight in your consecration, when you were ordained to the episcopate. I Cor. 9:16: *For if I preach the gospel, it is no glory to me, for a necessity lieth upon me: for woe is unto me if I preach not the gospel. For if I do this thing willingly, I have a reward: but if against my will, a dispensation is committed to me.* Or **a good confession,** namely, by preaching the faith, that you may guard it.

260. Then when he says, **I charge,** he obliges him by precept to preach: first, he posits it; second, he manifests certain things that had been said, when he says in verse fifteen [n. 262], **Which in His times.**

261. He first induces witnesses to the precept; second, he commends the precept; third, he shows how long he should preserve the precept. He induces as witness God the Father and our Lord, Jesus Christ.

Therefore he says: I have admonished you, but lest you believe it is allowable to do otherwise, **I charge you,** as you ought to charge your subjects, **before God.** He had brought in two things, namely, **lay hold on life** and **thou hast confessed,** etc., and therefore he brings in the author of life, **Who quickeneth all things.** Therefore he says, **God,** Who is the whole Trinity and Who is the author of life. Likewise he even induces the man, Christ, Who confesses Himself to be the Son of God, and this is the good confession of our faith.

Likewise, he commends the commandment, since it is in itself just, and right, and unable to be censured by others. Job 6:30: *You shall not find iniquity in my tongue.*

And until when must this be preserved? **Unto the coming of our Lord Jesus Christ.** The *unto* bespeaks the end of the intention, that is, that through the observance of this commandment you may order yourself unto His coming. Or *unto* your death, since such as you will be in that, so will you find yourself then. Mt. 24:13: *But he that shall persevere to the end,* etc.

Lecture Three

15 [n. 262] Which in His times He shall shew Who is the Blessed and only Mighty, the King of kings, and Lord of lords;
16 [n. 268] Who only hath immortality, and inhabiteth light inaccessible, Whom no man hath seen, nor can see: to Whom be honour and empire everlasting. Amen.

262. Above the Apostle, relating a warning to Timothy, instructed him that he ought to keep the command unto the coming of Christ [n. 260], and therefore he treats here about the coming of Christ, about which he makes known three things: first, what the suitable time will be; second, that it will be made manifest [n. 264]; third, the author of the coming [n.265].

263. Regarding the first he says, **Which in His times.** II Pet. 3:3: *Knowing this first, that in the last days there shall come deceitful scoffers,* etc. And therefore he wants to show that even if it might seem that the coming is delayed, nevertheless it will be shown in His own time. Eccles. 3:1: *All things have their season.* Eccles. 8:6: *There is a time and opportunity for every business.* The suitable time is the end of the world, because that time is the harvest time, and the gathering of the fruit. And therefore it is fitting that He will come in the end.

264. Regarding the second, he says **He shall shew,** that is, He shall make manifest. Although He may be visible regarding the flesh, nevertheless His power is hidden; but even so, then His divinity will be made manifest to the just, but the reprobate shall only see the glory of flesh.

265. Also, in regards to the third he says that God the Trinity will show Him. And concerning this he does two things: first, he describes the coming of Christ; second, he breaks forth in His praise, when he says [n. 271], **to Whom be honour,** etc. Likewise, the first is fashioned into three parts: first, he describes the author of the coming according to the perfection of operation; second, according to singular power [n. 267]; third, according to His incomprehensible nature [n. 268].

266. The first is when he says **Blessed.** Beatitude certainly is the perfect operation, which belongs to the highest operative power best disposed. And that is our beatitude. However, to God, beatitude is that by which He knows Himself. Indeed if He did not know Himself, God would not exist. Blessed Gregory: "As long as God has the full enjoyment of Himself, He is perfectly glorious."

And he fittingly says of the author of this coming that He is **Blessed,** because the coming of Christ is for this reason, that He might lead us into beatitude. Tob. 13:20: *Happy shall I be if there shall remain of my seed, to see the glory of Jerusalem.*

267. Concerning the second he says, **only Mighty.** Ps. 88:9: *Thou art mighty,*

O Lord, etc. But why does he say **only**? Is it possible that not all have power? No, more correctly they have it through participation, but only God possesses it in Himself essentially. Whence he says, **the King of kings, and Lord of lords.** Ambrose: "Lord is the name of power," and similarly king. Therefore, he who has the Lord and King above himself is subject to power, and such is not power in itself, but through another. If therefore Christ is **the King of kings, and the Lord of lords,** it is necessary that He alone ought to have power not by another, but everyone else by Him.

Also, the power of God is described in a twofold manner, namely, the governance of the world, when he says **King of kings,** as it were from the aforementioned power. Prov. 20:8: *The king, that sitteth on the throne of judgement, scattereth away all evil with his look.* Similarly, the power of creating, when he says **Lord of lords.** Ps. 99:3: *Know ye that the Lord He is God: He made us.* Apoc. 19:16: *And He hath on His garment, and on His thigh written: King of kings and Lord of lords.*

268. He says regarding the third, **Who only hath immortality, and inhabiteth light inaccessible.** The incomprehensibility of God is clear in two ways. First, He transcends everything in creatures that is comprehensible; second, this very thing which God is, exceeds the comprehension of all.

The first, when he says **only.** For in any change, there is a certain corruption, because all that is changed, inasmuch as it is such, ceases to be such. Therefore, that is properly and truly incorruptible which is thoroughly unchangeable. However, any creature, considered in itself, has some kind of change or changeability: God, however, is altogether unchangeable. Not to mention, if another creature is unchangeable, it is so from a gift of grace. And from this it is shown that the nature of God transcends all that is created in nature. Above 1:17: *To the king of ages, immortal,* etc.

Regarding the second he says, **light inaccessible,** etc. Light in sensible things is the principle of seeing; whence that is called light by which something is known in whatever way. However, each thing is known through its own form, and according as it is in act. Whence, as much as it has form and act, so much does it have light. Therefore, things which are of a certain act, but are not pure act, are illumined, but not light. But the divine essence, which is pure act, is itself light. Jn. 1:8: *He was not the light,* etc. However, God dwells with Himself, and that light is inaccessible, that is, not visible to the eyes of the flesh, but of the intellect. And yet, no created intellect is able to approach Him.

269. Nevertheless, it ought to be noted that the intellect is able to approach the knowledge of something's nature in two ways: to know it and to comprehend it. However, it is impossible for the intellect to arrive at comprehending God, because thus it would know God as He is knowable: God, however, is perfectly knowable, insofar as He has existence and light; but they are infinite, and so He

is infinitely knowable. However, the power of a created intellect is finite. And for that reason even the intellect of Christ does not comprehend God.

But the other way to know God is by reaching God. And according to this, no created intellect by its own nature reaches the knowledge of what God is. And the reason for this is that no power is able to attain to anything higher than its own object, as vision to higher knowledge. The proper object of the intellect is the essence of something; hence that which surpasses essence exceeds the proportion of every intellect. But in God to exist is not something other than His essence.

Then, in what way is He knowable? Therefore, let us approach the knowing of Him, here through grace, and in the future through glory. Ps. 33:6: *Come ye to Him and be enlightened.*

270. But then how does God dwell in light inaccessible? Ps. 96:2: *Clouds and darkness are round about Him.* Ex. 20:21: *But Moses went to the dark cloud wherein God was.*

Dionysius responds, "All darkness is inaccessible light." It is therefore the very same thing which here is light, and there darkness; but He is darkness inasmuch as He is not seen, and light inasmuch as He is seen.

But something is invisible in two ways. The first way is on account of itself, as a dark object; the other way on account of its exceeding the one seeing, as the sun does the eye of the owl. Thus, to us certain things are not clearly seen on account of a defect of their being, and certain others on account of their being excessive; and in this way God is inaccessible to us to a certain degree.

Whom no man hath seen. If this is understood concerning comprehension, then it is the absolute truth, even for the angels, because God alone comprehends Himself. However, if it is concerning the vision by which one arrives at the knowledge of God, it is understood thus in three ways. In one way, no one sees His essence with the eyes of the body. In another way, according to His essence He is seen with the eye of the mind by a man living in the flesh, which no one does except Christ. Ex. 33:20: *For man shall not see Me and live.* By the third way, no one sees through himself what God is. Mt. 11:27: *Neither doth any one know the Father*, etc. Mt. 16:17: *Flesh and blood hath not revealed it to thee.*

271.[3] Next he breaks out in praise of God, saying **to Whom be honour.** And he posits two things. The first pertains to the showing of reverence, saying **honour,** which is a showing of reverence. Mal. 1:6: *If then I be a father, where is My honour,* etc. The second pertains to governance, when he says, **empire everlasting.**

Lecture Four

17 [n. 272] Charge the rich of this world not to be highminded, nor to trust in the uncertainty of riches, but in the living God, (Who giveth us abundantly all things to enjoy,)
18 [n. 277] To do good, to be rich in good works, to give easily, to communicate to others,
19 To lay up in store for themselves a good foundation against the time to come, that they may lay hold of the true life.
20 [n. 278] O Timothy, keep that which is committed to thy trust, avoiding the profane novelties of words, and oppositions of knowledge falsely so called.
21 Which some promising, have erred concerning the faith. Grace be with thee. Amen.

272. Above the Apostle treated the instruction of persons of the lowest status [n. 232]; here he returns to his own material, and instructs Timothy to instruct the rich. First, he does this; second, he treats the instruction of Timothy when he says [n. 278], **O Timothy.**

And always when he instructs him to teach others, he warns that he should not neglect himself. And concerning the first, he first excludes vices which are accustomed to abound in the rich; second, he induces to good works when he says [n. 277], **to do good.** Likewise, regarding the first he proposes the vices which are accustomed to be in the rich; second, he excludes them by returning to his thought when he says [n. 276], **in the uncertainty.**

273. Therefore he says, **the rich.** Riches signify abundance. It is however the abundance of spiritual things, and these are true riches. Is. 33:6: *Riches of salvation, wisdom and knowledge: the fear of the Lord is his treasure.* Certain riches are corporeal, and these are not true riches since they do not suffice. And for this reason he adds with certain diminution, **of this world.** Bar. 3:18: *That hoard up silver and gold, wherein men trust.*

To this he therefore says, **Charge.** When he treated slaves, he did not give a command, because this is virtue, that a man uses authority for the more powerful, not for the weaker. And for that reason he said: Do not give up because of their wealth or their high station; in fact, you should command them.

274. And what ought to be warned? **Not to be highminded,** that is, not to think of himself as exalted above others.

Can it be that this is evil?

I respond that it is possible to be rendered evil in two ways. First, if a man thinks highly of himself on account of those things which do not possess true excellence. And such it is, if it is of the things of this world; whence, he who on account of external excellence thinks highly of himself inordinately thinks so; and this is pride. And yet carnal men do not care for any other exaltation except that one, and he can acquire these things through riches. Eccles. 10:19: *And all things obey money.* Hence, because the rich of this world have this, they are vainly extolled.

Second, there are some things which have a high place, such as spiritual gifts. Ecclus. 25:13: *How great is he that findeth wisdom and knowledge,* etc. Indeed, in this other way one is able to taste grandeur inordinately, not from the nature of the gifts, but by either attributing to himself what he does not have, or not acknowledging that what he has is from God.

Whence, in the first the disorder is because of the defect of things; in the second place, because of an inordinate affection.

275. The second vice in the rich is trust in the things of the world. Whence he says, **nor to trust.** Job 31:24: *If I have thought gold my strength, and have said to fine gold: My confidence.* Prov. 10:15: *The substance of a rich man is the city of his strength.*

276. Then when he says, **in the uncertainty of riches,** he assigns the reason for the warning.

Indeed, anyone trusts in that from which he believes to have help; but help is had by a strong man, and riches are fragile; therefore, they are not to be hoped in. Mt. 6:19: *Lay not up to yourselves treasures on earth: where the rust, and moth consume,* etc.

But in the living God, where true hope is to be placed. Jer. 17:7: *Blessed be the man that trusteth in the Lord, and the Lord shall be his confidence.* Jas. 1:5: *Who giveth to all men abundantly.*

But when he says, **abundantly...to enjoy,** this is able to be explained in two ways. In one way, so that fruition is taken for joy, and in this way it is also in corporeal things. Or so that through this we may come to the enjoyment of God.

277. Then when he says, **To do good,** he admonishes the doing of good works. Now, those who have affection for riches must first strive to acquire those not had; second, to use what they have; third, to arrive at the end of riches. The Apostle admonishes these three things.

First, to acquire spiritual riches which they do not posses. And for that reason he says, **To do good,** etc. Is. 1:17: *Learn to do well.*

Regarding the second, it must be known that there is a twofold use of riches. The first is to keep and the other is to give, but the chief one is to give. And therefore he posits two things: first, that they give, hence he says **to give easily,** that is, without a heavy heart within. II Cor. 9:7: *Not with sadness, or of necessity,* etc. Also without sluggishness. Prov. 3:28: *Say not to thy friend: Go, and come again: and to morrow I will give to thee: when thou canst give at present.* Job 31:16: *If I have... made the eyes of the widow wait.* Second, that he certainly take heed not so much for his own advantage, but for the common good; wherefore he says, **to communicate,** that is, to have them as if in common. Rom. 12:13: *Communicating to the necessities of the saints.*

Regarding the third, that they might come to the end of gathering treasure, he says, **To lay up in store,** etc. Spiritual treasure is the gathering of merits, which are the foundation of the future edifice prepared for us in heaven, because the whole preparation of future glory is through merit, which we acquire through grace, the principle of meriting. Mt. 6:21: *But lay up to yourselves treasures in heaven: where neither the rust nor moth,* etc. I Cor. 9:24: *So run that you may obtain.*

278. Then when he says **O Timothy,** he instructs Timothy himself: first, to conserve the good; second, to avoid evil, when he says [n. 280], **avoiding.**

279. Therefore he says: **O Timothy, keep that which is committed to thy trust.** Every good which is entrusted to man, whoever it is that has it, has been committed to him by God to guard and multiply it. Ecclus. 17:18: *Shall preserve the grace of a man as the apple of the eye.* I Cor. 15:10: *And His grace in me hath not been void...but His grace hath remained always in me.*

And thus he tells him to keep what is entrusted to him, that is, that he guard and multiply himself in the grace of God. Indeed, he who hid the talent was punished. Mt. 25:28.30: *Take ye away therefore the talent from him, and give it to him that hath ten talents. And the unprofitable servant cast ye out into the exterior darkness,* etc. And prelates especially have something entrusted to them, namely, the care of their neighbors and of the faithful. Jn. 21:17: *Feed My sheep.* Heb. 13:17: *For they watch as being to render an account of your souls.* II Tim. 1:14: *Keep the good thing committed to thy trust.*

280. Likewise, he should avoid evil, especially those which by nature befoul faith. The reason for which is that just as a secular prince is set for keeping the unity of the kingdom, so a spiritual prince is set for guarding the unity of the spirit. Now, the peace of the kingdom consists in justice, and therefore it is ordered towards justice; but the unity of the Church is in faith, and therefore he principally warns him to guard the faith. Luke 22:32: *But I have prayed for thee, that thy faith fail not: and thou, being once converted, confirm thy brethren,* etc.

However, faith is likewise able to be corrupted through deceit, as is any knowledge. But, as it is said in Book I of *On Sophistical Refutations,* deceit is sometimes made with words, at other times with the reality. Hence, there is deceit in speech and outside of speech. And so, faith is sometimes corrupted through inordinate words; Jerome says that from words uttered inordinately heresies are made. So therefore he says, **avoiding the profane novelties of words,** since not to want to hear anything new at all is to bark against the traditions. But rather, new profanities are not to be heard. But a novelty is profane when it introduces something contrary to faith. And it is called new through comparison to that which is ancient. Nestorius did this, when he said concerning the Virgin Mary that she was *Christotokos* (mother of Christ), in order to infer that she is not the mother of God. And therefore the Fathers established by the Council of Ephesus that she ought to be called *Theotokos* (mother of God). II Tim. 1:13: *Holding the form of sound words, which thou hast heard of me in faith, and in the love which is in Christ Jesus.* And in 2:16: *But shun profane and vain babblings,* etc.

But sometimes the faith is corrupted through sophistic reasoning in things. And this is to be avoided. And he says, **and oppositions of knowledge falsely so called,** because it is not true knowledge, but only apparent knowledge. Indeed, knowledge according to its proper notion regards nothing other than truth. However, it is impossible that truth could be contrary to truth, although sometimes two fallacies are contrary to themselves; and therefore it is impossible that what opposes divine truth, which is the summit of truth, could be true. Col. 2:8: *Beware lest any man cheat you by philosophy, and vain deceit; according to the tradition of men, according to the elements of the world, and not according to Christ.* **Promising**, that is, saying that they have it. Jer. 10:14: *Every man is become a fool for knowledge;* which knowledge is not of God, because *when he speaketh a lie, he speaketh of his own,* as it says in Jn. 8:44. Jer. 2:16: *The children also of Memphis and of Taphnes have deflowered thee, even to the crown of the head.* Is. 47:10: *Thy wisdom, and thy knowledge, this hath deceived thee.*

Grace be with thee. Amen.

The Commentary of St. Thomas Aquinas on
The Second Epistle of St. Paul to Timothy

Synoptical Outline of II Timothy

I. Greeting [n. 3]

II. Epistolary Narrative [n. 7]: a treatment about pastoral solicitude being so great that it should sustain even martyrdom for the care of the flock.

    A. Fortification of Timothy against present persecutions [n. 7]

        1. Insistence in preaching [n. 7]

            a. Timothy's goodness [n. 7]

                i. the affection which he had for Timothy [n. 7]

                ii. the good things which provoke him to such an affection [n. 9]

            b. exhortation to use his goodness [n. 12]

                i. general admonition to use the grace given to him [n. 12]

                ii. specific use of that grace [n. 15]

            c. the example of the Apostle [n. 24]

                i. he gives the example [n. 24]

                ii. he leads Timothy to follow himself [n. 29]

                iii. he shows the necessity of following him [n. 32]

        2. Exhortation to bear tribulations for Christ's sake [n. 35]

            a. enduring suffering for the salvation of faithful [n. 35]

                i. a preparation for undergoing martyrdom [n. 35]

                ii. an exhortation for martyrdom [n. 48]

            b. how to resist the infidels [n. 59]

                i. the manner of resisting them [n. 59]

                ii. what things are to be resisted [n. 63]

    B. Fortification of Timothy against future persecutions [n. 89]

        1. Future dangers [n. 89]

            a. foretelling the dangers of the last times [n. 89]

                i. the dangers of the last times [n. 89]

                ii. how their vices are even now to be avoided [n. 102]

            b. how their vices are even now to be avoided [n. 102]

                i. an admonition to avoid them [n. 102]

                ii. in which men the aforementioned dangers may appear now [n. 104]

        2. His suitability to resist them [n. 113]

            a. his education by the Apostle [n. 113]

                i. that he was sufficiently instructed by the Apostle [n. 113]

                ii. his education by others in general [n. 116]

            b. his experience with the Scriptures [n. 119]

                i. on the part of the teacher [n. 119]

Prologue

Day and night was I parched with heat, and with frost, and sleep fled from my eyes.[1] – Gen. 31:40

1. These are the words of Jacob showing and commending pastoral care and the pastoral office. And in these words, three things are laid down concerning this office, namely, assiduousness, patience, and solicitude.

The first is because the pastor must bear the care of the flock without intermission. For this reason, he says, **Day and night.** By night in praying, by day in instructing. Is. 21:8: *I am upon the watchtower of the Lord, standing continually by day: and I am upon my ward, standing whole nights.* Or through the day, that is, in time of prosperity, and through the night, that is, in time of adversity; for in these times the prelate must look after the care of the flock. II Cor. 6:7: *By the armour of justice on the right hand and on the left.* Prov. 17:17: *He that is a friend loveth at all times.*

The second is because patience is especially necessary to a prelate. For a prelate must sustain all things for the sake of the salvation of the flock. Jn. 10:11: *The good shepherd giveth his life for his sheep.* Prov. 19:11: *The learning of a man is known by patience.* For this reason he says, **with heat,** that is, in the heat of pressing persecution. Jas. 1:11: *For the sun rose with a burning heat, and parched the grass.* **And with frost,** that is, in the fear of future things. II Cor. 7:5: *Combats without, fears within.*

The third is because he is set over others in solicitude, as is said in Rom. 12:8. And the sleep of negligence expels this. For this reason, it is added in Gen. 31:40, **and sleep fled from my eyes.** Prov. 6:3–4: *Run about, make haste, stir up thy friend: Give not sleep to thy eyes.*

2. Rightly therefore do these words befit the matter of this epistle. For in the first epistle to Timothy, the Apostle instructs him about the ordering of the Church. In this second, however, he treats about pastoral solicitude being so great that he should sustain even martyrdom for the care of the flock, as is clear in the prologue.

Chapter One

Lecture One

1 [n. 3] Paul, an apostle of Jesus Christ, by the will of God, according to the promise of life, which is in Christ Jesus,
2 [n. 5] to Timothy my dearly beloved son, grace, mercy, and peace, from God the Father, and from Christ Jesus our Lord.

3. This epistle then is divided into a salutation and a narration. The second begins when he says [n. 7], **I give thanks.** Likewise, there is first put the person saluting; second, the person saluted [n. 5]; third, the good wishes [n. 6].

4. The person saluting is described from his name, **Paul,** which betokens littleness. And this is befitting because of humility of mind and tribulation, which make a man small. To that degree, Christ is said to be lessened on account of His sufferings. Heb. 2:9: *Who was made a little lower than the angels, for the suffering of death.*

Likewise, the person saluting is described from his dignity, which he puts first; second, the origin of this dignity; third, the fruit of it. His dignity is great, since he is **an apostle of Jesus Christ**, that is, one sent by Christ. Lk. 6:13: *And He chose twelve of them (whom also he named Apostles).* He obtained this dignity since he *laboured more abundantly than all they,* as it says in I Cor. 15:10; and Gal. 2:8: *For He Who wrought in Peter to the apostleship of the circumcision, wrought in me also among the Gentiles.*

The origin of this apostleship is the will of God. For this reason he says, **by the will of God,** which certain men anticipate, since they impose themselves. Against these people, it is said in Heb. 5:4, *Neither doth any man take the honour to himself, but he that is called by God, as Aaron was.* Likewise, certain of these are permitted on account of the sins of the people. Job 34:30: *Who maketh a man that is a hypocrite to reign for the sins of the people.* But this is **by the will of God,** since it is not by his own will.

The fruit, however, is not something earthly, but something **according to the promise of life, which is in Christ Jesus,** that is, for obtaining the eternal life promised by Christ. This must be the end of prelates. I Cor. 9:25: *They indeed that they may receive a corruptible crown; but we an incorruptible one.* Dan. 12:3: *They that instruct many to justice, as stars for all eternity.*

5. The person saluted is Timothy, his son converted by him, as it says in Acts 16:1. **Dearly beloved,** since he is of one mind with him. Phil. 2:19–20: *And I hope in the Lord...to send Timothy unto you shortly...for I have no man so of the same mind.*

6. The good wishes are three things, namely, **grace,** through which there is the remission of sins; **mercy,** through which we obtain the final good; **and peace.** As the Gloss says, "that is, the tranquility of the mind." And this befits a prelate, since he is put over others for the very purpose that he may procure peace. The Lord said in Jn. 26:26, *Peace to you;* and He commanded those entering a house to offer their peace, as is said in Mt. 10:32. And this **from God the Father,** Who is the Giver of every good, as it says in Jas. 1:5. Likewise, from **Jesus Christ,** Who, insofar as He is man, is the mediator of God and men. II Pet. 1:4: *By Whom He hath given us most great and precious promises.*

Lecture Two

3 [n. 7] I give thanks to my God,[2] Whom I serve from my forefathers with a pure conscience, that without ceasing, I have a remembrance of thee in my prayers night and day.

4 Desiring to see thee, [n. 9] being mindful of thy tears, that I may be filled with joy,

5 [n. 11] Calling to mind that faith which is in thee unfeigned, which also dwelt first in thy grandmother Lois, and in thy mother Eunice, and I am certain that in thee also.

7. Here begins the epistolary narration, in which he first fortifies Timothy against present persecutions; second, against future dangers to the Church, in verse one of chapter three, where he says [n. 89], **Know also this.** Likewise, first he persuades him to insistence in preaching, which was then the cause and occasion of persecution; second, he exhorts him to bear his tribulations for Christ's sake when he says [n. 35], **Thou therefore, my son,** in verse one of chapter two. Likewise, first he recalls the good things of Timothy himself; second, he exhorts him to the use of these good things through insistence in preaching, when he says in verse six [n. 12], **For which cause,** etc.; third, he puts himself as an example, when he says in verse eleven [n. 24], **Wherein I am appointed a preacher, and an apostle, and a teacher,** etc. Likewise, first he posits the affection which he had for Timothy; second, his good things which provoke him to such an affection, when he says [n. 9], **Being mindful of thy tears.**

8. Affection is shown through two things, namely, through prayer and desire. And therefore he gives thanks to God for the affection which he has for Timothy, since it is one of charity, and charity is the principal gift; as if he were to say: I consider myself to have received grace, because I have so sincere an affection toward you. And he says, **to my God, Whom I** especially **serve from my forefathers,** not from my carnal parents, since, as he says in I Tim. 1:15, *Christ Jesus came into this world to save sinners, of whom I am the first;* but by a service derived from my forefathers, namely, the patriarchs and prophets, who sincerely served God. And is said, **from my forefathers,** since children more easily imitate their father's perfection, both since they are instructed by them, as Tobias was, and also since they more easily imitate friends. And how do I serve him? **With a pure conscience;** since, as it is said in Hab. 1:13, *Thy eyes are too pure to behold evil, and thou canst not look on iniquity;* II Cor. 1:12: *For our glory is this, the testimony of our conscience.* About this he gives thanks, since **without ceasing,** whether in the day of prosperity, or in the night of adversity, I pray for you.

Likewise, from desire; and therefore he says, **Desiring to see thee,** namely, for the sake of the consolation of both of them. Rom. 1:11: *For I long to see you,* etc.

9. Then when he says, **being mindful,** he shows the good things which were in Timothy. And first, he recalls Timothy's affection toward himself;   second, his faith toward God, when he says [n. 11], **Calling to mind that faith,** etc.

10. Therefore he says, **being mindful of thy tears,** which Timothy shed when he departed from him at Ephesus, prepared for martyrdom. Or **thy tears** which he shed in his prayers. And this **that I may be filled with joy,** that is, this recollection fills me with joy. Phil. 2:2: *Fulfil ye my joy,* etc.

11. Likewise, being mindful of his faith toward God. First, he recalls his faith; second, he shows it to be derived from his parents and not a novelty.

Therefore, he says, **Calling to mind that faith,** etc. Faith is necessary to a prelate, who is a guardian of the faith. Heb. 11:6: *But without faith it is impossible to please God.* And he says, **unfeigned,** for it is true through good works. Jas. 2:18: *Shew me thy faith without works; and I will shew thee, by works, my faith.* I Tim. 1:5: *Now the end of the commandment is charity, from a pure heart, and a good conscience, and an unfeigned faith.* Wis. 1:5: *For the Holy Spirit of discipline will flee from the deceitful.*

And this faith is not new, but **dwelt first in thy grandmother Lois,** etc. In Acts 16:1, it is said that he was the son of a Jewish woman. **And I am certain,** either by revelation or by indications, **that in thee also.**

Lecture Three

6 [n. 12] For which cause I admonish thee, that thou stir up the grace of God which is in thee, by the imposition of my hands.

7 [n. 14] For God hath not given us the spirit of fear: but of virtue,[3] and of love, and of sobriety.

8 [n. 15] Be not thou therefore ashamed of the testimony of our Lord, nor of me His prisoner: but collaborate in the gospel,[4] according to the power of God.

9 Who hath delivered us and called us by His holy calling, [n. 20] not according to our works, but according to His own purpose and grace, which was given us in Christ Jesus before the times of the age.[5]

10 [n. 23] But is now made manifest by the illumination of our Saviour Jesus Christ, Who hath destroyed death, and hath brought to light life and incorruption by the gospel.

12. Above the Apostle commended him about his goods of grace [n. 7]; here he exhorts him to the use of the gratuitous goods given to him, principally in the preaching of the Gospel. And first, he admonishes him generally to use the grace given to him; second, he specifies how that use of grace should be when he says [n. 15], **Be not thou therefore ashamed.** Likewise, first, he puts the admonition; second, the reason for it, when he says, [n. 14] **For God hath not given us,** etc.

13. Therefore, he says first: There is *an unfeigned faith* in your mother and your grandmother and in you, **For which cause I admonish thee.** The grace of God is like a fire, which, when it is covered over with ashes, does not shine; so grace is covered over in man through sluggishness, or human fear. Wherefore, even Timothy, having become pusillanimous, had grown sluggish with regard to preaching. And therefore he says, **that thou stir up the grace of God** which has been put into slumber. I Thess. 5:19: *Extinguish not the spirit.* And he adds, **which is in thee, by the imposition of my hands,** by whom, namely, he had been ordained a bishop. In this imposition of hands, the grace of the Holy Spirit was given to him.

14. Then when he says, **For God hath not given,** etc., there is put the reason for the admonition, and it is taken from the characteristic of divine offices. For he who receives an office must work according to the fittingness for that office; therefore, we must serve God according to the characteristic of the divine offices.

However, there are two kinds of spirit: one of this world, the other, of God. And between these, there is a distinction; for spirit signifies love, since the word *spirit* implies an impulse, and love impels. However, there are two kinds of love, namely, of God, and this is through the spirit of God; and a love of the world, and this is through the spirit of the world. I Cor. 2:12: *Now we have received not the spirit of this world, but the Spirit that is of God.*

The spirit of the world, however, makes one love the good things of the world and fear temporal evils; and for that reason he says, **For God hath not given us the spirit of fear,** namely, of worldly fear, since God takes this away from us. Mt. 10:28: *And fear ye not them that kill the body.*

There is another spirit of the fear of the Lord, and this is holy; and it makes it such that God be feared, but this is without punishment and without offense. And this fear is from God. Mt. 10:28: *Fear Him that can destroy both soul and body in hell.* And he adds, **but of virtue,** since through the Holy Spirit, we are directed in the midst of evil things; and that through virtue, namely, the virtue of fortitude against the adversities of the world. Lk. 24:49: *But stay you in the city till you be endued with power from on high.* Likewise, we are directed in good things, since as regards affection, we are directed through the love of charity, when someone refers to God all the things that he loves. Wherefore, he also says, **and of love.** I Jn. 3:14: *He that loveth not, abideth in death.* Likewise, as regards exterior goods; and therefore he says, **and of sobriety,** that is, of all temperance, by keeping the due mode and measure, so that we use the goods of the world temperately. Tit. 2:12: *We should live soberly, and justly, and godly in this world.* I Tim. 3:2: *It behoveth therefore a bishop to be blameless, the husband of one wife, sober.*

15. Then, when he says, **Be not thou therefore ashamed,** he specifies the use of grace: and first, he excludes the things contrary to this use; second, he exhorts him to the use of grace when he says [n. 17], **But collaborate in the gospel.**

16. However, Timothy could have been impeded from his usual preaching because of two things. First, through shamefulness; second, from the punishment of the Apostle, which he was suffering for the sake of the Gospel. And therefore, as to the first, he says, **Be not thou therefore,** namely, from the fact that you possess the spirit of fortitude, **ashamed of the testimony of our Lord.** For if one refer to the wisdom of the world, the preaching of Christ seemed foolish; wherefore, he seemed to have a shamefulness about it. I Cor. 1:23: *We preach Christ crucified, unto the Jews indeed a stumblingblock, and unto the Gentiles foolishness.* Rom. 1:16: *For I am not ashamed of the gospel.* Lk. 9:26: *For he that shall be ashamed of Me and of My words, of him the Son of man shall be ashamed.*

As to the second, it must be known that if a thief see someone hung, he is ashamed to confess himself as his companion. So here, since the Apostle was a prisoner, Timothy could have been ashamed of him; and therefore he says **nor of me His prisoner.** Eph. 6:20: *For which I am an ambassador in a chain.* Ecclus. 4:27: *Be not ashamed of thy neighbour*[6] *in his fall.*

17. Then when he says, **but collaborate in the gospel,** he exhorts him to the use of grace; and first in general; second, he shows from what trust he should approach this use of grace when he says [n. 19], **according to the power of God.**

From there, he manifests why he says **but collaborate in the gospel,** when he says [n. 20], **not according to our works,** etc.

18. Therefore, he says: Be not ashamed, **but collaborate,** that is, labor together with me. I Cor. 3:8: *And every man shall receive his own reward, according to his own labour.*

And he says, **in the gospel,** which can be in the ablative case; and in that case, it means, "in preaching the Gospel." Or in the dative case, and thus it would be "for the praise of the Gospel," so that, namely, it might grow. Wis. 3:15: *For the fruit of good labours is glorious.*

19. And this with trust, not in himself, since we are not sufficient to think anything done by us as if from our own power, as it says in II Cor. 3:5, but **according to the power of God,** that is, having trust in the power of God. Is. 40:29: *It is He that giveth strength to the weary, and increaseth force and might to them that are not.*

This power is manifested through two things, namely, that we are liberated from evils so far as concerns affection, and therefore he says, **Who hath delivered us.** Esd. 8:31: *And the hand of our God was upon us, and delivered us from the hand of the enemy, and of such as lay in wait by the way.* Jn. 8:36: *If therefore the Son shall make you free, you shall be free indeed.* And this power is also manifested inasmuch as He calls us to good things. Wherefore, he continues, **and called us by His holy calling,** since He called us to be sanctified. Rom. 8:30: *And whom He predestinated, them He also called.* I Pet. 2:9: *Who hath called you out of darkness into His marvellous light.*

20. And he manifests some of the things which he said, saying, **not according to our works,** where he shows that we have been delivered and called through the power of God, and not through any human power. And first, he shows that the cause of our calling and deliverance is from God; second, he shows the progression of that cause, when he says [n. 22], **which was given us;** third, he commends the giver of the cause, when he says [n. 23], **Who hath destroyed death.**

21. Therefore, he says: He called, not by our virtue, since it was not by our works which are the effects of virtue. Tit. 3:5: *Not by the works of justice, which we have done, but according to His mercy, He saved us.*

Now, the cause of human salvation, which is from God, is twofold: one is eternal, which is His predestination; the other is temporal, which is justifying grace.

Regarding the first he says, **according to His own purpose,** that is, predestination, which is His purpose of having mercy. Eph. 1:11: *Who worketh all things according to the counsel of His will.* Rom. 8:28: *And we know that to them that love God, all things work together unto good, to such as, according to His purpose, are called to be saints.*

Regarding the second he says, **and grace.** Rom. 3:24: *Being justified freely by His grace.*

22. For the progression of grace he first shows how grace is prepared; second, how it is conveyed; third, through Whom.

He shows the first when he says, **which was given us in Christ Jesus,** that is, foreseen to be given to us, **before the times of the age.** As the Philosopher says, a time is nothing other than the measure of the duration of things; hence, diverse times are the diverse ages of men. Wherefore, one age lasts a thousand years since a man is said to live as long as he is in the memory of men, which does not exceed a thousand years. The times of the age measure changeable things, and these began with the world; predestination, however, is before the world. Eph. 1:4: *He chose us in Him before the foundation of the world.*

And he says, **in Christ Jesus,** for we are not saved by our own merits but through the grace of Christ. Just as He predestinated our salvation itself, so also the mode of our salvation. Jn. 1:17: *Grace and truth came by Jesus Christ.*

But before this predestination was secret, but now it is manifest. And how? Just as a conception of the heart is manifest by actions, just so now in the effect of the action He manifested it to His elect **by illumination.** Properly speaking, to manifest something is to bring it into the light. Job 28:11: *Hidden things He hath brought forth to light.* Thus it **is now made manifest** through this, that He sent Christ, Who illuminates us. Is. 60:1: *Arise, be enlightened, O Jerusalem: for thy light is come.* Lk. 1:79: *To enlighten them that sit in darkness, and in the shadow of death.*

23. Then when says, **Who hath destroyed death,** he commends Christ the illuminator: first, His power regarding the evils which He took away; second, regarding the good things He bestowed.

He says, **Christ,** on account of this, that He suffered for us, **hath destroyed death,** that is, He made satisfaction to God for our sins. I Pet. 3:18: *Christ also died once for our sins.* And sin was the cause of our bodily death. Rom. 6:23: *For the wages of sin is death.* And so by destroying sin He destroyed death. Os. 13:14: *O death, I will be thy death,* etc.

He also bestowed perfect goods, first to the soul in the present through the grace of faith. Hab. 2:4: *The just shall live in his faith.* It is imperfect in this life, but it shall be perfected in glory. Jn. 17:3: *Now this is eternal life: That they may know Thee.* Second, immortality of the body resulting from the glory of the soul. I Cor. 15:53: *For this corruptible must put on incorruption,* etc. Jn. 10:10: *I am come that they may have life,* now through grace, *and may have it more abundantly,* through glory in the future. Jn. 11:26: *And every one that liveth, and believeth in Me, shall not die for ever.*

Lecture Four

11 [n. 24] **Wherein I am appointed a preacher, and an apostle, and teacher of the Gentiles.**

12 [n. 26] **For which cause I also suffer these things: but I am not ashamed. For I know Whom I have believed, and I am certain that He is able to keep my deposit until that day.**[7]

13 [n. 30] **Holding the form**[8] **of sound words, which thou hast heard of me in faith, and in the love which is in Christ Jesus.**

14 [n. 31] **Keep the good thing committed to thy trust by the Holy Ghost, Who dwelleth in us.**

15 [n. 32] **Thou knowest this, that all they who are in Asia, are turned away from me: of whom are Phigellus and Hermogenes.**

16 [n. 34] **The Lord give mercy to the house of Onesiphorus: because he hath often refreshed me, and hath not been ashamed of my chain:**

17 **But when he was come to Rome, he carefully sought me, and found me.**

18 **The Lord grant unto him to find mercy of the Lord in that day: and in how many things he ministered unto me at Ephesus, thou very well knowest.**

24. Above the Apostle admonished Timothy unto solicitude for the preaching of Christ [n. 7]; here he gives him an example: first, he gives it; second, he leads him to follow himself when he says [n. 29], **Holding the form;** third, he shows the necessity of following him when he says [n. 32], **Thou knowest this.** Again, he first posits his duty; second, he shows what he suffers for the execution of his office when he says [n. 26], **For which cause;** third, the certitude of hope, when he says [n. 27], **For I know.**

25. He describes his office in three ways, for he calls himself a **preacher,** to move others to good morals. Below 4:2: *Preach the word: be instant in season, out of season.* Mk. 16:15: *Preach the gospel to every creature.* **Apostle,** to rule the Church. Gal. 2:8: *He Who wrought in Peter to the apostleship of the circumcision, wrought in me also among the Gentiles.* **Teacher,** instituted to teach the sanctity of the faith and the knowledge of God. I Tim. 2:7: *A doctor of the Gentiles in faith and truth.* Joel 2:23: *And you, O children of Sion, rejoice, and be joyful in the Lord your God: because He hath given you a teacher of justice.*

But he says, **Wherein I am appointed,** where three things must be noticed. First, that he did not assume it to himself, but it was placed on him by another. Heb. 5:4: *Neither doth any man take the honour to himself, but he that is called by God, as Aaron was.* Second, in position there is signified order. Third, stability, since, having been instituted according to the order of reason, he endured with stability. Jn. 15:16: *I have chosen you; and have appointed you, that you should go, and should bring forth fruit; and your fruit should remain.* Judg. 5:20: *The stars remaining in their order and courses.*

26. Then when he says, **For which cause,** he shows what he suffered for the execution of his office by saying, **I also suffer,** namely, chains and weariness, and this for the faith of Christ. Below 2:9: *Wherein I labour even unto bands.* And he says, **For which cause,** since simply to suffer is not praiseworthy, but to do so for a just cause is. Mt. 5:10: *Blessed are they that suffer persecution for justice' sake.* And so, **but I am not ashamed** since it is not unto his confusion who suffers for the sake of justice. I Pet. 4:15–16: *But let none of you suffer as a murderer, or a thief, or a railer, or a coveter of other men's things. But if as a Christian, let him not be ashamed,* etc. Acts 5:41: *And they indeed went from the presence of the council, rejoicing that they were accounted worthy to suffer reproach for the name of Jesus.*

27. Then when he says, **For I know,** he posits the certitude of hope, which makes him not to be confounded; this also comes forth from the greatness of God Who makes the promise. And so he says, **Whom I have believed.**

And note that in one way to believe is an act of faith; and the sense is, **I know,** that is, I know that He Who promised is truthful and powerful to grant eternal life which He promised the man remaining faithful.

But against this it follows that knowledge and faith are the same, and what is known is the same as what is believed, which is impossible since the notion of the known is what is seen while that of what is believed is not.

I respond that in faith there are two things: what is believed and He Who is believed. About that which is believed there cannot be knowledge since this would destroy the notion of faith. But about Him Who is believed there is knowledge since through the most evident reason it is known that God is truthful. And so he says, **Whom I have believed.** I Jn. 4:1: *Believe not every spirit, but try the spirits if they be of God.* Prov. 14:15: *The innocent believeth every word.*

In another way someone is said to entrust his cause to the faith of the one to whom he has committed it, and this sense is truer; it is as if to say: Myself, my labors and my sufferings I have entrusted, that is, I have committed, to God, Whom I know **is able to keep my deposit,** etc.

28. And note that something is called a deposit in two ways. In one way, what I have deposited. And thus man deposits his salvation with God when he commits himself totally to God. I Pet. 5:7: *Casting all your care upon Him, for He hath care of you.* Ps. 54:23: *Cast thy care upon the Lord, and He shall sustain thee.* Likewise, to deposit one's works, when he does not immediately receive remuneration until later. And so, he who does a good work deposits it with God. And this **until that day** when He shall judge the secrets of men, to whom the Lord will

render *the wages of their labours,* as it says in Wis. 10:17. Is. 3:10: *Say to the just man that it is well, for he shall eat the fruit of his doings.*

Or, **my deposit,** that is, what is placed in my power is the office of evangelization. Acts 9:15: *This man is to Me a vessel of election, to carry My name before the Gentiles.* Also, God is able to keep him as an Apostle until his death.

29. Then when he says, **Holding the form,** he leads him to follow him, and there is a twofold text. One says *Hold,* and the other says, *Holding.* If he says, *Holding,* then first he gives the suitability which he proposes to Timothy for imitating the example of the Apostle; second, he exhorts him unto that imitation when he says [n. 31], **Keep the good thing.**

30. Now, the Apostle had good suitability in two ways. First, according to his learning regarding knowledge; and so he says, **of sound words.** Likewise, according to virtue; hence he says, **in faith, and in the love.**

He says therefore: You cannot excuse yourself, if you do not remain patiently unto chains as I do, for you are **Holding the form of sound words,** which do not contain the corruption of falsity. Tit. 2:1: *But speak thou the things that become sound doctrine.* And it is called sound doctrine, not effectively corrupted, because it makes us sound. And he adds, **which thou hast heard of me,** as if to say: You are not deceived since what I heard from Christ I have handed on to you. I Cor. 11:23: *For I have received of the Lord that which also I delivered unto you.* Lk. 10:16: *He that heareth you, heareth Me.* And this **in faith, and in the love,** since if someone knew all sound words and did not believe them, he would not be suitable, neither would he love, since he would easily fall away from doctrine, either through adversities or through prosperities. Heb. 11:6: *But without faith it is impossible to please God.* I Jn. 3:14: *He that loveth not, abideth in death.* And this **in Christ Jesus,** since the true faith is of those things which Christ taught, and true love is in Christ since He gave the Holy Spirit through Whom we love God.

31. Therefore, having these things, **Keep the good thing committed to thy trust,** which I have given to you, that is, the office of preaching, lest you ever fall away from the truth or at any time lay down the office of preaching on account of fear. Prov. 4:23: *With all watchfulness keep thy heart, because life issueth out from it.* I Tim. 6:20: *O Timothy, keep that which is committed to thy trust.* And **Keep** this with excellent assistance, namely, through **the Holy Ghost, Who dwelleth in us.** I Cor. 3:16: *Know you not, that you are the temple of God, and that the Spirit of God dwelleth in you?*

According to the other text, *Hold,* he admonishes him unto two things: sound doctrine and persevering in it.

32. Then when he says, **Thou knowest this,** he shows the necessity of an admonition from the defect and progress of others. For when someone sees some

of his friends progress and others fall away, he struggles to follow the good. And so, he first recalls those who are falling away; second, those who are progressing, when he says [n. 34], **The Lord give mercy.**

33. He shows him, then, what to beware; otherwise there is danger. I Cor. 10:12: *Wherefore he that thinketh himself to stand, let him take heed lest he fall.* And so he says, **all they who are in Asia, are turned away from me.** The Gloss: "These were filled with treachery, for they had pretended to be with the Apostle in order to learn how to calumniate him." These, therefore, who **are turned away from me** are now **in Asia,** among whom chiefly are these two who were converted by James.

34. Then when he says, **The Lord give mercy,** he shows the progress of others, and chiefly of one Onesiphorus, recalling the good things he had done for him first in Rome and then in Asia. Again, he first wishes the mercy of God upon him; second, he shows the merit of this mercy; third, the time of mercy.

He does the first when he says, **The Lord give mercy.** He rightly wishes mercy upon him because this present life is a misery.[9] Job 14:1: *Man born of a woman, living for a short time, is filled with many miseries.* He says, **The Lord give mercy to the house of Onesiphorus,** not only to his person but to his whole family, for on account of the goodness of one man grace devolves upon the whole family. Mt. 10:13: *And if that house be worthy, your peace shall come upon it.*

The merit of this mercy is the mercy which they showed to the Apostle. Hence he says, **because he hath often refreshed me** by giving him rest. Mt. 5:7: *Blessed are the merciful: for they shall obtain mercy.* Ecclus. 18:16: *Shall not the dew assuage the heat?* Philem. 1:7: *The bowels of the saints have been refreshed by thee, brother.* **And hath not been ashamed of my chain.** Below 2:9: *Wherein I labour even unto bands, as an evildoer.* **But when he was come to Rome, he carefully sought me,** as a friend does. Ecclus. 6:7: *If thou wouldst get a friend, try him before thou takest him.* Prov. 17:17: *He that is a friend loveth at all times.*

And he wishes him the mercy of the future age when he says, **in that day,** in which the Lord shall judge all men, when mercy is necessary not only in Rome but also in Ephesus. And so he is worthy of the divine mercy.

Chapter Two

Lecture One

1 [n. 35] **Thou therefore, my son, be strong in the grace which is in Christ Jesus:**
2 [n. 37] **And the things which thou hast heard of me by many witnesses, the same commend to faithful men, who shall be fit to teach others also.**
3 [n. 38] **Labour as a good soldier of Christ Jesus.**
4 [n. 40] **No man, being a soldier to God, entangleth himself with secular businesses; that he may please Him to Whom he hath engaged himself.**
5 [n. 44] **For he also that striveth for the mastery, is not crowned, except he strive lawfully.**
6 [n. 45] **The husbandman, that laboureth, must first partake of the fruits.**
7 [n. 47] **Understand what I say: for the Lord will give thee in all things understanding.**

35. Above the Apostle led Timothy to love the preaching of the Gospel [n. 7], and here he leads him to a constant endurance of martyrdom. First, he leads him to endure suffering for the salvation of the faithful; second, he teaches him how to resist the infidels when he says in verse fourteen [n. 59], **Contend not in words.** Again, first he brings in a preparation for undergoing martyrdom; second, an exhortation for martyrdom, when he says in verse eight [n. 48], **Be mindful that the Lord Jesus Christ.** The preparation for martyrdom is given regarding three things: first, fortitude of mind; second, the distribution of good things, when he says [n. 37], **And the things which thou hast heard;** third, the fruitful labor of military service, when he says [n. 38], **Labour as a good soldier.**

36. Now, fortitude is required for martyrdom since it regards the dangers of death. And so he says, **Thou therefore, my son,** whom I have begotten through the Gospel, **be strong in the grace.** Ps. 30:25: *Do ye manfully, and let your heart be strengthened.* **Which is** not in you, for such fortitude is vain, but **in Christ Jesus.** Eph. 6:10: *Finally, brethren, be strengthened in the Lord, and in the might of His power.*

Or, **in the grace,** etc., that is, the gift of God given gratis through Christ. Jn. 1:17: *Grace and truth came by Jesus Christ.*

37. Second is the dispensation of good things.

Regarding this it must be known that when someone approaches death, he makes arrangements for what is his. Not less, therefore, should the saints be anxious about spiritual goods credited to them, which should not perish after they die but be lent to others; thus, he admonishes him that if he is to come to martyrdom, he must dispense the doctrine of faith.

And first he posits how he received it, namely, through hearing. Hence he says, **which thou hast heard of me,** as I did of Christ. And I say not **of me** alone, but confirmed **by many witnesses,** that is, by the Law and the prophets. Rom. 3:21: *Being witnessed by the law and the prophets.* Or by the Apostles. I Cor. 15:11: *For whether I or they, so we preach, and so you have believed.* **The same commend,** inasmuch as these things have been accepted. Wis. 7:13: *Which I have learned without guile, and communicate without envy.* **To faithful men,** so that they may not seek temporal gain but the glory of God. I Cor. 4:2: *Here now it is required among the dispensers, that a man be found faithful.* Mt. 24:45: *Who, thinkest thou, is a faithful and wise servant, whom his lord hath appointed over his family, to give them meat in season.*

Likewise, those who are suitable to dispense; hence he says, **who shall be fit to teach others also.**

They ought to be suitable in three ways. First, in intellect, that they may be wise for understanding. Lk. 21:15: *For I will give you a mouth and wisdom, which all your adversaries shall not be able to resist and gainsay.* And in speech, that they may be eloquent for teaching. Is. 50:4: *The Lord hath given me a learned tongue, that I should know how to uphold by word him that is weary.* And in works, since Jesus began to do and to teach, as it says in Acts 1:1.

38. Then when he says, **Labour as a good soldier,** he gives the third thing, which is the legitimate work of military service: he first makes an exhortation for this; second, he gives the reward for the labor when he says [n. 44], **For he also that striveth;** third, the wage of this warfare, when he says [n. 45], **The husbandman.** Again, he first exhorts him to legitimate labor; second, he explains what labor is legitimate when he says [n. 40], **No man.**

39. He says therefore, **Labour as a good soldier of Christ Jesus.** There are three ways in which someone is a soldier of Christ. First, inasmuch as he fights

against sin. Job 7:1: *The life of man upon earth is a warfare;* and 14:14: *All the days in which I am now in warfare,* etc. And this fight is against the flesh, the world, and the devil. Eph. 6:12: *For our wrestling is not against flesh and blood,* etc.

Second, someone is a soldier of Christ by fighting against errors. II Cor. 10:4: *For the weapons of our warfare are not carnal, but mighty to God unto the pulling down of fortifications, destroying counsels,* etc.

Third, the military service of martyrs is against tyrants. And this is more laborious. Job 25:3: *Is there any numbering of his soldiers?* And a soldier (*miles*) ought not to rest since he is named from the warfare to be endured (*militia sustinenda*).

40. Then when he says, **No man,** he explains what legitimate labor is. First, he leads him to labor; second, he shows what a good soldier ought to be like when he says [n. 43], **that he may please Him.** He does two things regarding the first: first, he gives an example; second, he makes it clear [n. 44].

41. He says therefore, **No man, being a soldier to God,** etc. Regarding this it must be known that there is one end for a spiritual warfare, and another for a corporal warfare. The end of the latter is that they obtain victory against the enemies of the homeland, and so the soldiers have to abstain from those things which withdraw them from fighting, for example, business and pleasures. I Cor. 9:25: *And every one that striveth for the mastery, refraineth himself from all things.* But the end of the spiritual army is to have victory over men who are against God, and so spiritual soldiers must abstain from all things which withdraw one from God. Such are secular businesses, since anxiety for this world suffocates the word. And so he says, **entangleth himself.**

42. But on the contrary, secular businesses are temporal things. But the Apostle did this when he lived by the labor of his own hands.

I respond that the Apostle says, **entangleth himself,** but he does not say, "exercise himself." He is entangled in them whose care and solicitude is tied around them. And then these things are properly forbidden to the soldiers of Christ, in whom it is shown that being entangled is not necessary. Likewise, he does not say simply, "entangle," but **entangleth himself,** since sometimes someone is entangled but does not entangle himself. For he entangles himself when without godliness and necessity he takes up business; but when the necessity of the duty of godliness and authority is exercised, then he does not entangle himself, but is entangled by such necessity. Rom. 16:2: *Assist her in whatsoever business she shall have need of you.*

43. The reason why he ought not entangle himself is **that he may please Him to Whom he hath engaged himself.** I Jn. 2:15: *If any man love the world, the charity of the Father is not in him.* For he is a soldier of Christ who devotes himself to war for God. And so he ought to try to **please Him to Whom he hath engaged himself.**

44. Then when he says, **For he also that striveth,** he gives the reward for labor. And since someone would say: O Paul, you impose great things, but what is the fruit of them? He responds: Take the example of secular fights where not all but only those who fight lawfully receive the crown. Thus also shall it be in spiritual matters, that no one is crowned unless he keep the due laws of war. I Cor. 9:25: *They indeed that they may receive a corruptible crown; but we an incorruptible one.* Wis. 4:2: *It triumpheth crowned for ever.*

45. Then when he says, **The husbandman,** he shows the wages and forbids secular business. First, he proposes the wages under a metaphor; second, he explains it when he says [n. 47], **Understand what I say.**

46. Now, the office of preachers and teachers is the office of soldiers, inasmuch as they rise up against enemies and vices. So also farmers, inasmuch as they make a harvest by promoting good things. The field is the Church, and the chief farmer is God, working interiorly and exteriorly. Jn. 15:1: *I AM the true vine; and My Father is the husbandman.* Men work on the external ministry. I Cor. 3:6: *I have planted, Apollo watered, but God gave the increase.* These are the exterior farmers. Job 31:39: *If I have...afflicted the soul of the tillers thereof.*

Therefore, such a farmer ought to receive fruits, and the fruits are the works of virtue. Ecclus. 24:23: *My flowers are the fruit of honour and honesty.*[1] Gal. 5:22: *But the fruit of the Spirit is, charity, joy, peace, patience, benignity, goodness, longanimity.* Among these fruits there are also the fruits of almsgiving. Acts 9:36: *This woman was full of good works and almsdeeds which she did.* Therefore, these chiefly should perceive the fruits so that they may rejoice. First, from the fruits of subjects. Phil. 4:1: *Therefore, my dearly beloved brethren, and most desired, my joy and my crown.* Second, from temporal assistance, not as the chief reward but as wages. Gal. 6:6: *And let him that is instructed in the word, communicate to him that instructeth him, in all good things.* Mt. 10:10: *The workman is worthy of his meat.*

47. Then when he says, **Understand what I say,** he explains what he had said, using parables after the manner of Christ. Mt. 13:9: *He that hath ears to hear, let him hear.* This is as if to say: Take these things with a spiritual understanding. Dan. 10:1: *There is need of understanding in a vision.*

It is as if someone were to say: You say: receive the wage, O Timothy, but you yourself do not do this for you wish to live from the work of your hands. Hence, **Understand what I say,** since discretion is necessary for they are not to be received where there is occasion for avarice against the Gospel, whether on account of cupidity or on account of leisure. And this you will be able to understand because **the Lord will give thee in all things understanding.** I Jn. 2:27: *His unction teacheth you of all things.*

Lecture Two

8 [n. 48] Be mindful that the Lord Jesus Christ is risen again from the dead, of the seed of David, according to my gospel.

9 [n. 50] Wherein I labour even unto bands, as an evildoer; but the word of God is not bound.

10 [n. 52] Therefore I endure all things for the sake of the elect, that they also may obtain the salvation, which is in Christ Jesus, with heavenly glory.

11 [n. 53] A faithful saying: for if we be dead with Him, we shall live also with Him.

12 If we suffer, we shall also reign with Him. If we deny Him, He will also deny us.

13 If we believe not, He continueth faithful, He can not deny Himself.

14 [n. 58] Of these things put them in mind, charging them before the Lord. [n. 59] Contend not in words, for it is to no profit, but to the subverting of the hearers.

15 [n. 60] Carefully study to present thyself approved unto God, a workman that needeth not to be ashamed, rightly handling the word of truth.

48. Above the preparation for martyrdom was given [n. 35], and here is the exhortation to it. First, he offers an example of the reward; second, an example of martyrdom, when he says [n. 50], **Wherein I labour;** third, he makes manifest the logical consequence of the reward and martyrdom when he says [n. 53], **A faithful saying.**

49. For the reward of the precious death of martyrdom is a glorious resurrection, the example of which goes before us in Christ our head. And so he says, **Be mindful,** etc., as if to say: Keep our Lord Jesus Christ in mind against tribulations. Prov. 3:6: *In all thy ways think on Him, and He will direct thy steps.* Now, there are many things to be considered in Him, but especially the resurrection. To this many things are ordered, and chiefly the whole state of the Christian religion. Rom. 10:9: *For if thou confess with thy mouth the Lord Jesus, and believe in thy heart that God hath raised Him up from the dead, thou shalt be saved.*

And note that he says that He is raised, since even if the Father raised Him, yet He also rose by His own power, and He is the first of those who rise, as it says in I Cor. 15:20. But since it was according to His human nature that He rose and died, he says, **of the seed of David.** Rom. 1:3: *Who was made to Him of the seed of David, according to the flesh.*

According to my gospel, that is, the one preached by me. I Cor. 15:1: *I make* *known unto you, brethren, the gospel which I preached to you.* He who preaches the Gospel is a minister of the Gospel, just as he who baptizes is a minister of baptism. Nevertheless, it cannot be said to be my baptism, but it can be said thus of the Gospel since exhortation and solicitude avail much.

50. Then when he says, **Wherein I labour,** he shows himself as an example of martyrdom: first, his punishment; second, the reason for it, when he says [n. 52], **Therefore I endure all things.**

51. He shows that there are three things in punishment: severity, reproaches, and perseverance.

Severity when he says, **Wherein,** namely, in preaching the Gospel, or for which **I labour,** that is, I am afflicted, and this **even unto bands,** since when he wrote this epistle he was in fetters in Rome. Eph. 6:19–20: *The mystery of the gospel for which I am an ambassador in a chain.*

Reproaches from the infidels when he says, **as an evildoer,** for Christians were then considered the worst of men. Lk. 6:22: *Blessed shall you be when men shall hate you, and when they shall separate you, and shall reproach you,* etc. Christ also was condemned as an evildoer. Is. 53:12: *And was reputed with the wicked.*

Perseverance when he says, **but the word of God is not bound.** For although the body be bound, yet the word of God is not, since preaching came from the will of the Apostle, which was free, chiefly on account of the efficacy of charity, which fears nothing. Rom. 8:38: *For I am sure that neither death, nor life,* etc. I Jn. 3:20: *God is greater than our heart.* And it is said that while he was in chains he converted many.

52. Then when he says, **Therefore I endure all things,** he shows the cause; for punishment does not make a martyr, but the cause does.

Now, the cause of martyrdom is twofold: divine honor and the salvation of one's neighbor. For God, because it says in Rom. 8:36, *For Thy sake we are put to death all the day long.* For the salvation of our neighbor since he says, **for the sake of the elect.** Jn. 15:13: *Greater love than this no man hath, that a man lay down his life for his friends.*

And he says, **for the sake of the elect,** since whatsoever good comes about happens especially for the good of the elect and not the reprobate.

And how? **That they also may obtain the salvation.** But is not the passion of Christ sufficient? It must be said to this that it is effectively, but the sufferings of the Apostle were expedient in two ways. First, he gave an example of persevering in the faith; second, faith was strengthened, and from this they were led to salvation. And this **in Christ Jesus,** that is, the grace which comes to us through Him. Mt. 1:21: *He shall save His people from their sins.* And this brought not only the present salvation of grace but also **with heavenly glory.** Mt. 5:12: *Be glad and rejoice, for your reward is very great in heaven.*

53. Then when he says, **A faithful saying,** he posits the logical consequence of the reward for the merit of martyrdom. First, he gives an attestation; second, the logical consequence, when he says [n. 55], **for if we be dead with Him;** third, he confirms this through a witness, when he says [n. 58], **Of these things put them in mind.**

54. He says therefore, **A faithful saying,** that is, the word which I speak is faithful. Apoc. 22:6: *These words are most faithful and true.*

55. Then when he says, **for if we be dead with Him,** etc., he posits the logical consequence: first, the recompense of the good; second, the punishment of the evil, when he says [n. 57], **If we deny Him.**

56. There are two things in the reward of the good: restoration through the resurrection and the addition of glory to which they rise. And so he shows the first, through which one arrives at Christ through the restoration of life; second, he shows that through Him one comes to the resurrection when he says, **If we suffer.**

He says therefore: **if we be dead with Him,** namely, with Christ, and this through the reception of a sacrament in baptism. Rom. 6:4: *For we are buried together with Him by baptism into death.* Likewise, by wearing ourselves down with penance. Gal. 5:24: *And they that are Christ's, have crucified their flesh, with the vices and concupiscences.* Likewise, by dying for the confession of the truth, just as Christ did. Ps. 115:6: *Precious in the sight of the Lord is the death of His saints.* If, therefore, we die with Christ, **we shall live also with Him,** that is, just as He rose, so we shall also. Rom. 6:5: *For if we have been planted together in the likeness of His death, we shall be also in the likeness of His resurrection.*

Then he treats of the glory which the saints merit through the ignominy of death. Lk. 24:26: *Ought not Christ to have suffered these things, and so to enter into His glory?* And so he says, **If we suffer,** namely, suffering afflictions and reproaches, **we shall also reign with Him,** that is, we shall attain the kingdom together with Him. Mt. 5:10: *Blessed are they that suffer persecution for justice' sake: for theirs is the kingdom of heaven.*

57. Then when he says, **If we deny Him,** he shows the consequence regarding punishment. Now, someone is able to sin against the faith in two ways: first, by denying it exteriorly; second, by giving it up interiorly.

Regarding the first he says, **If we deny Him,** namely, before others, **He will also deny us** in the judgment. Mt. 25:12: *Amen I say to you, I know you not.* To deny them is not to know them as members of His flock.

Regarding the second he says, **If we believe not,** that is, if we cast the faith away from our hearts, **He continueth faithful,** that is, He holds to His own faith. Hence, He remains faithful in His own faith since faith is nothing other than a participation in or adherence to the truth. But He is truth itself, which cannot deny itself.

Then He is not omnipotent.

I respond that from this is He omnipotent, that **He can not deny Himself.** For to fall away pertains more to impotence, since that something falls away from its own being is through weakness of its own power. But for Christ to deny Himself is to fall away from Himself; therefore, that He cannot deny Himself is by reason of His perfect power. Hence neither is sin in Him, as has been said, nor can He deny His power and justice – rather, He punishes. Mk. 16:16: *He that believeth not shall be condemned.*

But is not God able to remit someone's punishment? Indeed He can, according to the order of His wisdom; but against the order of His wisdom and justice, no.

58. Then when he says, **Of these things put them in mind,** he confirms what he said through a witness, as if to say: Together with others I admonish you to have these things always in your heart, **charging them before the Lord,** that is, bringing in the witness before Whom I speak.

59. Then when he says, **Contend not in words,** he shows how to resist infidels: first, he lays out the manner of resisting them; second, he shows what things are to be resisted when he says in verse sixteen [n. 63], **But shun profane and vain babblings.** Again, first he excludes the undue manner of resisting; second, he posits the correct manner when he says [n. 62], **Carefully study.** Regarding the first, first he excludes the inappropriate manner; second, he gives the reason why, when he says [n. 61], **for it is to no profit.**

60. He says therefore: **Contend not in words.** Contention signifies a conflict in words. Therefore, it can be understood in two ways since the one speaking sharpness is depraved in two ways. In one way, if through this one comes to favor what is false, as when someone, trusting in his loud voice, impugns the truth. In another way, on account of the disorder, as when sharpness is used either beyond the appropriate manner or against the character of the person. But if it be used moderately, both with due circumstances and for the truth, it is not a sin. And thus in rhetoric it is one instrument of exhortation. But in Sacred Scripture it is taken to mean the disorder. I Cor. 11:16: *But if any man seem to be contentious, we have no such custom, nor the church of God.*

And he says **in words,** since some debate only in words of sarcasm. And this is properly to contend. If it happens not in words only but with true arguments, this is to dispute, not to contend.

61. Then when he says, **for it is to no profit,** he gives the reason for his point. For moderate disputation, when it takes place with reason, is useful for instruction; but when it takes place with words only, then it is litigious. Therefore he says, **but to the subverting of the hearers,** and this in two ways. In one way, when that which is certain comes into doubt; in another way, when the hearers are scandalized. Prov. 14:23: *Where there are many words, there is oftentimes want.*

Hence Jas. 3:16: *For where envying and contention is, there is inconstancy, and every evil work.*

But ought not someone dispute about the faith before people without contention?

I respond that a distinction is necessary. On the part of the audience, either they are disturbed by infidels, and then a public disputation is useful, since through this the simple become more instructed when they see those in error confounded. But if they are not agitated by infidels, then a dispute is not useful but dangerous. Likewise, on the part of the disputant, if he be prudent, thus confuting his adversary manifestly, then he ought to dispute publicly. But if not, then he in no way ought to engage in dispute.

62. Then when he says, **Carefully study to present thyself,** he posits the appropriate manner of resisting. First, regarding a right intention; second, regarding a right operation; third, regarding right doctrine.

For he who would dispute ought first to scrutinize his intention, whether he be moved by good zeal. And so he says, **approved unto God,** Who scrutinizes the heart. II Cor. 10:18: *For not he who commendeth himself, is approved, but he, whom God commendeth.* Ps. 16:3: *Thou hast proved my heart, and visited it by night.*

Likewise, that the doctrine which he preaches with his mouth be made firm by his works, for unless he do this he is worthy of shame. Hence he says, **a workman that needeth not to be ashamed,** as if to say: Do this, if you would not be ashamed.

Likewise, that he treat the word of truth rightly, by teaching true and profitable things to his listeners. Hence he adds, **rightly handling the word of truth,** not seeking gain and glory. II Cor. 2:17: *For we are not as many, adulterating the word of God; but with sincerity, but as from God, before God, in Christ we speak.*

Lecture Three

**16 [n. 63] But shun profane and vain babblings: for they grow
much towards ungodliness.**

**17 [n. 67] And their speech spreadeth like a canker: of whom are
Hymeneus and Philetus:**

**18 Who have erred from the truth, saying, that the resurrection is
past already, and have subverted the faith of some.**

**19 [n. 69] But the sure foundation of God standeth firm, having this
seal: the Lord knoweth who are His; and let every one depart
from iniquity who nameth the name of the Lord.**

**20 [n. 72] But in a great house there are not only vessels of gold and
silver, but also of wood and earth: and some indeed unto honour,
but some unto dishonour.**

63. Above the Apostle instructed Timothy, showing the general manner in
which infidels are to be resisted [n. 59]; here he shows in particular who is to be
resisted. First, he shows who is to be resisted; second, why, when he says [n. 65],
for they grow much; third, how, when he says in verse twenty-two [n. 78], **But
flee thou youthful desires.**

64. He says therefore: **But shun profane and vain babblings.** Here he shows
that there are two things to be avoided, namely, **profane and vain babblings,** and
these refer either to the same thing or to diverse things. For profane things are so
called for being far from the temple,[2] that is, from divine cult, and these are
heretical arguments; these are to be avoided, and so he says, **shun profane** things.
It can also be said that these profane things are **vain babblings** which are repugnant to the faith. Ps. 11:3: *They have spoken vain things every one to his neighbour.*

65. Then when he says, **for they grow much,** he shows why they are to be
avoided, and this in two ways: first, from the harm which they bring; second, from
the fruit of avoiding them, when he says in verse twenty-one [n. 75], **If any man
therefore shall cleanse himself.** Regarding the first he does two things: first, he
shows how they can be harmful by bringing about a subversion of the faith; second, how they cannot completely subvert the faith, when he says [n. 69], **But the
sure foundation.** Again, he first gives his point; second, he adds a similitude,
when he says [n. 67], **And their speech;** third, an example, when he says [n. 68],
of whom are.

66. He says therefore: These things are to be avoided for they impede godliness, which is the worship of God. Hence the doctrine of the faith is the doctrine
of godliness. But ungodliness is doctrine contrary to the faith; hence he says, **for
they grow much towards ungodliness,** that is, they lead to error or erroneous

doctrine. But here error is taken metaphorically for evil men. Below 3:13: *But evil men and seducers shall grow worse and worse: erring, and driving into error.*

67. Then he posits their likeness by saying, **And their speech.**

For in the beginning heretics say some things true and profitable, but when they are given attention, they mix in certain deadly things which they vomit forth. And so he says, **And their speech spreadeth like a canker.** Ecclus. 11:34: *Of one spark cometh a great fire, and of one deceitful man much blood.*

68. Then when he says, **of whom,** he gives an example of this. For these two men at that time corrupted their faith. From them certain men who erred were turned to their babblings. About Philetus it is said above in 1:15, *Thou knowest this, that all they who are in Asia, are turned away from me: of whom are Philetus³ and Hermogenes.* About Hymeneus he says in I Tim. 1:20, *Of whom is Hymeneus.* And he says, **Who have erred.** I Jn. 2:19: *They went out from us.* And this is made worse because, as it says in II Pet. 2:21, *For it had been better for them not to have known the way of justice, than after they have known it, to turn back.*

Now, they erred by saying that the resurrection had already happened. Mt. 27:52: *Many bodies of the saints that had slept arose.* And they said that there is no other resurrection to wait for, but they rose then.

In another way, and better, just as there is a twofold death, so there is a twofold resurrection, namely, of the body and of the soul. About the resurrection of the soul it says in Apoc. 20:6, *Blessed and holy is he that hath part in the first resurrection.* They said, therefore, that all things which are said in the Scriptures were to be referred to the resurrection of the soul, which had already happened. Col. 3:1: *Therefore, if you be risen with Christ, seek the things that are above.* And this error exists even today among the heretics, and through it they still subvert some men.

And fittingly does he say that they **have subverted the faith of some** because they destroy the foundation of faith. Acts 13:10: *O full of all guile, and of all deceit, child of the devil, enemy of all justice, thou ceasest not to pervert the right ways of the Lord.*

69. Then when he says, **But the sure foundation,** he shows how the faith is not completely subverted by heresies: first, that the whole faith of the Church cannot be corrupted by heretical doctrines; second, he shows why God permits some to err when he says [n. 72], **But in a great house.** Again, first he shows the immovability of the faith of the elect; second, he adds a demonstration when he says [n. 71], **having this seal.**

70. He says therefore: They subvert, **But the sure foundation of God standeth firm.** For these are the foundations, by which the grace of standing immovably is given. Mt. 7:25: *For it was founded on a firm⁴ rock.* **Firm,** because it is immobile. For this reason it says earlier in the same place, *And the rain fell,*

and the floods came, and the winds blew, and they beat upon that house, and it fell not.

71. This firmness depends first on divine providence; second, on our free will.

And so regarding the first he says: This firm foundation, **having this seal,** that is, this is the sign of its firmness. Jn. 3:33: *He that hath received His testimony, hath set to His seal that God is true.* This is the first part of the seal, namely, that from divine predestination **the Lord knoweth who are His.** And this is the knowledge of divine predestination. Jn. 10:14.16: *I know Mine, and Mine know Me. And other sheep I have, that are not of this fold.* Mt. 7:23: *I never knew you.*

But regarding the second he says, **and let every one depart from iniquity who nameth the name of the Lord.** It is as if to say: If they have been predestinated by God, through free will they will be saved, since this, that someone in the end does not cling to sin, shows him to be predestinated.

And he posits two things which pertain to the ordination in the state of salvation. First, that he profess the faith, and so he says **every one...who nameth,** etc. Rom. 10:10: *With the mouth, confession is made unto salvation.* Second, that he fall away from sin. Mt. 7:21: *Not every one that saith to me, Lord, Lord, shall enter into the kingdom of heaven,* etc. And so he says, **let** him **depart from iniquity.** Is. 55:7: *Let the wicked forsake his way,* etc.

But that he says, **nameth the name,** is not to be understood that he only names Him with his mouth, but interiorly with faith and exteriorly with deeds.

72. Then when he says, **But in a great house,** he gives the reason why God permits some to err, although He loves all.

And this can be understood in two ways: in general, or in particular to this or that man. For if you ask in particular why He gives to this man the gift of perseverance, and not to that man, no reason can be had but the will of God alone. Augustine says, "Why He draws this one and does not draw that one, do not judge if you do not want to err."

But if you seek why in general He gives it to some and not to others, there is the reason which the Apostle assigns in Rom. 9:16. And it is the same reason as this one, though with different examples. So he says in Rom. 9:22 that God *endured with much patience vessels of wrath, fitted for destruction,* etc. For according to this all things which God does in nature and in grace are deeds to manifest the glory of God – Ecclus. 42:16: *Full of the glory of the Lord is His work* – thus also He makes diverse creatures so that the perfection of divine goodness, which cannot be manifested by one thing, is sufficiently manifested by another. The same consideration holds for one craftsman: in one house there is one window more beautiful than another. Therefore, if someone asks why the whole house is not a window, the reason is that the whole house would then be imperfect. Likewise, the Apostle says in I Cor. 12:17, *If the whole body were the eye, where would be the hearing?* Therefore the Apostle says of the effect of grace that God must manifest justice and mercy. For if He were to save all, there would only be His mercy; but if He were to damn all, there would only be His justice. And so God, willing to manifest His wrath, that is, His justice, etc.

73. And a similar reason holds regarding the perfection of the Church, that there must be diversity in it for it to be perfect. In it there is a threefold diversity: of good men and evil, of good men and better, and of bad men and worse. And imputing this last he says, **But in a great house,** that is, the Church – Bar. 3:24: *O Israel, how great is the house of God, and how vast is the place of His possession! –* **there are not only vessels of gold and silver but also of wood and earth,** where gold and silver are distinguished from earth; likewise, silver from gold, and earth from wood. In the first we see the comparison of the good and evil; in the second, the good and the better; in the third, the bad and the worse. For the gold and the silver are the good men, but the gold are the better men and silver the less good men. In the same way the wood and the earth are the wicked men, but the earth are the worse men while the wood are the less evil men.

74. Consequently he designates a diversity regarding use, so that the good are vessels of honor, as it were deputed for honorable use; the evil are earth and wood, as it were deputed for dishonor, that is, vile use. In the same way among men, some, namely the saints, are as it were precious vessels. Ecclus. 50:10: *As a massy vessel of gold, adorned with every precious stone.* Acts 9:15: *This man is to Me a vessel of election.* But some are useless vessels, namely the evil. Is. 32:7: *The vessels of the deceitful are most wicked.* Ecclus. 21:7: *The heart of a fool is like a broken vessel.* The first vessels are in honor, to whom is due eternal life. Rom. 2:7: *To them indeed, who according to patience in good work, seek glory and honour and incorruption, eternal life.* The second are vessels for dishonor. I Kg. 2:30: *They that despise Me, shall be despised.*

And the aforementioned diversity can be applied in another way to the diversity of the Church, such that golden vessels are the prelates, but silver, wood and earth hold a lesser grade. And that he adds, **and some indeed unto honour,** etc., is not then to be understood to mean that all gold and silver vessels are for honor while earthen vessels are for dishonor, since some are saved from whatever state, while others are damned.

Lecture Four

21 [n. 75] If any man therefore shall cleanse himself from these, he shall be a vessel unto honour, sanctified and profitable to the Lord, prepared unto every good work.

22 [n. 78] But flee thou youthful desires, and pursue justice, faith, hope,[5] charity, and peace, with them that call on the Lord out of a pure heart.

23[n. 81] And avoid foolish questions without discipline,[6] knowing that they beget strifes.

24 [n. 83] But the servant of the Lord must not wrangle: but be mild towards all men, apt to be taught,[7] patient,

25 [n. 85] With modesty admonishing them that resist the truth: if peradventure God may give them repentance to know the truth,

26 [n. 88] And they may recover themselves from the snares of the devil, by whom they are held captive at his will.

75. Above the Apostle showed that profane things are to be avoided by a reason taken from their harm [n. 65]; here he shows the same thing by a reason taken from the fruit of their avoidance: first, he proposes the avoidance of them; second, the fruit of it, when he says [n. 77], **he shall be a vessel.**

76. He calls avoidance a cleansing. He says therefore: There are certain vessels for dishonor, **If any man therefore shall cleanse himself from these,** etc., since association with them defiles. Ecclus. 13:1: *He that toucheth pitch, shall be defiled with it.* And so they are to be avoided. II Cor. 6:17: *Wherefore, Go out from among them, and be ye separate, saith the Lord, and touch not the unclean thing.*

77. And the fruit following is fourfold. The first is from the order to glory, since **he shall be a vessel unto honour;** for if he were defiled by them, he would be a vessel unto dishonor; if he cleanse himself, unto honor. Ps. 138:17: *Thy friends, O God, are made exceedingly honourable.* Prov. 25:4: *Take away the rust from silver, and there shall come forth a most pure vessel.*

Other effects are those of grace, of which the first is the sanctification of man; the second is the ordering of man through a right intention; the third is through the execution of the work. Regarding the first he says, **sanctified.** I Cor. 6:11: *But you are washed, but you are sanctified.* Regarding the second he says, **profitable to the Lord.** But surely the Lord does not need our service? Of course not. Ps. 15:2: *Thou hast no need of my goods.* But he says, **profitable to the Lord,** that is, being profitable means acting for the honor of the Lord. Acts 9:15: *To carry My name before the Gentiles, and kings, and the children of Israel.* Regarding the third he says, **prepared unto every good work.** Ps. 118:60: *I am ready, and am not troubled.*

And he says, **prepared unto every good work,** because the affirmative precepts do not always bind. And so he ought to say **prepared,** so that he may act when necessary.

78. Then [n. 63] when he says, **But flee thou,** he shows how profane things are to be avoided. And he posits two things to be avoided: first, base conversation; second, evil doctrine, when he says [n. 81], **And avoid foolish questions without discipline.** Regarding the first he does two things: first, he shows what is to be avoided; second, what is to be followed, when he says [n. 80], **pursue justice.**

79. He says therefore: I say that you ought to avoid these things so that you may be a purified vessel; therefore, **flee thou youthful desires.**

It must be considered that he says this since Timothy was young. And these are the desires of exterior vanities and carnal pleasures. For it is natural for youth to desire these things. Eccles. 11:10: *For youth and pleasure are vain.* The reason for this is twofold. First, since they have not experienced different things; second, since such natural delights are ordered as medicine against toils. And nature toils in youth, and so they are inclined to these delights.

80. Then when he says, **pursue justice, faith, hope, charity, and peace,** he shows what things are to be pursued. And there are four, of which the first orders one to his subjects, and this is justice, since the prince is the guardian of justice. Prov. 20:8: *The king, that sitteth on the throne of judgment, scattereth away all evil with his look.* The second orders one to Him, and this is faith, for without faith it is impossible to please God, as it says in Heb. 11:6. Third is hope. The fourth orders each to his neighbor, namely charity, and peace, which extends itself to enemies. I Cor. 13:2: *And if I should have all faith, so that I could remove mountains, and have not charity, I am nothing.* From charity follows joy. And peace signifies ordered harmony.

That he adds, **with them that call on the Lord,** etc., can be explained in one way as referring to what he said immediately before. Then it is as if to say: Follow peace **with them,** etc. And that he says, **out of a pure heart,** is given because it is not specious praise, but that **out of a pure heart.**

But Heb. 12:14 says, *Follow peace with all men.* Why then is it said here, **with them that call on the Lord out of a pure heart?**

I respond that as much as it is in us, we must have peace with all men, if this be possible; but there cannot be peace between the good and the wicked for peace bespeaks harmony, which cannot be had with evil men.

In another way, **with them that call on the Lord,** is read to refer to all that preceded. Then it is as if to say: So pursue justice, peace, and all things as do those who call on the Lord, etc.

81. Then when he says, **And avoid foolish,** he exhorts him to avoid evil doctrine: first, he teaches him what to avoid; second, what to pursue, when he says [n. 83], **but be mild.** Regarding the first he does two things: first, he posits his

point; second, he assigns a reason when he says [n. 82], **knowing that they beget strifes.**

82. **Foolish questions** are to be avoided, for they regard stupid things, that is, things which are contrary to wisdom, that is, things which are against divine wisdom. A man ought not put these forward but resist them. Jer. 10:14: *Every man is become a fool for knowledge.*

And he says **without discipline** regarding the manner, which is noisy. Or **without discipline** on the part of those things about which a doubt arises, such that, for example, if a man makes a doubt out of that which the whole Church holds. Job 34:35: *But Job hath spoken foolishly, and his words sound not discipline.*

But questions are to be loved inasmuch as they lead to the truth: it is through this that all men say one thing. But stupid questions do not lead to the truth, but to quarrels, which are to be avoided. Is. 58:4: *Behold you fast for debates and strife.* And so he says, **But the servant of the Lord,** that is, he who gives himself to the service of the Lord, **must not wrangle.** I Tim. 3:3: *Not quarrelsome.*

83. Then when he says, **but be mild,** he shows what must be pursued: first, he states his point; second, the reason for it, when he says [n. 85], **if peradventure God may give them.** Again, the first is in two parts: first, he proposes something general for all; second, something necessary for each, when he says [n. 84], **apt to be taught.**

84. A general thing necessary for him who would dispute is that he be meek. Ps. 24:9: *He will teach the meek His ways.* For meekness is a virtue restraining anger, which disturbs the judgment of the reason, something necessary in a question and judgment of the truth. Mt. 11:29: *Learn of Me, because I am meek, and humble of heart.*

Specifically a man ought to have docility with respect to his superiors, patience with respect to his adversaries, and admonition with respect to false teachers.

Regarding the first he says, **apt to be taught,** that is, prepared to be corrected by whomever. And this is heavenly wisdom. Jas. 3:17: *But the wisdom, that is from above, first indeed is chaste, then peaceable, modest, easy to be persuaded,* etc. Regarding the second he says, **patient.** Ps. 91:15: *They...shall be well patient,*[8] *that they may shew, that the Lord our God is righteous, and there is no iniquity in Him.* Prov. 19:11: *The learning of a man is known by patience.* Regarding the third he says, **With modesty admonishing them,** since correction ought to be modest. Gal. 6:1: *You, who are spiritual, instruct such a one in the spirit of meekness.*

85. Then when he says, **if peradventure,** he gives the reason for this avoidance and responds to a certain tacit question. For someone could say: They resist the truth, and so the need to correct them is imminent. I respond that God the

Father can bring them to repentance, and for this the just man should strive. First, he puts forth the repentance which he ought to intend against his adversaries; second, the fruits of repentance [n. 87]; third, the necessity of repentance [n. 88].

86. He says therefore, **if peradventure,** that is, at some time, **God may give them repentance,** since they resist out of pride, and to such it seems difficult that repentance could be given.

Here he excludes the error of Pelagius who said that the gifts of grace are from our own merits, which is manifestly false through this, since even the principle of good things, namely, repentance, is given by God. Lam. 5:21: *Convert us, O Lord, to thee, and we shall be converted.* Prov. 19: *From Thy fear we have conceived.*[9]

87. The fruit of repentance is twofold: knowledge of the truth and freedom from the power of the devil.

Regarding the first he says, **to know the truth,** since when truth is resisted out of malice, that very malice blinds them; when, therefore, the malice is removed, they know the truth. Jn. 8:32: *And you shall know the truth.*

Regarding the second he says, **And they may recover themselves from the snares of the devil,** that is, from occasions for errors on the part of the intellect, such as false imaginations, and on the part of the affection, such as envy, pride, and suchlike.

88. The necessity for repentance is great; if they have it not, the devil rules over them. Hence he says, **by whom they are held captive,** since he who commits sin is a slave to sin, as it says in Jn. 8:34. And he says, **at his will,** namely, to follow his will. Or that he does his will concerning men.

On the contrary, he does not immediately cast man down headlong as he would want to do.

It must be said that he overtakes a man only when it is permitted him; but it is difficult that what he holds be taken from him. Is. 49:24: *Shall the prey be taken from the strong? or can that which was taken by the mighty be delivered?*

Chapter Three

Lecture One

1 [n. 89] Know also this, that, in the last days, shall come dangerous times.
2 [n. 91] Men shall be lovers of themselves, covetous, haughty, proud, blasphemers, disobedient to parents, ungrateful, wicked,
3 [n. 98] Without affection, without peace, slanderers, incontinent, cruel,[1] without kindness,
4 [n. 101] Traitors, shameless,[2] puffed up, and lovers of pleasures more than of God:
5a Having an appearance indeed of godliness, but denying the power thereof.

89. Above the Apostle instructed Timothy how to resist tribulations and present dangers; here he shows him how to stand against future dangers. First, he foretells future dangers; second, he shows his suitability to resist them when he says in verse ten [n. 113], **But thou hast fully known;** third, he shows how to resist them when he says in chapter four, verse one [n. 129], **I charge thee.** Regarding the first he does two things: first, he foretells the dangers of the last times; second, he shows how their vices are even now to be avoided when he says in verse five [n. 102], **Now these avoid.** Again, the first is in two parts: first, he foretells that there will be dangers in the last times; second, the cause of these dangers, when he says [n. 91], **Men shall be lovers of themselves.**

90. He says therefore: I have told you to avoid profane things, but not only are these to be avoided now, but in the future there remain certain other things to be shunned. They are called the last days because of their proximity to the last day. Jn. 6:55: *I will raise him up in the last day.* Gen. 49:1: *Gather yourselves together that I may tell you the things that shall befall you in the last days.* And

he adds that there **shall come dangerous times.** Mt. 24:9: *And you shall be hated by all nations for My name's sake.*

91. The cause of these things is the abundance of iniquity. Mt. 24:12: *And because iniquity hath abounded, the charity of many shall grow cold.* Faith and charity will either be obliterated or perish totally, for as much as something is removed from its principle, so much does it wane. And so at that time faith and charity shall wane the greater since they will be far from Christ. Lk. 18:8: *But yet the Son of man, when He cometh, shall He find, think you, faith on earth?* And regarding this he first gives the root of their iniquity; second, its diverse species [n. 93].

92. Now, the root of all iniquity is the love of self. A twofold love makes a twofold city.[3]

On the contrary, each man naturally loves himself.

I respond that in man there are two things: rational nature and corporeal nature. Regarding the intellectual or rational, which is called the interior man, as said in II Cor. 4:16, a man ought to love himself more than all others because he would be stupid who would will to sin so that he might withdraw others from sin. But regarding the exterior man, it is praiseworthy that he love others more than himself. Hence, those who in this way love themselves so much are blameworthy. Phil. 2:21: *For all seek the things that are their own; not the things that are Jesus Christ's.*

93. From this root there are diverse species of iniquity. Hence he says, **covetous, haughty,** etc. Regarding this he does three things: first he gives the sins which are an abuse of exterior things; second, those which pertain to the disorder of a man towards others, when he says [n. 95], **blasphemers;** third, those which pertain to the disorder of a man within himself, when he says [n. 98], **incontinent.**

94. There are two things in exterior things: the abundance of riches and the excellence of goods.

Regarding the first he says, **covetous.** Now, cupidity is given first because it is the root of all evils, or because it is near to that love of self which respects exterior goods.

Regarding the second he says, **haughty.** Haughtiness is a species of pride, of which there are four. One is when one attributes to himself what in fact he lacks. The second is when what he has from another he attributes to himself as if he had it from himself. I Cor. 4:7: *Or what hast thou that thou hast not received?* The third is when he attributes to himself by his own merits what he has from another. Lk. 18:12: *I fast twice in a week,* etc. The fourth is when with singularity he wishes to be seen above everyone else, and this is haughtiness. Ps. 130:1: *Lord, my heart is not exalted,* etc.

That he says **proud** is reduced to the other species of pride. Jas. 4:6: *God resisteth the proud, and giveth grace to the humble.*

95. Then he posits the vices regarding others: first, regarding superiors; second, regarding equals, when he says [n. 97], **wicked.**

96. Superiors are threefold. First is God, against this he says, **blasphemers.** Is. 1:4: *They have forsaken the Lord, they have blasphemed the Holy One of Israel, they are gone away backwards.* Then parents, and regarding this he says, **disobedient to parents.** I Kg. 15:23: *Because it is like the sin of witchcraft, to rebel: and like the crime of idolatry, to refuse to obey.* Prov. 30:17: *The eye that mocketh at his father, and that despiseth the labour of his mother in bearing him, let the ravens of the brooks pick it out, and the young eagles eat it.* Lastly, a benefactor inasmuch as he is such; regarding this he says, **ungrateful.** Ps. 37:21: *They that render evil for good,* etc. Col. 3:15: *And be ye thankful.* Wis. 16:29: *For the hope of the unthankful shall melt away as the winter's ice, and shall run off as unprofitable water.*

97. Then he gives the evils which are against an equal and neighbor, of which there are three.

The first pertains to deeds, and so he says, **wicked,** that is, those who perpetrate gravely wicked deeds against their neighbors. Is. 1:4: *Woe to the sinful nation, a people laden with iniquity, a wicked seed, ungracious children,* etc. The second pertains to the affections; hence he says, **Without affection,** that is, without the affection of charity, and **without peace.** The third pertains to speech; hence he says, **slanderers.** Lev. 19:16: *Thou shalt not be a detractor nor a whisperer among the people.*

98. Regarding a man himself he shows three other sins: first, regarding the corruption of the concupiscible part; second, of the irascible part [n. 100]; third, of the rational part [n. 101].

99. Regarding the first he says, **incontinent.** Hence he is said to be incontinent who does not keep himself in his good resolution on account of vile desires. Ecclus. 26:20: *And no price is worthy of a continent soul.*

100. Regarding the irascible he says properly, **cruel,** that is, not meek, for this virtue of meekness moderates the passions of anger. Mt. 11:29: *Learn of Me, because I am meek, and humble of heart.* Ps. 24:9: *He will teach the meek His ways.*

Then he places that which pertains to the effect of the irascible, namely, the exclusion of kindness; hence he says, **without kindness.** For it is natural that when one contrary rules, it excludes the other. Eph. 4:32: *And be ye kind one to another.*

101. Then he posits vices which are unto the corruption of the rational. Now, this power is perfected through prudence, and opposed to prudence are a vice through the abuse of prudence and one through its lack. He gives both.

Regarding the first he says, **Traitors.** Shrewdness, which certain men abuse unto evil, pertains to prudence, and traitors are shrewd. Prov. 11:13: *He that* *walketh deceitfully, revealeth secrets.* Likewise, constancy, which some abuse while being impudent; hence he says, **shameless.** Prov. 3:5: *Lean not upon thy own prudence.*

Then he posits vices which respect the lack of due prudence. First, he gives the cause of this privation when he says, **puffed up.** For the proud are inflated in what they need to do since they do not measure their own powers; thus they fail. Prov. 11:2: *Where pride is, there also shall be reproach: but where humility is, there also is wisdom.* Second, he gives the effect of the privation, that temporal things are placed before the eternal. Hence he says, **and lovers of pleasures more than of God.** Is. 13:22: *Sirens in the temples of pleasure.*

But is it not the same to be incontinent and a lover of pleasure?

I respond that it is not, since properly speaking he is called incontinent who has the hope of fleeing but is conquered by pleasures; properly the lover of them, who has a corrupt judgment, is intemperate.

Then he gives a similitude, saying, **Having an appearance indeed of godliness** – II Cor. 11:13: *Deceitful workmen* – **but denying the power thereof,** namely, the power of godliness, which is said here in two ways. In one way, the power of godliness itself, that is, the virtue of it. Hence he says, **denying,** that is, not having the truth. Tit. 1:16: *They profess that they know God: but in their works they deny Him.* In another way, the power of a thing is said to be that upon which the whole thing depends. Now, the whole power of godliness depends on charity; hence he says, **denying the power thereof,** namely, charity.

Lecture Two

5a [n. 102] Now these avoid.
6 [n. 104] For of these sort are they who creep into houses, and lead captive silly women laden with sins, who are led away with divers desires:
7 Ever learning, and never attaining to the knowledge of the truth.
8 [n. 108] Now as Jannes and Mambres resisted Moses, so these also resist the truth, men corrupted in mind, reprobate concerning the faith.
9 [n. 110] But they shall proceed no farther; for their folly shall be manifest to all men, as theirs also was.
10 [n. 113] But thou hast fully known my doctrine, manner of life, purpose, faith, longsuffering, love, patience,
11 Persecutions, afflictions: such as came upon me at Antioch, at Iconium, and at Lystra: what persecutions I endured, and out of them all the Lord delivered me.

102. Above the Apostle described the dangers of the last days and gave the cause for them [n. 89]; here he teaches that such dangers are also to be avoided in the present: first, he gives an admonition to avoid them; second, he shows in which men in the present the aforementioned dangers may appear when he says [n. 104], **For of these sort are they.**

103. He says therefore: I have said that in the last times there will be the worst of men. But do not believe that being in the present you are safe, for even now they are here. Avoid such men lest you fall into a similar error. Tit. 3:10: *A man that is a heretic, after the first and second admonition, avoid.* And although they are to be avoided in some ways, not with regards to giving them a word of exhortation.

104. And then he shows that even now there are such men: first, he shows the harm they bring; second, the defect they suffer, when he says [n. 109], **men corrupted in mind;** third, the impediment by which they are constrained, when he says [n. 110], **But they shall proceed no farther.** Regarding the first he does two things: first, he shows the harm they bring to subjects; second, the harm they bring to prelates, when he says [n. 108], **Now as Jannes and Mambres resisted Moses.** Again, the first is in two parts: first, he shows their imprudence; second, their cunning, when he says [n. 106], **and lead captive.**

105. Regarding the first he says, **Now these avoid,** since already there are some such, **For of these sort,** that is, from their number, **are they.** I Jn. 2:18: *Even now there are become many Antichrists.* Nor are you to understand that they have been of this sort, namely, wicked and ungrateful, for sinners who have already

converted ought not be called sinners. Ps. 15:4: *Nor will I be mindful of their names by my lips.*

106. Then when he says, **who creep into houses,** he shows their malice. And it can be explained literally, as it were forcing themselves inordinately and going about for the sake of gain. Against which it is said in Ecclus. 21:25, *The foot of a fool is soon in his neighbour's house.* But not on this account are some prohibited from visiting the ill in their homes. Jas. 1:27: *Religion clean and undefiled before God and the Father, is this: to visit the fatherless and widows in their tribulation.*

Or metaphorically it can be explained that **houses** are consciences. Wis. 8:16: *When I go into my house, I shall repose myself with her.* Therefore, they penetrate houses who with cunning wish to know the secrets of the conscience, in order to deceive others. Ecclus. 13:14: *By much talk he will sift thee, and smiling will examine thee concerning thy secrets.* Nonetheless, those who have care for them ought to inquire into the state of their consciences. Prov. 27:23: *Be diligent to know the countenance of thy cattle, and consider thy own flocks.*

107. Then when he says, **and lead captive,** he shows their cunning. And first their malice is touched upon, since they lead them away from freedom and the state of grace. Jas. 1:25: *But he that hath looked into the perfect law of liberty,* etc. And they lead them into the state of slavery, which is the state of sin. Ps. 125:1: *When the Lord brought back the captivity of Sion,* etc. For captivity signifies this. Is. 5:13: *Therefore is My people led away captive, because they had not knowledge.*

Second, he shows upon which persons they exercise their malice, whom he describes first by the fragility of their sex; second, from the malice of their conversation; third, from the vanity of their affections; fourth, from the defect of their discretion.

Regarding the first he says, **silly women,** who are of less discretion and the weaker sex. And he says, **silly women,** since great ladies have counselors so that they may not be seduced. But these are destitute of such assistance. Mt. 23:14: *You devour the houses of widows.* I Mach. 1:34: *And they took the women captive,* etc.

Regarding the second he says, **laden with sins.** Sin is a burden since it does not allow one to walk freely nor to stand erect, but bends one down. Ps. 37:5: *For my iniquities are gone over my head: and as a heavy burden are become heavy upon me.* And so they especially deceive these women since sin prepares the way for seduction. Likewise, since these women are evil, they fear to resist lest they be destroyed.

Regarding the third he says, **who are led away with divers desires,** that is, they are fit to be seduced because of the various desires which they have. Jas. 1:8: *A double minded man is inconstant in all his ways.* And so the first woman was seduced because she did not stand with constancy in the word of the Lord but said, *Lest perhaps we die.* Ecclus. 9:3: *Look not upon a woman that hath a mind for many.*

Regarding the fourth he says, **Ever learning, and never attaining to the knowledge of the truth.** Curiosity always seeks to discover novelties and does not want to stop. Hence he says, **Ever learning.** Prov. 9:13: *A foolish woman and clamorous, and full of allurements, and knowing nothing at all.*

Yet when he says, **Ever learning,** this can refer to those entering their houses.

108. Then when he says, **Now as Jannes and Mambres resisted Moses,** he shows the harm which they offer to prelates and the harm of resisting their doctrine. And he brings in an example from Exodus, when the magi of Pharao resisted Moses, since from the beginning of the world there was always a fight between truth and falsity. II Pet. 2:1: *But there were also false prophets among the people, even as there shall be among you,* etc. In Exodus these magi are not named, but they are here; perchance he received them from some words of the Jews.

So these also resist the truth which we preach. Job 24:13: *They have been rebellious to the light.* Acts 7:51: *You always resist the Holy Ghost.*

109. Then when he says, **men corrupted in mind,** etc., he shows their defect in faith and in deed. In deed, **men...reprobate.** The Gloss: "In their deeds, that is, through their works, they show themselves to be reprobate." Jer. 6:30: *Call them reprobate silver.*

And in faith, **corrupted in mind,** that is, the power of reason. For each thing is called corrupt when it fails of its proper power. And the proper perfection of the mind is the knowledge of the truth. Hence, he is called corrupt in mind who has fallen away from the knowledge of the faith.

110. Then when he says, **But they shall proceed no farther,** he shows how they are constrained: first, he shows them about to be hindered; second, he teaches the manner of hindering them when he says [n. 112], **for their folly shall be manifest.**

111. It must be known regarding the first that the will to harm is a man's from himself, but the power to harm is by God's permission. And God does not permit harm as much as an evil man wills but imposes a limit. Job 38:11: *Here thou shalt break thy swelling waves.* Thus also the devil did not injure Job except inasmuch as God permitted him to do so. Apoc. 7:3: *Hurt not the earth, nor the sea, nor the trees, till we sign the servants of our God in their foreheads.*

And he says, **they shall proceed no farther,** namely, than God permits.

112. The manner of hindering them is to take their cloak and secrecy away, for these are harmful. Job 41:4: *Who can discover the face of his garment?* And so he says, **for their folly shall be manifest,** by God revealing it when He *both*

will bring to light the hidden things of darkness, and will make manifest the coun-
sels of the hearts, as it says in I Cor. 4:5. **As theirs also was,** namely, the magi of
Pharaoh, which was manifest when they were not able to perform signs.

113. Then when he says, **But thou,** etc., he shows Timothy's suitability for
resisting such dangers: first, he shows this from his education by the Apostle; second, from his experience with the Scriptures, when he says in verse fifteen [n.
119], **And because from thy infancy.** Again, first he shows he was sufficiently
instructed by the Apostle; second, how he was able to be educated by others in
general, when he says in verse twelve [n. 116], **And all that will live,** etc.
Regarding the first, he first shows how he was instructed in word; second, by
example, when he says [n. 115], **purpose.**

114. But it must be known that someone is educated in word in two ways: in
one way, about truth to be acknowledged; second, about justice to be performed.
Regarding the first he says, **But thou hast fully known my doctrine,** that is, you
were instructed in the Catholic faith; therefore, you are quite able to avoid these
dangers. Regarding the second he says, **manner of life.** One's manner of life is
instruction about some things to be done which are subject to human operation.
Phil. 4:12: *Everywhere, and in all things I am instructed.*

115. And then how he was instructed by example. And first regarding good
things to be done; second, evils to be tolerated, when he says, **patience.**

Among good things to be done he places two. The first is the intention for a
due end, and regarding this he says, **purpose,** which is of the end. Wis. 8:9: *I pur-*
posed therefore to take her to me to live with me. And to this one arrives through
good works, which are derived from three virtues: faith, hope, and charity. And
first he posits faith when he says, **faith.** Heb. 11:6: *But without faith it is impos-*
sible to please God. Second, hope, when he says, **longsuffering,** which waits for
a long time. II Cor. 6:6: *In longsuffering.* Third, charity, when he says, **love.** I Jn.
3:14: *He that loveth not, abideth in death.*

Then regarding evils to be endured he teaches him about three things by
recalling them to mind. First is the patience which he had; second the evils he sustained; third, the divine aid which came to him.

First, then, he posits **patience,** which has a perfect work, as it says in Jas. 1:4.
And first he gives the matter of patience, namely, **Persecutions** in general. Mt.
10:23: *And when they shall persecute you in this city, flee into another.* Then
specifically, when he says, **afflictions,** which he suffered in his own body. II Cor.
11:25: *Thrice was I beaten with rods,* etc. Third, in particular, when he says, **such**
as came upon me at Antioch, at Iconium, and at Lystra, as it says in Acts 16
and 17. The Jews persecuted him while Timothy was there.

But the divine assistance was present. And so he says, **out of them all the**
Lord delivered me. II Cor. 1:4: *Who comforteth us in all our tribulation.*

Lecture Three

12 [n. 116] And all that will live godly in Christ Jesus, shall suffer persecution.

13 [n. 118] But evil men and seducers shall grow worse and worse: erring, and driving into error.

14 [n. 119] But continue thou in those things which thou hast learned, and which have been committed to thee: knowing of whom thou hast learned them;

15 [n. 121] And because from thy infancy thou hast known the holy scriptures, which can instruct thee to salvation, by the faith which is in Christ Jesus.

16 [n. 124] All scripture, inspired of God, is profitable to teach, to reprove, to correct, to instruct in justice,

17 [n. 128] That the man of God may be perfect, furnished to every good work.

116. Above [n. 113] the Apostle proposed as an example to Timothy the persecutions he had suffered. And lest it seem that he alone had passed through such suffering, he shows that they are common to the saints: first, he teaches how the saints suffer here penal defects; second, how the evil progress through the defect of fault, when he says [n. 118], **But evil men.**

117. He says therefore: I have endured persecutions, and not only I, but also **all. Godly** is taken in two ways: sometimes for the virtue of piety with respect to divine worship, as it says above in verse five, *Having an appearance indeed of godliness;* sometimes for mercy to one's neighbor. I Tim. 4:8: *But godliness is profitable to all things.* **And all that will live godly in Christ Jesus,** etc., that is, who wish to observe the worship of the Christian religion. Tit. 2:12: *We should live soberly, and justly, and godly in this world,* etc. And such **shall suffer persecution,** especially in the primitive Church, when Christ was everywhere impugned by the Jews and Gentiles. And so Jn. 16:2: *Yea, the hour cometh, that whosoever killeth you, will think that he doth a service to God.* Mt. 24:9: *You shall be hated by all nations for My name's sake.*

And all that will live godly, etc., that is, those who through faith in Christ will to show mercy to their neighbors must suffer persecutions, and if not without, then at least within, when they suffer the defects of their neighbors, whose faults and punishments they see. II Cor. 11:29: *Who is scandalized, and I am not on fire?* II Pet. 2:8: *Dwelling among them, who from day to day vexed the just soul with unjust works.* Ps. 118:158: *I beheld the transgressors, and I pined away,* etc.

And there are other persecutions which cannot be lacking to all the saints: those of the flesh, those of the world, and those of the devil. Gal. 5:17: *For the flesh lusteth against the spirit.* Rom. 7:24: *Unhappy man that I am, who shall deliver me from the body of this death?* Ps. 33:20: *Many are the afflictions of the just.*

118. Then when he says, **But evil men,** he shows that evil men fall into worse evils, namely faults. He calls them **evil** in themselves, inasmuch as they cling to sin. Mt. 21:41: *He will bring those evil men to an evil end.* **And seducers** to their neighbors' harm, inasmuch as they lead them apart from the way of truth, which is common to all. Rom. 16:18: *And by pleasing speeches and good words, seduce the hearts of the innocent.* But these, not content with the evils they have committed, **shall grow worse and worse.** Apoc. 22:11: *He that is filthy, let him be filthy still.*

But on the contrary it says above in verse nine, *But they shall proceed no farther.* It must be said to this that those who grow worse are permitted by God to do so. Or it means here that they grow worse by the intention of their malice; but according to divine providence they are prohibited lest they be able to complete what they have begun. The evil grow worse in themselves, inasmuch as they err regarding the truth. Mt. 22:29: *You err, not knowing the Scriptures, nor the power of God.* They likewise err in action, and in this way all the evil err. Prov. 14:22: *They err that work evil.* Likewise among their neighbors, for they are seducers; hence he says, **driving into error,** namely, by suggesting that they could come to the kingdom of heaven through success, against which it said above, **And all that will live godly in Christ Jesus, shall suffer persecution.** Is. 3:12: *O My people, they that call thee blessed, the same deceive thee.*

119. Then when he says, **But continue thou,** he admonishes him to remain in his instruction. And he exhorts him in three ways: first, on the part of the teacher; second, on the part of Timothy himself [n. 121]; third, on the part of those things which he received [n. 122].

120. He says therefore: *Thou hast fully known my doctrine,* as it says above in verse ten; therefore **continue thou in those things.** Eccles. 10:4: *If the spirit of Him that hath power, ascend upon thee, leave not thy place.* I Cor. 15:58: *Therefore, my beloved brethren, be ye steadfast and unmoveable.*

Therefore he says, **which thou hast learned and which have been committed to thee,** for every Christian learns what is of faith, and this is the doctrine of salvation. Jn. 6:45: *Every one that hath heard of the Father, and hath learned, cometh to Me.* But especially the lessons of faith are entrusted to prelates, inasmuch as they ought to dispense them to others. Gal. 2:7: *They had seen that to me was committed the gospel of the uncircumcision.*

And why must he continue? Because I have it from the Master of knowledge Who could not err. II Cor. 13:3: *Do you seek a proof of Christ that speaketh in me?* And so continue in these firmly, **knowing of whom thou hast learned them,** namely, from Paul, who learned it neither by man nor through man, as it says in Gal. 1:12.

121. Second, from his own character. For it is vile for a man, nourished in the good from his youth, to fall away in his age. Ecclus. 26:27: *And he that passeth over from justice to sin, God hath prepared such an one for the sword.* And thus was Timothy raised. Prov. 22:6: *A young man according to his way, even when he is old he will not depart from it.* Hence he says, **And because from thy infancy thou hast known the holy scriptures,** which are the texts of the Old Testament which he learned from his infancy since he was the son of a Jewish woman, as it says in Acts 16:1. Therefore his mother made him learned in these. This is against Manichaeus, since the Apostle here calls the Old Testament **holy scriptures,** which cannot be understood about the New Testament since he was not taught the writings of the New Testament from his infancy.

122. Third, on the part of those things which he had received. For if someone has knowledge in which there is no profit, he deserts it and passes to another. But if the knowledge is very useful, it is stupid to leave it. First, he gives the reason; second, he makes it clear when he says [n.124], **All scripture,** etc.

123. He says therefore: I say that you received the Holy Scriptures, which are not to be despised for they are profitable. Is. 48:17: *I am the Lord thy God that teach thee profitable things.* Hence he adds, **which can instruct thee.** Jn. 6:69: *Lord, to whom shall we go? Thou hast the words of eternal life.* Jn. 5:39: *Search the scriptures, for you think in them to have life everlasting; and the same are they that give testimony of Me.* And these Scriptures can instruct you **to salvation,** but not without **the faith which is in Christ Jesus.** Rom. 10:4: *For the end of the law is Christ, unto justice to every one that believeth.* Heb. 11:6: *But without faith it is impossible to please God.*

124. And he makes the reason clear by saying, **All scripture.** Here he shows that the Holy Scriptures are the way to salvation. And he posits three things: he commends Scripture by reason of its principle [n.125], by reason of its profitable effect [n.127], and by reason of its ultimate fruit and success.

125. For if you consider its principle, it is privileged over all other writings: all others were handed down by human reason, but Sacred Scripture is divine; and so he says, **All scripture, inspired of God.** II Pet. 1:21: *For prophecy came not by the will of man at any time: but the holy men of God spoke, inspired by the Holy Ghost.* Job 32:8: *The inspiration of the Almighty giveth understanding.*

126. But you will say: How are not all the other writings divinely inspired when according to Ambrose everything true, by whomsoever it is said, is from the Holy Spirit?

It must be said that God works anything in a twofold manner: immediately, as His own work, such as a miracle, and through the mediation of inferior causes, such as natural works. Job 10:8: *Thy hands have made me,* etc. Which things yet happen by the operation of nature. And thus in man He instructs the understanding both immediately through the Sacred Scriptures and mediately through other writings.

127. The effect of Sacred Scripture is twofold: it teaches man to know the truth and persuades him to work justice. Jn. 14:26: *But the Paraclete, the Holy Ghost...will teach you all things* to be known, *and bring all things* to be done *to your mind.* And therefore it is profitable to know the truth and direct it into action.

For there is the speculative reason and the practical reason. And in each two things are necessary: that it know the truth and refute errors. For this work is the work of the wise man, namely, not to lie and to refute the liar. Regarding the first he says, **is profitable to teach,** namely, the truth. Ps. 118:66: *Teach me goodness and discipline and knowledge.* Regarding the second he adds, **to reprove.** Tit. 1:9: *That he may be able to exhort in sound doctrine, and to convince the gainsayers.*

Again, regarding the practical reason two things are necessary: to lead one back from evil and into the good. Ps. 33:15: *Turn away from evil and do good.* Regarding the first he says, **to correct,** which is to correct from evil. Mt. 18:15: *But if thy brother shall offend against thee, go, and rebuke him between thee and him alone.* Job 5:17: *Blessed is the man whom God correcteth.* Regarding the second he says, **to instruct in justice.** And all these things Sacred Scripture does. Is. 8:11: *He hath taught me, with a strong arm,* etc.

Thus the effects of Scripture are fourfold: regarding the speculative reason, to teach the truth and to reprove falsity; regarding the practical reason, to free one from evil and to lead him to the good.

128. Its ultimate effect is that it leads men to perfection. For it does good not in whatever manner, but it perfects. Heb. 6:1: *Let us go on to things more perfect.* And so he says, **That the man of God may be perfect,** since a man cannot be perfect unless he is a man of God. For something is perfect which lacks nothing. Therefore, then is a man perfect when he is **furnished,** that is, prepared, **to every good work,** not only for those which are necessary for salvation but also for those which are of supererogation. Gal. 6:9: *And in doing good, let us not fail.*

Chapter Four

Lecture One

1 [n. 129] I charge thee, before God and Jesus Christ, Who shall judge the living and the dead, by His coming, and His kingdom:
2 [n. 132] Preach the word: be instant in season, out of season: reprove, entreat, rebuke in all patience and doctrine.
3 [n. 138] For there shall be a time, when they will not endure sound doctrine; but, according to their own desires, they will heap to themselves teachers, having itching ears:
4 [n. 140] And will indeed turn away their hearing from the truth, but will be turned unto fables.
5 [n. 141] But be thou vigilant, labour in all,¹ do the work of an evangelist, fulfil thy ministry. Be sober.

129. With the dangers of the last times having been dealt with, and the suitability of Timothy for dealing with them [n. 89], the Apostle shows how he ought to resist. And first, he gives an admonition; second, the necessity for it, when he says [n. 138], **For there shall be a time.** Likewise, first is given his testimony; second, an admonition, when he says [n. 132], **Preach the word.**

130. In a witness two things are to be considered: before whom one appeals and through whom [n. 131].

He appeals before two, namely, before Him Who is our beatitude, and before Him Who leads us into beatitude. Now, God is our beatitude. Ps. 21:12: *Blessed is the nation whose God is the Lord.* And so he says, **I charge thee, before God,** that is, I call God as witness that I make this admonition. For this witness is not deceived. II Cor. 1:23: *I call God to witness upon my soul.*

And Jesus Christ, to Whom it belongs to introduce us into beatitude. Rom. 5:2: *By Whom also we have access through faith into this grace.* Or otherwise, He leads us in since He **shall judge the living and the dead.** And then he calls those **living** who will be found alive at His coming; truly they will be dead, but since they will rise in but a brief time, they are called **living.** I Thess. 4:15: *We who are alive, who remain unto the coming of the Lord, shall not prevent them who have slept.* Or, he calls the good **alive,** for they are alive with the life of grace; the **dead** are the evil ones. I Jn. 3:14: *He that loveth not, abideth in death.* And He also judges these. Acts 10:42: *It is He Who was appointed by God, to be judge of the living and of the dead.*

But since Christ is God, why does the Apostle use here the phrase **before God and Jesus Christ?**

I respond that it can be said that **before God** means the Father, and **Jesus Christ** means the Son. For the Father is the font of the divinity.

131. Then when he says, **by His coming,** etc., he witnesses through two things desirable to the saints. The first is His coming. Lk. 12:36: *And you yourselves like to men who wait for their lord, when he shall return from the wedding.* Apoc. 22:20: *Come, Lord Jesus.*

The second is His kingdom. Mt. 6:10: *Thy kingdom come.* He rules according to a general power over all creatures. Mt. 28:18: *All power is given to Me in heaven and in earth.* But specially and spiritually He reigns in the saints now through grace and in the future through glory. Those who are saints are not of this world. Jn. 18:36: *My kingdom is not of this world.* But this kingdom is begun here, and in the future it will be consummated, when all kingdoms will be subjected to Him, whether they will or no. Ps. 109:1: *Until I make Thy enemies Thy footstool.*

132. Consequently when he says, **Preach the word,** the admonition is given, and this that he pursue doctrine, which is twofold. One is for all, which he gives first. The other is for some, and this he gives second, when he says [n. 135], **reprove.** Likewise, he first admonishes him to follow the general teaching; second, the manner of following it [n. 134].

133. He says, therefore, **Preach the word,** namely, the word of the Gospel. Mk. 16:15: *Go ye into the whole world, and preach the gospel to every creature.* There are two things in preaching: announcing the truth and the instruction of morals; these two things a preacher ought to do. Lk. 24:27: *And beginning at Moses and all the prophets, He expounded to them in all the scriptures, the things that were concerning Him.*

134. The manner is urgent and continual; hence he says, **be instant in season, out of season.** II Cor. 11:28: *My daily instance.*

But he says, **out of season.** On the contrary, Ecclus. 20:22: *A parable coming out of a fool's mouth shall be rejected: for he doth not speak it in due season.* Likewise, Prov. 15:23: *A word in due time is best.*

It must be said that a preacher according to truth ought always to preach in season, but according to the false opinion of those listening he ought to preach out of season, since the preacher of the truth is always in season for the good and out of season for the wicked. Jn. 8:47: *He that is of God, heareth the words of God. Therefore you hear them not, because you are not of God.* Ecclus. 6:21: *How very unpleasant is wisdom to the unlearned.* For if a man would wish to preserve this opportuneness so that he would only speak to those who want to hear, this would profit only the just. But he must also preach sometimes to the wicked to convert them. And for this does he add, **out of season.**

135. Then when he says, **reprove,** he posits his teaching in particular: first, he posits it; second, the manner, when he says [n.137], **in all patience.**

136. Now, when educating someone, one can specially educate him either regarding those things pertaining to the faith, so that he might teach the truth, for example, and remove error. And regarding this first he says, **reprove,** namely errors. Tit. 2:15: *Rebuke with all authority.* Or about those things pertaining to good morals, and for this he must sometimes lead him to the good, even if he be a superior, and then he must kindly and peacefully admonish him; and so he adds, **entreat.** I Tim. 5:1: *An ancient man rebuke not, but entreat him as a father.* Gal. 6:1: *You, who are spiritual, instruct such a one in the spirit of meekness,* especially if he sins not out of malice. But if he instructs or establishes evil, one ought to rebuke him, and so he says, **rebuke.** Tit. 1:13: *Wherefore rebuke them sharply, that they may be sound in the faith.* Job 5:17: *Refuse not therefore the chastising of the Lord.*

137. But what is the manner? **In all patience,** lest you appear irate and instruct out of anger when it ought to be done with tranquility. Prov. 19:11: *The learning of a man is known by patience.* Ps. 91:15–16: *They...shall be well patient,*[2] *that they may shew, that the Lord our God is righteous, and there is no iniquity in Him.* **And doctrine,** namely, about those things which pertain to faith, and those which pertain to morals. Jer. 3:15: *They shall feed you with knowledge and doctrine.*

138. Then when he says, **For there shall be,** he shows the necessity of the foregoing admonition. And it is a threefold necessity: first, on the part of the listeners; second, on the part of Timothy, when he says [n. 141], **But be thou vigilant;** third, on the part of the Apostle, when he says in verse six [n. 145], **For I am even now.** Regarding the first he does two things: first, he proposes its necessity; second, he explains what he said, when he says [n. 140], **And will indeed turn away.**

139. The first necessity is the perversity of the hearers in hearing, such that they do not want to hear useful things but curiosities. He says therefore regarding the first: **Be instant,** while they do not want to hear sound doctrine, **For there shall be a time, when they will not endure sound doctrine,** when there shall be evil teachers. Acts 20:29: *I know that, after my departure, ravening wolves will enter in among you, not sparing the flock.* Hence he says, **they will not endure,** that is, your teaching, or rather that of Christ, will be odious to them. Prov. 8:8: *All my words are just, there is nothing wicked nor perverse in them.*

Another perversity is that they want to hear curious and harmful things inordinately. Prov. 1:22: *O children, how long will you love childishness, and fools covet those things which are hurtful to themselves, and the unwise hate knowledge?* Therefore he says, **but, according to their own desires, they will heap to themselves,** that is, multiply, **teachers.** Against this it says in Jas. 3:1, *Be ye not many masters, my brethren, knowing that you receive the greater judgment.* And it is a heaping to oneself when those who are unworthy or insufficient are multiplied; and it is more of a heaping if there be four who are unworthy than if there be a hundred good men, since, as it says in Wis. 6:26, *Now the multitude of the wise is the welfare of the whole world.* Is. 30:10: *Speak unto us pleasant things.*

And this is according to their own desires since one wants to hear one thing, and another something else, and so they seek different teachers. Thus he says, **teachers having itching ears.** He is said to have an itch in his feet who does not want to rest, and in his ears who always wants to hear news, unheard things, curiosities, and sometimes harmful things. In Acts 17:21 the Athenians had leisure for nothing else than to learn or hear something new. And in this way is heretical teaching multiplied. Prov. 9:17: *Stolen waters are sweeter, and hidden bread is more pleasant.*

140. Then when he says, **And will indeed turn away,** he explains what he said. First, he posits what he had said, that they do not endure sound doctrine, when he says, **And will indeed turn away their hearing from the truth.** Sound doctrine is when there is no admixture of falsity; therefore they do not endure sound doctrine who do not want to hear the truth. Os. 4:1: *There is no truth, and there is no mercy, and there is no knowledge of God in the land.* Jn. 8:45: *But if I say the truth, you believe Me not.* Second, what he had said, **they will heap to themselves,** he explains when he says, **but will be turned unto fables.** A fable is composed from wonders in which truth is lacking. And such things men having itching ears want to hear. I Tim. 4:7: *But avoid foolish and old wives' fables.*

141. Then when he says, **But be thou vigilant,** he gives the necessity on the part of Timothy, to whom this office was entrusted; and so it was necessary that he preach. First, he admonishes him to vigilance; second, to labor [n. 143]; third, the labor is regulated [n. 144].

142. He says, then, **But be thou vigilant.** It is as if he had said: They act thus, **But be thou vigilant.** Mt. 24:42: *Watch ye therefore, because ye know not what hour your Lord will come.* Lk. 2:8: *And there were in the same country shepherds watching, and keeping the night watches over their flock.* Rom. 12:8: *He that ruleth, with carefulness.*

143. But since carefulness without labor is useless, he first brings him to labor in general; second, he determines in what he is to labor; third, the necessity of laboring.

He says, therefore, **be thou vigilant,** but in such a way that you may do something; and so, **labour.** Wis. 3:15: *For the fruit of good labours is glorious.* And this **in all,** that is, among every kind of man. Is. 32:20: *Blessed are ye that sow upon all waters.* Mk. 16:15: *Preach the gospel to every creature.*

Hence, he next determines in what he is to labor, saying, **do the work of an evangelist,** that is, evangelize. For this is a noble work, since Christ was sent for this. Lk. 4:43: *To other cities also I must preach the kingdom of God: for therefore am I sent.* Is. 41:27: *The first shall say to Sion: Behold they are here, and to Jerusalem I will give an evangelist.* Sometimes a man is called an evangelist when he writes a Gospel, and thus there are four evangelists; sometimes, when he preaches it, and in this way it is said here and in Eph. 4:11.

Now, the necessity of this labor, which is **thy ministry,** has been entrusted to you. And so, **fulfil** it by preaching. Col. 4:17: *And say to Archippus: Take heed to the ministry which thou hast received in the Lord, that thou fulfil it.* And he fulfills the office of evangelist who preaches in word and fulfills in deed. Acts 1:1: *All things which Jesus began to do and to teach.*

144. Then he leads him to moderation, saying, **Be sober,** either with corporeal sobriety which befits a preacher – Eccles. 2:3: *I thought in my heart, to withdraw my flesh from wine* – or sobriety is given here for discretion, which is better. Acts 26:25: *I speak words of truth and soberness.* I Pet. 5:8: *Be sober and watch.*

Lecture Two

6 [n. 145] For I am even now being offered as a pre-libation:[3] and the time of my dissolution is at hand.

7 [n. 148] I have fought a good fight, I have finished my course, I have kept the faith.

8a [n. 150] As to the rest, there is laid up for me a crown of justice, which the Lord the just judge will render to me in that day: and not only to me, but to them also that love His coming.

145. Above the Apostle warned Timothy to be instant in doctrine, for the sake both of those listening and of Timothy himself [n. 138]. Here he brings in a third necessity, on the part of the Apostle, and it is that in a short time he would be taken from the world. And first he foretells his imminent death; second, he commands him to visit him, when he says in verse eight [n. 154], **Make haste.** He does two things regarding the first: first, the immediacy of his death is described; second, the safety of the one dying, when he says [n .148], **I have fought.** Regarding the first he does two things: first, he tells the sufferings he experienced; second, he foretells his death, which was expected, when he says [n. 147], **and the time.**

146. Regarding the first he says, **For I am even now being offered as a pre-libation,** as if to say: I shall be sacrificed immediately. Phil. 2:17: *Yea, and if I be made a victim upon the sacrifice and service of your faith, I rejoice, and congratulate with you all.* Ps. 115:8: *I will sacrifice to Thee the sacrifice of praise,* by suffering for Thee. In ancient times, in the sacrifices which were offered from liquids, certain ones became foretastes, and these were called pre-libations. Rom. 11:16: *For if the pre-libations[4] be holy, so is the lump also.* And so he calls his imminent sufferings pre-libations.

147. And although I may have experienced them for a long time now, **the time of my dissolution is at hand.** And dissolution is twofold: body and soul. Eccles. 12:7: *And the dust return into its earth, from whence it was, and the spirit return to God, Who gave it.* Likewise there is a dissolution of the body into dust. Gen. 3:19: *For dust thou art, and into dust thou shalt return.*

148. Then when he says, **I have fought,** he shows the security of his death. But it must be known that there is a difference between the death of a just man and that of a sinner, since, as it says in Prov. 11:7, *When the wicked man is dead, there shall be no hope any more.* For, since he has hope in these transitory things, he does not have hope in eternal things. But the just man has hope in eternal things and not in transitory things.

First, he gives the merit of this security; second, his security regarding his reward, when he says [n. 150], **As to the rest.**

149. The merit of this life is in three things: in resisting evils, making progress in doing good, and in using well the gifts of God.

The first is called a certain fight; hence he says, **I have fought a good fight.** But a fight is called good, first, if it be for a good reason, for example, for the faith or justice, as in the case of the Apostle. Jude 1:3: *I was under a necessity to write unto you: to beseech you to contend earnestly for the faith.* Ecclus. 4:33: *Strive for justice for thy soul, and even unto death fight for justice.* Second, according to the manner of the fight, if it be fought legitimately and carefully. Above 2:5: *For he also that striveth for the mastery, is not crowned, except he strive lawfully.* I Cor. 9:26–27: *I so fight, not as one beating the air: But I chastise my body.* Third, because of the difficulty of the fight. Wis. 10:12: *And gave him a strong conflict, that he might overcome.*

The second, which is progress in the good, is called the course; hence he says, **I have finished my course.** I Cor. 9:24: *So run that you may obtain.* And the course is called profit for the saints, for they run with haste so that, always improving, they may attain perfection, stirred up by the prod of charity. Heb. 4:11: *Let us hasten therefore to enter into that rest.* Ps. 118:32: *I have run the way of Thy commandments.*

But as yet the fight and course of death remained; therefore, he had not fought or consummated the course. But it must be said that just as a man who begins well and intends to finish manages the work perfectly, so also the Apostle: for he had already begun and intended to finish.

Good use of the gifts of God is twofold. One is keeping the faith, and so he says, **I have kept the faith,** which he does who uses the gifts of God for the glory of God and the salvation of his neighbor. Mt. 24:45: *Who, thinkest thou, is a faithful and wise servant, whom his lord hath appointed over his family, to give them meat in season.* I Tim. 1:12: *He hath counted me faithful, putting me in the ministry.* Or, I have kept in me the power of faith. Rom. 14:23: *For all that is not of faith is sin.*

On account of which, Mt. 10:16: *Be ye therefore wise as serpents,* that is, keep the faith as the head and foundation of the virtues.[5]

150. Then when he says, **As to the rest,** his hope for a reward is given: first, he gives the hope; second, he shows the giver of it when he says [n. 152], **which the Lord the just judge will render;** third, he gives the sharers of the reward when he says [n. 153], **but to them also.**

151. He says therefore: From this, that I have fought and finished the course, nothing remains except that I be crowned. It is called a crown of justice which the Lord renders from His justice.

But on the contrary, eternal life is given by grace. Rom. 6:23: *But the grace of God, life everlasting;* and 8:18: *For I reckon that the sufferings of this time are not worthy to be compared with the glory to come.* Therefore, it is not given out of justice.

I respond that it is a grace for you regarding the root of meriting, but justice regarding the act, which proceeds from the will. Or, **a crown of justice** is what is given out of justice, since it is given to the just according to their works. Is. 3:10: *Say to the just man that it is well, for he shall eat the fruit of his doings.*

This crown is twofold: the first principal, the other secondary. The first is the essential reward, which is nothing else than rejoicing in the truth. Is. 28:5: *In that day the Lord of hosts shall be a crown of glory, and a garland of joy to the residue of His people.* Therefore, God is our crown. The second is a crown which is owed for special works, and this is an aureola. One is given to martyrs. Above 2:5: *For he also that striveth for the mastery, is not crowned, except he strive lawfully.* And it is for this that he says, **I have fought a good fight.** Another is due to virgins. Wis. 4:2: *And it triumpheth crowned for ever, winning the reward of undefiled conflicts.* And so he says, **I have finished my course.** Apoc. 14:4: *These are they who were not defiled with women: for they are virgins. These follow the Lamb whithersoever He goeth.* The third is for doctors. Prov. 4:9: *She shall give to thy head increase of graces, and protect thee with a noble crown.* And for this does he say, **I have kept the faith.**

And he says, **there is laid up,** that is, reserved according to eternal predestination. Above 1:12: *For I know Whom I have believed, and I am certain that He is able to keep my deposit until that day.*

152. God is the giver of this, and so he says, **which the Lord the just judge will render to me,** that is, through His justice, **in that day.** For this is the crown of glory, and it is twofold: that of the soul, and this is rendered to the saints on that day, namely, on the day of death. Hence he says, **the time of my dissolution is at hand.** II Cor. 5:1: *For we know, if our earthly house of this habitation be dissolved, that we have a building of God.* And that of the body, and this is given **in that day,** namely, the day of judgment. I Cor. 15:43: *It is sown in dishonour, it shall rise in glory. It is sown in weakness, it shall rise in power.*

153. The sharers of this are all the saints; hence he says, **and not only to me** is it held in store. Apoc. 22:20: *Come, Lord Jesus.* Cant. 5:1: *Let my beloved come into his garden, and eat the fruit of his apple trees.* Those who do not love God have no reason to love His coming. Amos 5:18: *Woe to them that desire the day of the Lord,* for the reward is only given for charity. Jn. 14:21: *And he that loveth Me, shall be loved of My Father: and I will love him, and will manifest Myself to him.*

Lecture Three

8b[n. 154] Make haste to come to me quickly.
9 [n. 156] For Demas hath left me, loving this world, and is gone to Thessalonica:
10 Crescens into Galatia, Titus into Dalmatia.
11 [n. 157] Only Luke is with me. Take Mark, and bring him with thee: for he is profitable to me for the ministry.
12 But Tychicus I have sent to Ephesus.
13 [n. 158] The cloak that I left at Troas, with Carpus, when thou comest, bring with thee, and the books, especially the parchments.
14 [n. 159] Alexander the coppersmith hath shewn[6] me much evil: the Lord will reward him according to his works:
15 [n. 162] Whom do thou also avoid, for he hath greatly withstood our words.
16 [n. 163] At my first answer no man stood with me, but all forsook me: may it not be laid to their charge.
17 [n. 166] But the Lord stood by me, and strengthened me, that by me the preaching may be accomplished, and that all the Gentiles may hear: and I was delivered out of the mouth of the lion.
18 The Lord hath delivered me from every evil work: and will preserve me unto His heavenly kingdom, to whom be glory for ever and ever. Amen.
19 [n. 169] Salute Prisca and Aquila, and the household of Onesiphorus.
20 Erastus remained at Corinth. And Trophimus I left sick at Miletus.
21 Make haste to come before winter. Eubulus and Pudens, and Linus and Claudia, and all the brethren, salute thee.
22 The Lord Jesus Christ be with thy spirit. Grace be with you. Amen.

154. The Apostle asks [n. 145] to be visited: first, he calls Timothy to himself; second, he indicates his state, when he says [n. 159], **Alexander the coppersmith;** third, he concludes his epistolary salutation, when he says [n. 169], **Salute Prisca and Aquila.** Again, he first commands that he come; second, he gives him a companion when he says [n. 157], **Take Mark;** third, he shows what to bring, when he says [n. 158], **The cloak that I left.** Regarding the first he does two things: first, he calls him; second, he gives the reason for calling him, when he says [n. 156], **For Demas hath left me.**

155. He says, therefore: Since I am shortly to quit this world, **Make haste to come to me quickly.** And this so that they may console each other and help him in preaching the Gospel, for which he was anxious and in chains. Prov. 18:19: *A brother that is helped by his brother, is like a strong city.*

156. The reason for calling him is this, that he was destitute of due companionship. And first by one who left on account of his own fault; second, since he had sent them to preach.

He says, then, **For Demas hath left me,** etc., that is, he put the love of this world before my love. I Jn. 2:15: *If any man love the world, the charity of the Father is not in him.* **Crescens,** a certain disciple, was sent **into Galatia. Titus** the Apostle sent **into Dalmatia,** where he is said finally to have been the bishop. Job 38:35: *Canst thou send lightnings, and will they go?* **Only Luke is with me,** whom he retained for preaching the Gospel, in which he was pleasant and agreeable. II Cor. 8:18: *Whose praise is in the gospel through all the churches.*

157. Then when he says, **Take Mark, and bring him,** he assigns a companion to him. And regarding this he does two things: first, he gives him a companion; second, the reason for it.

This Mark was also called John, and he was a cousin of Barnabas. Acts 15:37–39 says that Barnabas wanted to take Mark, but Paul did not want him. And because of this dissension between them, they parted ways. Col. 4:10: *Mark, the cousin german of Barnabus, touching whom you have received commandments; if he come unto you, receive him.*

The reason for this is **for he is profitable to me,** etc.

158. Then when he says, **The cloak that I left,** etc., he tells him what to bring. **Carpus** was a certain saint.

A **cloak,** according to Jerome, was a certain volume of the Law, which had paper rolled up, and this was called a cloak. Or a **cloak** is an article of clothing; according to Chrysostom it was common. And since the Apostle of Rome was poor, not taking things from others, he wanted his clothing to be brought to him. Haymo says that it was a special vestment as a sign of nobility. Hence in Acts 22:25 Paul says that he is a citizen of Rome. For Paul's father served the Romans in Tarsus of Cilicia, for which reason he was made a Roman citizen; and the cloak was a sign of a consul. And perhaps his father was the consul there. Or, a **cloak** was a knapsack in which were books, as it seems since what follows is **and the books.**

But why does the Apostle, filled with the Holy Spirit, need books? Moreover, his own dissolution was approaching.

I respond that he wanted them for two reasons. First, to have consolation in reading. I Mach. 12:9: *Having for our comfort the holy books.* For in books is found a remedy for trials. Or he says this lest they be lost, but rather saved for the faithful. Again, as much as his death drew near, so much did he draw close to the service of the Scriptures, just as it is said about Ambrose that unto his final illness he ceased not to write. Hence, writing on Ps. 47:2, *Great is the Lord, and exceedingly to be praised,* etc., he died.

Especially the parchments. Parchments are paper without writing, or documents where he had written letters or his preaching.

159. Then when he says, **Alexander,** etc., he shows how things were and are with him: first, on the part of men; second, on the part of God, when he says [n. 166], **But the Lord stood by me.** Again, the first is in two parts: first, he tells him about one who was against him; second, about negligence of those who did not help him, when he says [n. 163], **At my first answer.** Again, first he gives the fault of one assailing iniquitously; second, he shows his future punishment when he says [n. 161], **the Lord will reward him;** third, he shows how he may also be punished by the Church, when he says [n. 162], **Whom do thou also avoid.**

160. It seems that this Alexander was a coppersmith, or a guardian of the treasury, and he was from those who said that it was necessary for salvation to keep the legal observances. I Tim. 1:19–20: *Having faith and a good conscience, which some rejecting have made shipwreck concerning the faith. Of whom is Hymeneus and Alexander.* And some say that it is he about whom it says in Acts 19:24 that he started a sedition against the Apostle. But the names differ, since in that place was Demetrius, and in this Alexander; and the location, since that was in Ephesus, and this in Rome.

And he adds, **hath shewn me much evil.** And notice that he did not say *done,* but **shewn,** for the wicked can show their mind against the just, but not always satisfy it. Jer. 1:19: *And they shall fight against thee, and shall not prevail: for I am with thee.* Job 5:12–13: *Who bringeth to nought the designs of the malignant, so that their hands cannot accomplish what they had begun: Who catcheth the wise in their craftiness, and disappointeth the counsel of the wicked.*

161. Then when he says, **the Lord will reward him,** etc., he gives his future punishment.

But notice that he does not say *May the Lord reward him,* but **the Lord will reward him,** signifying that his punishment is prepared by God, which the Apostle foresaw because of the other's obstinacy. Ps. 61:13: *Thou wilt render to every man according to his works.* Nevertheless, although punishment is reserved for him in the future, the Church ought still to punish him by excommunicating him.

162. Hence he adds, **Whom do thou also avoid,** namely, as a heretic. Tit. 3:10: *A man that is a heretic, after the first and second admonition, avoid.* He also gives the reason for this instruction by saying, **for he hath greatly withstood our words.** Acts 7:51: *You always resist the Holy Ghost.*

163. Next he posits the negligence of those who helped him not: first, he reprehends their fault; second, he begs pardon for them when he says [n. 165], **may it not be laid.**

164. He says, therefore, **At my first answer,** etc. The Gloss says that the Apostle fought often against a perversely teaching Alexander and no one aided him in person. But this does not seem to be the sense of it, since this Alexander was not so great that the Apostle needed others to dispute with him. But it must be said that, as it is said in Acts 25:21, *Paul appealing to be reserved unto the hearing of Augustus,* he had to be sent to Caesar to discuss the reason for his mission, and the Jews came against him. And this the Apostle called his first defense, in which his disciples did not aid him, fearing punishment from the cruel Nero. Ecclus. 51:10: *I looked for the succour of men, and there was none.* Is. 63:3: *I have trodden the winepress alone, and of the Gentiles there is not a man with me.*

But it could be said that this was the case because from the beginning no one knew it. But this is false; rather, they fell away from a certain pusillanimity. Ps. 87:19: *Friend and neighbour Thou hast put far from me: and my acquaintance, because of misery.* Job 6:15: *My brethren have passed by me, as the torrent that passeth swiftly in the valleys.*

165. But since they acted thus out of weakness, he prays for them and does not excommunicate them, saying, **may it not be laid to their charge.** Lk. 6:28: *Pray for them that calumniate you.*

166. Then when he says, **But the Lord stood by me,** he shows what was done for him on the part of God: first, His aid; second, the effect of this aid, when he says [n. 168], **that all the Gentiles may hear.**

167. He says, therefore: All have left me, but where man is lacking, the Lord offers Himself. Ps. 26:10: *For my father and my mother have left me: but the Lord hath taken me up.* Hence he says, **But the Lord stood by me,** to help me. Jer. 20:11: *But the Lord is with me as a strong warrior.* Ps. 15:8: *I set the Lord always in my sight: for He is at my right hand, that I be not moved.* And how? **And strengthened me**, by giving strength of mind so that I might not be stupified before Caesar. Ez. 3:14: *The hand of the Lord was with me, strengthening me.* And this **that by me the preaching may be accomplished,** which is the case when it is diffused to many and when what is said with the mouth is done in works. Acts 9:15: *This man is to Me a vessel of election, to carry My name before the Gentiles.*

168. Then when he says, **that all the Gentiles may hear,** the effect of divine aid is given: first, regarding the past; second, regarding the future; third, he gives thanks. But the favors of the past are twofold: freedom from fault and punishment.

He says, therefore: The Lord stood by me, and so in that calling I was freed, since I was not condemned by Caesar, but it was permitted me to go where I wanted. And so he says, **that all the Gentiles may hear,** so that, namely, others might be strengthened to come to him. Ps. 95:5: *Declare His glory among the Gentiles.* And so that the insults of the Jews might be silenced. And he adds, **I was delivered out of the mouth of the lion,** that is, from the cruelty of Nero. Prov. 19:12:

As the roaring of a lion, so also is the anger of a king. Prov. 28:15: *As a roaring lion, and a hungry bear, so is a wicked prince over the poor people.* Second, he was freed from fault; hence he says, **The Lord hath delivered me from every evil work.** But some are freed from pain and fall into the fault of a denial of the faith. Ps. 17:18: *He delivered me from my strongest enemies, and from them that hated me.* And this is through God. Wis. 8:21: *And as I knew that I could not otherwise be continent, except God gave it,* etc.

In the future He **will preserve me.** Is. 45:17: *Israel is saved in the Lord with as eternal salvation.* And he says, **unto His heavenly kingdom.** Lk. 22:29: *And I dispose to you, as My Father hath disposed to Me, a kingdom.* Mt. 5:12: *Your reward is very great in heaven.*

And so he gives thanks by saying, **to Whom be glory for ever and ever.** I Tim. 1:17: *Now to the king of ages, immortal, invisible, the only God, be honour and glory for ever and ever. Amen.*

169. Then when he says, **Salute,** etc., he enjoins to Timothy a greeting to others; second, he greets him on the part of others; third, on his own part. Again, regarding the first he enjoins their greeting; second, he determines the time of his coming.

He says, therefore: **Salute Prisca,** a woman, **and Aquila,** her husband, whom he puts first perhaps because they were more devout, **and the household of Onesiphorus.** Why not him but rather his house? Perhaps because he was dead, and so he greets the family; or perhaps he was with the Apostle in Rome.

Determining the time of his coming, he first shows its necessity; second he describes its manner. The necessity is on account of others remaining in other places and because of sea storms.

Then he gives the persons greeting, as is clear.

And in his usual way, lest the epistle be falsified, he writes with his own hand, **Grace be with you. Amen.**

The Commentary of St. Thomas Aquinas on
The Epistle of St. Paul to Titus

Synoptical Outline of Titus

I. Greeting [n. 3]

II. Epistolary Narrative [n. 10]: he intends to fortify the Church against heretics.

    A. Admonition of Titus to instruct others to resist heretics [n. 10]

        1. Admonition to institute bishops, who resist the heretics [n. 10]

            a. the commission made to Titus of instituting bishops [n. 10]

            b. what the bishops ought to be like [n. 13]

            c. manifestation of the point [n. 16]

        2. The necessity of this commission [n. 25]

            a. on the part of false teachers [n. 25]

                i. the condition of the false teachers [n. 25]

                ii. the perversity of their study [n. 28]

            b. on the part of evil listeners [n. 29]

                i. their condition [n. 29]

                ii. the remedy [n. 33]

    B. How he ought to resist them [n. 47]

        1. In general [n. 47]

        2. More particularly [n. 49]

            a. sound doctrine against perversity of life [n. 49]

                i. the individual conditions of men [n. 49]

                ii. all of them generally [n. 77]

            b. sound doctrine against heretics and errors [n. 98]

                i. what things to avoid in doctrine [n. 98]

                ii. certain familiar things said to Titus [n. 104]

Prologue

If the householder did know at what hour the thief would come,
he would surely watch, and would not suffer his house to be bro-
ken open. – Lk. 12:39

1. The prelate of the church is signified by the householder on account of three things which he ought to show forth, namely generation unto faith, erudition unto salvation, and protection unto security.

The first because just as corporeal life is through the soul, so the spiritual life is through faith. Hab. 2:4: *The just shall live in his faith.* And just as someone is generated unto carnal life through the emission of corporeal seed, so also unto spiritual life through the infusion of spiritual seed, which is the word of God, as it says in Mt. 13:3–17. I Cor. 4:15: *By the gospel, I have begotten you.* Likewise through erudition. Ecclus. 7:25: *Hast thou children? instruct them.* Is. 48:17: *I am the Lord thy God that teach thee profitable things.* In the same manner through protection and defense. Deut. 32:10: *He led him about, and taught him.* For to each prelate is committed the care of his subjects. I Kg. 20:39: *Keep this man: and if he shall slip away, thy life shall be for his life, or thou shalt pay.* And Heb. 13:17: *For they watch as being to render an account of your souls.*

But knowledge is required for this generation. Os. 4:6: *Because thou hast rejected knowledge, I will reject thee, that thou shalt not do the office of priesthood to Me.* And therefore he says, **If the householder did know.** For it is required that he know.

Likewise, beyond erudition, it is required that he be solicitous. Rom. 12:8: *He that ruleth, with carefulness.* Lk. 2:8: *And there were in the same country shepherds watching, and keeping the night watches over their flock.* But to guard them, fortitude is required, in order to protect. It is said in I Mach. 3:3 of Judas Machabeus, *And he got his people great honour, and put on a breastplate as a giant, and girt his warlike armour about him in battles, and protected the camp with his sword.* And therefore it is said that he **would not suffer his house,** that is, the Church, **to be broken open.** I Tim. 3:15: *That thou mayest know how thou oughtest to behave thyself in the house of God, which is the church of the living God.* This is the house of God as the lord, and of a prelate as a servant. Heb. 3:5: *And Moses indeed was faithful in all his house as a servant.* This is penetrated by a thief, that is, a heretic. Abd. 1:5: *If thieves had gone in to thee, if robbers by night, how wouldst thou have held thy peace?* He is called a thief, because he comes in a hidden manner, and walks in the shadows. Wherefore *thief* comes from *oven,*[1] which is dark; such are these through obscure dogmas. Prov. 9:17: *Stolen waters are sweeter, and hidden bread is more pleasant.* Likewise from a perverse intention, because they intend to kill. Jn. 10:10: *The thief cometh not, but for to steal, and to kill, and to destroy.* In the same manner from the mode of entering, because they do not do so through the gate. I Jn. 4:3: *And every spirit that dissolveth Jesus, is not of God: and this is Antichrist,* etc.

2. In such a manner therefore, the intention of this epistle is fittingly drawn from the things having been set forth, in which the Apostle instructs Titus how he ought to rule the Church, as is clear in the argument.

Chapter One

Lecture One

1 [n. 3] Paul, a servant of God, and an apostle of Jesus Christ, according to the faith of the elect of God and the acknowledging of the truth, which is according to godliness:
2 [n. 6] Unto the hope of life everlasting, which God, Who lieth not, hath promised before the ages[1] of the world:
3 [n. 8] But hath in due times manifested His word in preaching, which is committed to me according to the commandment of God our Saviour:
4 [n. 9] To Titus my beloved son, according to the common faith, grace and peace from God the Father, and from Christ Jesus our Saviour.

3. This epistle is divided into the salutation and the epistolary narration, when he says in verse five [n. 10], **For this cause.**

4. In the first part, there is first set forth the person saluting, who is made known in three ways, namely, from his name, when he says **Paul,** which signifies humility. I Cor. 15:9: *For I am the least of the apostles.*

Likewise from his condition, when he says, **a servant.** Ps. 115:7: *O Lord, for I am Thy servant.*

Against this is Jn. 15:15: *I will not now call you servants.* I respond that the saints are sometimes called servants, sometimes not, but sons. For servitude is twofold. One is from fear, which does not befit the filiation of God, but is distinguished from it. Rom. 8:15: *For you have not received the spirit of bondage again in fear,* etc. The other is from love, which is consequent to the filiation of God. And the reason for this distinction is that the free man is he who is for his own sake, who does what he wills; but the servant is he who is for the sake of another.

But the cause, which is the principle of the work, is threefold, namely the final, formal and efficient causes. If, therefore, on account of the final cause, thus all the saints are servants of God, because they do all things on account of God. I Cor. 10:31: *Therefore, whether you eat or drink, or whatsoever else you do, do all to the glory of God.* And this is out of love, from which it proceeds that we operate all things on account of God. But if on account of a moving cause, which is extrinsic and compels, in such a manner it is the servitude of fear, and it is of evil men. If on account of the formal cause, in such a manner it is a habit inclining, and in such a manner certain men are called servants of sin, certain men servants of justice, who according to habit are inclined to evil or to good.

5. Likewise from authority, since he says, **an apostle.** Lk. 6:13: *He chose* over all the other faithful *twelve of them (whom also He named apostles).* Eph. 4:11: *And He gave some apostles.*

And this is described first from the founder, when he says **of Jesus Christ,** because he was chosen by Him. Gal. 1:1: *Not of men, neither by man, but by Jesus Christ,* etc. In like manner because he announced Christ alone. I Cor. 4:5: *For we preach not ourselves, but Jesus Christ our Lord; and ourselves your servants through Jesus.* Again, because he was an ambassador of Christ, Whose authority he used. II Cor. 5:20: *For Christ therefore we are ambassadors.* Eph. 6:20: *For which I am an ambassador.* II Cor. 2:10: *If I have pardoned any thing, for your sakes have I done it in the person of Christ.*

Second, the apostleship is described from fitness; for the apostle is an announcer. Mt. 28:19: *Teach ye all nations.*

A doctor, moreover, ought to have the foundation and perfection of doctrine. The first pertains to all, but the second pertains to preachers and to doctors. And just as in the other sciences there are principles, so in this there are the articles of faith, which are made known to all the faithful according to an infused light; and the articles are the foundations of faith, which is *the substance of things to be hoped for,* etc., as it says in Heb. 11:1. And therefore he says, **according to the faith of the elect of God.**

In the same manner, there is required the perfection of doctrine. Wherefore he says, **and the acknowledging of the truth.** But the cognition of truth is twofold: as perfect in the fatherland, when we will see face to face; as imperfect through faith, and this the saints have. Jn. 8:32: *And you shall know the truth, and the truth shall make you free.*

But the truth of what? In the acknowledgment of the truth **which is according to godliness.** For religion and piety, according to Cicero, are parts of justice; and they differ, because religion is the worship of God. But because God is not only the creator, but also a father, therefore we not only owe worship to Him as a creator, but love and worship as to a father. And therefore piety is sometimes taken for the worship of God. Job 28:28: *Behold piety,*[2] *that is wisdom,* according to another translation, whereas ours has it: *Behold the fear of the Lord, that is wisdom.*

6. Third, it is described from the end: first, he sets forth the end itself; second, its dignity, when he says [n. 8], **But hath in due times.**

The end, moreover, is the hope of eternal life, because although Moses is able to be called an apostle since he was sent by the Lord; nevertheless, not in the hope of eternal life but of the land of the Hevites and Ammorhites; but Paul is an Apostle in the hope of eternal life. Jn. 6:40: *And this is the will of My Father that sent Me: that every one who seeth the Son, and believeth in Him, may have life everlasting, and I will raise him up in the last day.* I Pt. 1:3: *Who according to His great mercy hath regenerated us unto a lively hope.* Rom. 5:2: *By Whom also we have access through faith into this grace, wherein we stand, and glory in the hope of the glory of the sons of God.*

7. But the promise is firm in two ways: first, on the part of the one promising; wherefore he says, **Who lieth not.** For God is truth, the contrary of which is a lie. Num. 23:19: *God is not a man, that He should lie.*

Second, from the divine intention of the one giving; wherefore he says, **before the ages of the world.** An age, according to the Philosopher, is the measure of the duration of any given thing. Temporal ages, therefore, are times distinct according to the diverse successions of things; as if he were to say: before successive time would have begun to be. And because this time begins with the world, therefore it was before the beginning of the world.

Another translation has *eternal times,* that is, ancient times. For sometimes an eternal time is taken thus, that is, as an ancient time. Or *eternal times,* not according to truth, but according to imagination. And before these God promises this, because these are successive. But to promise is to announce by word one's own desire concerning the giving of something. And God from eternity brought forth His Word, in Whom it was to be that the saints might have eternal life. Eph. 1:4: *He chose us in Him before the foundation of the world.*

8. This hope, moreover, is confirmed from the manifestation of the promise, whence he says, **But hath in due times manifested His word,** etc. And this manifestation is described from three things.

First, from time, wherefore He manifested it when He established that His word should become incarnate; so he says, **in due times,** that is, in a suitable time, in which man would be convinced of the pride through which he had sinned. And so in like manner does a doctor convince a sick man, so that he might more suitably heal him. For man was proud concerning knowledge, but he was convinced of his ignorance before the time of the Law, when he sinned in idolatry and in vices against nature. Likewise concerning the virtues; of these things also he was convinced in the time of the Law. Gal. 4:4: *But when the fulness of the time was come, God sent His Son,* etc.

Second, from its mode, because it was done through public preaching. Mk. 16:15: *Go ye into the whole world, and preach the gospel to every creature.* Therefore he says, **in preaching.** I Cor. 9:17: *A dispensation is committed to me.*

Third, from the author. And so he says, **according to the commandment of God our Saviour.** Mt. 1:21: *He shall save His people from their sins.* Acts 9:15: *This man is to Me a vessel of election, to carry My name before the Gentiles,* etc.

9. The person saluted is set forth when he says, **To Titus,** whom he describes in three ways: first, from his name; second, from his love; third, from his filiation.

He is a son, therefore, through love and faith, which ought to be common to all, so that all might say the same thing. And so he says, **common faith,** which is also called catholic, that is, universal. Wherefore he says in Eph. 4:5, *One Lord, one faith, one baptism.*

And the goods wished to him are **grace and peace.** This he wisely conjoins, because the principle of all spiritual gifts is grace; and the end, peace. Ps. 147:14: *Who hath placed peace in thy borders.* **From God the Father, and from Christ Jesus our Saviour.**

Lecture Two

5 [n. 10] For this cause I left thee in Crete, that thou shouldest set in order the things that are wanting, and shouldest establish presbyters[3] in every city, as I also appointed thee:

6 [n. 13] If any be without crime, the husband of one wife, having faithful children, not accused of lust,[4] or unruly.

7 [n. 16] For a bishop must be without crime, as the steward of God: not proud, not subject to anger, not given to wine, no striker, not greedy of filthy lucre:

8 [n. 20] But given to hospitality, gentle, sober, just, holy, continent.

10. He comes to the narration; and, as has been said [n. 3], he intends to fortify the Church against heretics. And first he admonishes Titus to instruct others to resist the heretics; second, he teaches how he ought to resist them when he says in verse one of chapter two [n. 47], **But speak thou the things that become sound doctrine.** So, first he admonishes him to institute bishops, who resist the heretics; second, he shows the necessity of this commission when he says in verse ten [n. 25], **there are also many.** First, he sets forth the commission made to Titus of instituting bishops; second, he shows what the bishops ought to be like when he says [n. 13], **If any be without crime;** third, he manifests that which he said, when he says [n. 16], **For a bishop must be without crime.**

11. And because the Apostle has the universal commission of the Church of the Gentiles, and he was not able to carry everything out by himself alone, therefore he says, **For this cause I left thee in Crete,** on the island of Crete namely, so that in the place of the Apostle, Titus might bear the pastoral office in the Church of the Cretans. Prov. 18:19: *A brother that is helped by his brother, is like a strong city.*

But that he says, **that thou shouldest set in order the things that are wanting,** it seems that he should have said, "that thou shouldest supply."

I respond that the Gloss thus supplies: "So that all things which are in evil men you might correct; and those things which are wanting in good men you might add." I Thess. 3:10: *And may accomplish those things that are wanting to your faith.* Or it must be said that there is a certain sin of omission, and one of transgression, and each is in need of correction. But in the saints and in the perfect, as was Titus, transgressions did not abound; and therefore he does not say, that you might correct the transgressions, but, **things that are wanting,** that is, omissions.

12. **And shouldest establish presbyters,** that is, bishops, wherefore he says below, **For a bishop must be,** etc. And he uses the name of bishops and presbyters indifferently. From which a heretic, who sought after the episcopate,

because he was not able to attain it, divided himself from others and took occasion to teach many false things. Among which he said that the bishops in no way differ from the priests, which is contrary to Dionysius in *The Ecclesiastical Hierarchies*. The Apostle therefore uses the same name in each through the identity of the thing, because the presbyter is called an elder. Likewise, because it pertains to the elders to establish the bishop, although the canons elect him.

And he says, **thou…shouldest establish,** not in villages, but throughout the cities; just as in a republic the rulers are only in the cities, so also bishops in the spiritual regime. I Pet. 2:9: *A kingly priesthood.* In the same manner there ought to be elders. Eccles. 10:16: *Woe to thee, O land, when thy king is a child.* And understand elders not only in age, but also in habits. Num. 11:16: *And the Lord said to Moses: Gather unto Me seventy men of the ancients of Israel, whom thou knowest to be ancients and masters of the people,* etc. Likewise according to the form of the Church; whence he says, **as I also appointed thee.** Prov. 3:21: *My son, let not these things depart from thy eyes.*

13. Then, when he says, **If any be without crime,** he describes them in three ways, namely, as concerns themselves, on the part of the wife, and on the part of the children.

Of the first it is said, **without crime.** Is there someone thus? I Jn. 1:8: *If we say that we have no sin, we deceive ourselves, and the truth is not in us.* It must be said that a crime is one thing, and sin another. Every sin is called sin, whether great, small, or hidden. But a crime is great and infamous. Ps. 14:1: *Lord, who shall dwell in Thy tabernacle?* and afterwards he adds: *He that walketh without blemish,* etc. Not that he who mortally sins after baptism is not able to be chosen; but that the one to be chosen is not to be infamous.

14. With respect to the second he says, **the husband of one wife.** The Easterners set it forth thus, that is, that he not have at the same time two wives, as was the custom of some. But according to this it would not have been necessary that the Apostle say this; because according to Roman laws, by which the Apostle was writing, even before the faith it was not permitted them to have many wives at the same time. Likewise in I Tim. 5:9 he says this also of the widow, namely, that she would not have had except one husband.

But Jerome says that it is necessary that he would have had only one wife after baptism, and that it would have held of no weight if before baptism he had already had other wives. But Augustine and Ambrose say that through baptism all crimes are abolished, but that matrimony is not abolished through baptism; therefore, it must be said according to them, and more correctly, that one only and not many wives, although he had already had them either before or after.

According to some, however, the reason for this is that it would be a sign of incontinence if he had many. But this is not true; because there would have been nothing repugnant if he had had many courtesans, who are more incontinent. But there is another reason of higher significance, namely, that he is the dispenser of the sacraments, and therefore no defect of the sacraments ought to be in him; but the sacrament of matrimony is significative of the union of Christ and the Church; therefore, so that the sign might correspond to the thing signified, just as Christ is one, and also the Church is one, so also here; which indeed would be deficient, if the bishop had many wives. In the Old Law, however, the patriarchs signified this union, not as having been conjoined to Christ, but as yet to be conjoined, and since the Church was to be from the many, therefore then they did not have one wife, but many. And so they signified this by the multitude of their wives.

15. Regarding the third, namely, on the part of sons, he adds, **having faithful children, not accused of lust,** etc. For a bishop is established as a superintendent, and he who is established for something ought to be experienced in it; otherwise, he would not be instituted prudently. He is presumed to be well experienced if he has ruled others well.

And a bishop is instituted for three things. First, that he teach the faith. Mt. 28:19: *Teach ye all nations,* etc. Second, it is required that he instruct the people unto virtue. Ecclus. 7:25: *Hast thou children? instruct them.* But the vices of wantonness do more to draw from virtue. Ecclus. 20:7: *A wanton,[5] and a fool, will regard no time.* And so he says, **not accused of lust.** In I Kg. 3:13 Heli is condemned for not correcting his sons. Third, he must correct the obstinate. Wherefore he says **or unruly,** that is, not obedient. Ecclus. 30:8: *A horse not broken becometh stubborn, and a child left to himself will become headstrong.*

16. Then when he says, **For a bishop,** he explains what he said: first, what he said, **without crime;** second, what things he ought to be without, when he says [n. 18], **not proud.**

17. The reason for the first is that he must dispense divine things. Ecclus. 10:2: *As the judge of the people is himself, so also are his ministers.* Ps. 100:6: *The man that walked in the perfect way, he served me.*

18. Then when he says, **not proud,** he shows from what he should be immune: first, he shows from what crimes; second, in what virtues he ought to shine, when he says [n. 20], **But given to hospitality.**

19. Now, certain sins are carnal, and others are spiritual. He makes no mention of the first since they ought to be altogether clean from these. Eph. 5:3: *But fornication, and all uncleanness, or covetousness, let it not so much as be named among you, as becometh saints.* But he only mentions the spiritual sins, which are five, of which two have no place among prelates. First, envy, which is a sin of children. Job 5:2: *Anger indeed killeth the foolish, and envy slayeth the little one.* But a prelate is at the height. Likewise, neither does sloth have place since all things follow his will. But pride does because he is at the height, as well as anger and cupidity because of the temporal goods of which he is the dispenser.

Regarding the first he says, **not proud.** Ps. 100:5: *With him that had a proud* *eye, and an unsatiable heart, I would not eat.* Ecclus. 32:1: *Have they made thee ruler? be not lifted up: be among them as one of them.*

Regarding the second, first he excludes anger when he says, **not subject to anger;** second, the fire of anger, which is wine, by saying, **not given to wine.** Prov. 23:29–30: *Who hath redness of eyes? Surely they that pass their time in wine, and study to drink of their cups.* Third, what follows anger, which is striking; and so he says, **no striker,** that is, not cruel. Is. 50:6: *I have given My body to the strikers, and My cheeks to them that plucked them.* Or, **no striker,** that is, not striking the consciences of others by depraved morals. I Cor. 8:12: *Now when you sin thus against the brethren, and wound their weak conscience, you sin against Christ.*

Regarding the third he says, **not greedy of filthy lucre.** I Tim. 3:8: *Deacons in like manner chaste, not double tongued, not given to much wine, not greedy of filthy lucre.* Wis. 15:12: *Yea and they have counted our life a pastime, and the business of life to be gain, and that we must be getting every way, even out of evil.*

20. Then he posits the good things which he ought to have: first, those which pertain to his conduct of life; second, those which regard the truth of his doctrine, when he says in verse nine [n. 21], **Embracing that faithful word.**

And all the rest is clear.

Lecture Three

9 [n. 21] Embracing that faithful word which is according to doctrine, that he may be able to exhort in sound doctrine, and to convince the gainsayers.
10 [n. 25] For there are also many disobedient, vain talkers, and seducers: especially they who are of the circumcision:
11 Who must be reproved, [n. 28] who subvert whole houses, teaching things which they ought not, for filthy lucre's sake.
12 [n. 29] One of them a prophet of their own, said, The Cretians are always liars, evil beasts, slothful bellies.
13a [n. 32] This testimony is true.

21. Above the Apostle taught how a bishop should be in his life [n. 20]; here he shows how he ought to be in his doctrine: first, he shows that he is required to be diligent in study; second, he posits the material of his study [n. 23]; third, the utility of it [n. 24].

22. Regarding the first he says, **Embracing that faithful word,** for those embracing something diligently hold fast to it, and it becomes an embrace of love. And he must adhere to knowledge with an embrace, that is, with a firm adherence of mind and love of the heart. Wis. 6:14: *She seizeth*[6] *them that covet her.* Prov. 4:8: *Take hold on her, and she shall exalt thee: thou shalt be glorified by her, when thou shalt embrace her.*

23. The material for study must not be fables or temporal matters, but a word faithful and true. Ps. 144:13: *The Lord is faithful in all His words.* Or the **faithful word,** that is, the word of faith in which a bishop ought to be instructed.

But some devote themselves to this in two ways, so that, namely, they only learn and act. But this is not sufficient for a bishop because he must instruct others. And so he says, **which is according to doctrine.** I Tim. 4:12: *Let no man despise thy youth: but be thou an example of the faithful in word, in conversation.*

24. The utility of this study is the ability to carry out his duty. Now, the duty of a prelate is as that of a pastor. Jn. 21:17: *Feed My sheep.* And the pastor has two things to do: to feed the flock – I Pet. 5:2: *Feed the flock of God which is among you* – and to ward off wolves. So also a bishop ought to feed the flock through true doctrine. Jer. 3:15: *And I will give you pastors according to My own heart, and they shall feed you with knowledge and doctrine.*

And so he says, **that he may be able to exhort.** He did not say, "that he may exhort," but **that he may be able to exhort.** This is when he has exhortations ready when it is necessary to give them. This is prefigured in Ex. 25:27 by the poles in the rings on the ark so that it was ready to be carried. Lk. 24:19: *Mighty in work and word.* And he says, **sound,** that is, without the corruption of falsity.

Below 2:1: *But speak thou the things that become sound doctrine.* I Thess. 2:3: *For our exhortation was not of error, nor of uncleanness, nor in deceit.*

Again, they must guard against heretics. And so he says, **and to convince the gainsayers.** And this is done through the study of Sacred Scripture. II Tim. 3:16: *All scripture, inspired of God, is profitable to teach, to reprove, to correct, to instruct in justice.* Job 6:10: *Nor I contradict the words of the Holy One.*

And according to the Philosopher these two pertain to the work of the wise man, namely, not to lie about what he knows, regarding the first; and to be able to make a liar known, regarding the second.

25. Consequently when he says, **For there are also many,** he posits the necessity of what has been said: first, on the part of false teachers; second, on the part of evil listeners, when he says [n. 29], **One of them.** Regarding the first he does two things: first, he describes the condition of the false teachers; second, the perversity of their study, when he says [n. 28], **who subvert whole houses.** Again, first he shows their condition; second, he teaches the remedy for them when he says [n. 27], **Who must be reproved.**

26. He shows their condition in four ways. First, from their number, when he says, **many.** Eccles. 1:15: *The number of fools is infinite.* Second, from the vice of disobedience, when he says, **disobedient,** regarding God and their superiors. Rom. 1:30: *Disobedient to parents.* I Kg. 15:23: *Like the crime of idolatry, to refuse to obey.* Third, from their empty speech, when he says, **vain talkers,** regarding themselves. Ps. 93:11: *The Lord knoweth the thoughts of men, that they are vain.* Wis. 13:1: *But all men are vain, in whom there is not the knowledge of God.* And chiefly the vain are heretics, and so he adds, **seducers,** that is, toward their inferiors. II Tim. 3:13: *Evil men and seducers shall grow worse and worse: erring, and driving into error.* Fourth, from their place, when he says, **especially they who are of the circumcision,** who forced men to become Judaizers. Phil. 3:2: *Beware of dogs, beware of evil workers, beware of the concision.*

27. Against whom he gives a remedy. They are not to be tolerated since the people would be corrupted and pastors charged for it. Ez. 13:5: *You have not gone up to face the enemy, nor have you set up a wall for the house of Israel, to stand in battle in the day of the Lord.* II Tim. 4:2: *Reprove, entreat, rebuke in all patience and doctrine.* And so he says, **Who must be reproved.**

28. Then when he says, **who subvert whole houses,** he describes their pursuit: first from the harm they bring; second, from the falsity they teach; third, from the gain they desire.

The harm is that they **subvert whole houses.** For the Catholic doctrine is proclaimed publicly in the churches, but heretics do so secretly, and so they seek hiding places. Prov. 9:17: *Stolen waters are sweeter, and hidden bread is more pleasant.* And so they go about through homes so that they may seduce chiefly the women. II Tim. 3:6: *For of these sort are they who creep into houses, and lead captive silly women laden with sins.* **Teaching things which they ought not,** that is, vain and useless things. Nor do they seek spiritual gain but temporal, and so he adds, **for filthy lucre's sake,** that is, temporal gain or their own glory. Wis. 15:12: *Yea and they have counted our life a pastime, and the business of life to be gain, and that we must be getting every way, even out of evil.*

29. Then when he says, **One of them,** he describes the listeners, since they were Cretans, to whom this work makes reference: first, he shows their condition; second, he gives the remedy when he says in verse thirteen [n. 33], **Wherefore rebuke them sharply.** Regarding the first, he first describes their condition through a witness; second, he confirms it [n. 32].

30. He says therefore: The teachers are such, but the listeners are likewise able to be seduced according to the testimony of one of their own poets, namely, Epimenides,[7] whom Paul here calls their prophet.

Here it must be noted that someone is called a prophet who is illuminated by God according to his intellect to know some things above the common knowledge of men. Num. 12:6: *If there be among you a prophet of the Lord, I will appear to him in a vision, or I will speak to him in a dream.* Likewise, he who explains the prophecies in the same spirit and in the same manner they were handed on. Likewise, he who offers something prophetic. Hence, something prophetic can be offered from a certain interior instinct, even beyond his understanding. Jn. 11:49: *But one of them, named Caiphas, being the high priest that year, said to them,* etc. For he did not prophesy according to his own intention who said that it was expedient for Him to die, understanding rather that he did not want Him to seduce the people. Nevertheless, he was moved to say this by the Spirit. And this manner of prophesying is among those who take the first word of some men for an omen, which also happens by demons.

And he says, **of their own,** since he properly described their condition.

31. Then when he says, **The Cretians,** he brings forth his witness and notes three things about them. First, their corruption of reason, when he says, **always liars.** Ps. 5:7: *Thou wilt destroy all that speak a lie.*

Then, the corruption of their irascible appetite, when he says, **evil beasts,** that is, cruel; they are called beasts, as it were ravagers, since they are cruel. Prov. 28:15: *As a roaring lion, and a hungry bear, so is a wicked prince over the poor people.* And he says, **evil,** since, according to the Philosopher in the *Politics,* man when he works according to his reason is the best of animals; but when he declines to evil he is the worst, since if he lowers himself on account of cruelty, no beast is so cruel. Hence he says that one evil man is ten thousand times worse than one evil beast.

Then, the corruption of the concupiscible appetite, when he says, **slothful**

bellies, that is, having sloth from the belly, for they were gluttons, and such seek relaxation. Lk. 12:19: *Soul, thou hast much goods laid up for many years, take thy rest; eat, drink, make good cheer.*

32. And he confirms the testimony when he says, **This testimony is true.** The Gloss: "By this we understand that the doctor of Sacred Scripture receives the testimony of the truth wheresoever he finds it." Hence the Apostle in many places recites the words of the Gentiles, as in I Cor. 15:33: *Evil communications corrupt good manners.* And Acts 17:28: *For in Him we live, and move, and are.* Nor is their whole teaching approved because of this, but the good is chosen since the truth, from wheresoever it is said, is from the Holy Spirit, and evil is spat out. Hence it is said in Deut. 21:11 as a figure of this that if a man sees a girl in the number of the captives, he ought to cut off her nails and hair, that is, the superfluities.

Lecture Four

13b [n. 33] Wherefore rebuke them sharply, that they may be sound in the faith;

14 [n. 36] Not giving heed to Jewish fables and commandments of men, who turn themselves away from the truth.

15 [n. 38] All things are clean to the clean: but to them that are defiled, and to unbelievers, nothing is clean: but both their mind and their conscience are defiled.

16 [n. 45] They profess that they know God: but in their works they deny Him; being abominable, and incredulous, and to every good work reprobate.

33. With the condition of the Cretan people having been laid down [n. 29], the Apostle posits here the remedy: first, he gives the remedy of rebuke; second, he assigns a reason for what had been told when he says [n. 38], **All things.** Regarding the first he does three things: first, he urges Titus to rebuke them; second, he shows the end of rebuking when he says [n. 35], **that they may be sound;** third, he teaches the due manner of attaining to the faith when he says [n. 36], **Not giving heed.**

34. He says therefore: Cretans are evil beasts, to whom are due but whip and scourge. And so he says, **Wherefore rebuke them sharply.** Prov. 6:23: *Reproofs of instruction are the way of life.* Ps. 67:31: *Rebuke the wild beasts of the reeds.* But against this it says in II Tim. 4:2, *Rebuke in all patience.*

I respond that the reason for this exhortation is twofold. One is on the part of those who are being rebuked. For Cretans were stubborn and obdurate, and so he commands them to be rebuked sharply. The Ephesians, however, were not, and Timothy was their archbishop. The other is on the part of those rebuking, since Titus was a man gentle and mild, and so he is led as it were to a contrary; but Timothy was stern, and so he was led to patience.

35. Then when he says, **that they may be sound,** he touches upon the goal of rebuking. For a man is sound in whom there is no corruption. And thus he is sound in the faith who in no way has it corrupted. But their faith was vitiated by heretics. I Cor. 11:3: *But I fear lest, as the serpent seduced Eve by his subtilty, so your minds should be corrupted, and fall from the simplicity that is in Christ.* I Tim. 6:3: *If any man teach otherwise, and consent not to the sound words of our Lord Jesus Christ,* etc.

36. The manner of arriving at soundness is if he avoid the errors of the Jews. Hence he says, **Not giving heed to Jewish fables.** For in the Law there were twofold propositions of faith. Some regarded what was to be believed, and some were the mandates of religion which were to be observed regarding the worship

of God. And he calls the first **fables;** the second, **the commandments of men,** and not of God.

From this it seems that he condemns the Old Testament, as the Manichaeans say. But that he says **fables** can be referred to their stories outside the doctrine of the Law, which were fables, such as the Talmud. I Tim. 1:4: *Not to give heed to fables and endless genealogies.* Or the doctrine itself, which was once the truth but now as they understand it is but fables, just as Is. 7:14: *Behold a virgin shall conceive,* etc., was the truth, but now since they say it has yet to be fulfilled, is a fable. Likewise, the commandments of men can be understood not of those things which are in the Law of Moses, but the traditions of the elders, as in Mt. 15:2.

37. But is not obedience to be given to the commandments of men?

I respond that assuredly it is, as long as they do not turn away from the truth of God. And so he adds, **who turn themselves away from the truth.** II Tim. 4:4: *And will indeed turn away their hearing from the truth, but will be turned unto fables.* The same is had in Mt. 15:9: *And in vain do they worship Me, teaching doctrines and commandments of men.* And the same thing is said in Mk. 7:7. Or it must be said that the commandments which are in the law of God have become the commandments of men. For when they are observed as a sign of a future truth, they are the mandates of God; but when men want to keep them after our body has died to the law, they are the mandates of men.

38. Then when he says, **All things are clean,** he specifically shows the reason for what he said, namely, how they turn aside from the truth, and how they speak fables and the commandments of men. This chiefly pertains to the discretion of foods according to the Law, which certain false brethren said had to be observed. First, he shows how these foods relate to the good; second, how to the evil, when he says [n. 42], **but to them that are defiled.**

39. He says therefore: Give no heed to the Jewish fables regarding food since **All things,** namely, all foodstuffs, **are clean to the clean.**

But one can infer: Therefore is adultery clean to the clean.

I respond that this is not the case since, because it is adultery, it defiles. But those things which do not defile of themselves are clean to the clean. To this speaks Mt. 15:11: *Not that which goeth into the mouth defileth a man: but what cometh out of the mouth, this defileth a man.* Therefore, everything that enters the mouth is clean.

40. But there is a twofold objection. One is Lev. 11:7, which says that when some animal does not chew the cud or does not split the hoof, it is unclean.

I respond according to Augustine in *Against Faustus.* Something is unclean either according to the nature of the thing or according to a signification. For example, the word *stupid* taken in itself, as a certain sound of the voice, is not unclean but good. But if is taken as a signification, it indicates a defect of wisdom, and thus it has uncleanness. Now, the acts of this people were prophetic.

Hence pork, inasmuch as it is a certain thing, is not unclean; but according as it signifies a man wrapped up in his desires, it is unclean. But now that truth has come, these things cease, and men use foods according to the nature of the food.

41. The other question is in Acts 15:28 where the Apostles commanded that they restrain themselves from things strangled and from blood. Therefore, it seems that it is not licit to eat these; thus also, not all things are clean to the clean.

I respond that some believe that this command may be understood literally and that it obliges even until now, as among the Greeks and at one time among the Latins. But some say that this is not understood literally but mystically, so that by blood homicide is understood, and by suffocated things the oppression of the poor. And this is good, but it is not the whole reason for the precept. And so I say that the precept is literal, and yet we are not bound. For certain things are forbidden because they are evil, and these are simply to be avoided. But other things, which are not evil simply speaking but for a time, are to be observed as long as the cause remains. And these things the Apostles prohibited, not because they were evil in themselves, since the Lord speaks in Mt. 15:11 to the contrary. But the reason is that some men had been converted from the Jews, and some from the Gentiles. And so it was necessary that, for one people to arise from them both, one would condescend to the other, so that the Jews, to whom to eat blood and something strangled was abominable, would be condescended to. And so to keep the peace the Apostles established this to be kept for that time.

42. Then when he says, **but to them that are defiled,** he shows how these foods relate to the evil. And regarding this he does three things: first, he shows this; second, he assigns the cause when he says [n. 44], **but both their mind;** third, he makes this clear through a sign when he says [n. 45], **They profess that they know God.**

43. He says therefore: These foods are clean to the clean, but unclean **to them that are defiled,** that is, to those who have a defiled conscience. Ecclus. 13:1: *He that toucheth pitch, shall be defiled with it;* **and to unbelievers,** that is, who have bad faith. Is. 21:2: *He that is unfaithful dealeth unfaithfully.*

But surely a sinner and unfaithful man does not give an unclean alms?

It must be said that the Apostle does not posit the affirmative but the negative. Hence he does say that all things are unclean to them, but that nothing is clean, which is true, since nothing is clean in actions except it be ordered to a right faith. But these are outside the faith.

But surely something is clean to them? Yes.

On the contrary, everything that is not of faith is a sin.

It must be said that evil never corrupts good entirely. For it is impossible that in whatever sinner there not be something good, namely, the good of nature, as it is even in the demons. When therefore a sinner does anything good according as he is a sinner and unfaithful, the whole of it is a sin from its root. But if what he does is from a principle of good which he has, such as unformed faith or nature, it is not unclean. And so he expressly says, **to them that are defiled, and to unbelievers,** that is, inasmuch as they are such. For they ate against their conscience and erred in the faith. And so, what is clean of its nature they made unclean to themselves.

44. The reason for this is that the cause of their actions is unclean, namely, their will and intellect, which in them were depraved. Hence he says, **but both their mind,** through infidelity, **and their conscience,** through sin, **are defiled.** Bar. 3:10–11: *How happeneth it, O Israel, that thou art in thy enemies' land? Thou art grown old in a strange country, thou art defiled with the dead,* etc.

45. Then when he says, **They profess that they know God,** he shows their faith by a sign. For if someone were to say that their words were true and that they have faith in the one God and confess Him – he excludes this.

And first he shows the good that was in them when he says, **They profess,** with their lips, **that they know God.** Is. 29:13: *Forasmuch as this people draw near Me with their mouth, and with their lips glorify Me, but their heart is far from Me, and they have feared Me.* Jer. 12:2: *Thou art near in their mouth, and far from their reins.*

Second, he shows their interior defect: first, regarding the present; second, regarding the future, when he says [n. 46], **and incredulous.**

Regarding the present, since **in their works they deny Him.** For he who sins, inasmuch as it is from himself, he denies Him with his deeds; he who confesses God confesses also His power, namely, that He must be obeyed. And so, if by sinning he does not obey, he denies in his deeds Him Whom he professes with his mouth.

But you say: Whosoever denies God is an infidel; sinners deny God with their deeds. Therefore, sinners are infidels.

I respond that just as one who has a science in general can err in particular, so one having the faith in general is yet corrupted in a particular thing to be done through the corruption of his affections. I Tim. 5:8: *But if anyone have not care of her own, and especially of those of her house, she hath denied the faith, and is worse than an infidel.*

46. But how are they deficient regarding the future? They not only deny God but are also indisposed to return to Him.

For there are three things by which a man returns to God. The first is God's grace. Below 3:7: *Justified by His grace.* The second is faith. Acts 15:9: *Purifying their hearts by faith.* Third, the exercise of good works. Rom. 2:13: *The doers of the law shall be justified.*

He excludes these three things from them. First, grace, when he says, **being abominable,** that is, not received unto grace. Second, faith, when he says, **and**

incredulous, that is, not apt to believe. Ez. 2:6: *Thou art among unbelievers and destroyers.* Third, the third, **and to every good work reprobate,** that is, they are to be reprobated. Jer. 6:30: *Call them reprobate silver, for the Lord hath rejected them.*

Chapter Two

Lecture One

1 [n. 47] But speak thou the things that become sound doctrine:
2 [n. 49] That the aged men be sober, chaste, prudent, sound in faith, in love, in patience.
3 [n. 53] The aged women, in like manner, in holy attire, not false accusers, not given to much wine, teaching well:
4 [n. 54] That they may teach the young women to be wise, to love their husbands, to love their children,
5 [n. 56] To be discreet, chaste, sober, having a care of the house, gentle, obedient to their husbands, that the word of God be not blasphemed.
6 [n. 58] Young men, in like manner, exhort that they be sober.

47. Above the Apostle instructed Titus which ministers to institute to ward off heretics [n. 10]; here he teaches what he should do regarding them: first, he proposes this in general; second, he distinguishes its parts when he says [n. 49], **That the aged men be sober.**

48. He says therefore: I have said to establish bishops, but lest you believe that because of this you are free from care, rather you must have a greater anxiety for teaching. And so, **speak thou the things that become sound doctrine,** namely, through which the incorrupt faith is edified. Above 1:9: *Embracing that faithful word which is according to doctrine, that he may be able to exhort in sound doctrine, and to convince the gainsayers.*

49. Then he shows the same thing in its parts: first is placed sound doctrine against perversity of life; second, against heretics and errors, when he says in verse nine of chapter three [n. 98], **But avoid foolish questions.** He does two things regarding the first: first, he teaches the individual conditions of men; second, all of them generally, when he says at the beginning of chapter three [n. 77],

Admonish them. Again, the first is in two parts: first, he shows how to instruct free men; second, slaves, when he says in verse nine [n. 63], **Exhort servants.** Again, first, he shows how to instruct free men in speech; second, by example, when he says in verse seven [n. 59], **In all things.** Regarding the first he does two things: first, he shows how to instruct the elderly; second, how to teach youth, when he says [n. 54], **That they may teach.** Again, the first is in two parts: first, he shows how to instruct old men; second, old women, when he says [n. 53], **The aged women.**

But it must be known that there are certain good things to which old age disposes a man; these he posits first. Second, there are certain goods which are contrary to old age; these he gives second when he says [n. 52], **sound in faith.**

50. Among the good things to which old age disposes a man, one is contempt for pleasures; another is the perfection of wisdom and prudence [n. 51].

Indeed, old age disposes a man to despise pleasures. For the bodies of the youth burn with natural heat, by which youth is urged to bodily pleasures which consist chiefly in food, drink, and venery. But old age disposes one to shun these. II Kg. 19:35: *I am this day fourscore years old, are my senses quick to discern sweet and bitter?* And so he says, **That the aged men be sober,** as regards food and drink, **chaste,** as regards venery. Gen. 18:12: *After I am grown old, and my lord is an old man, shall I give myself to pleasure?*

But if old age disposes to this, why does he admonish them?

I respond that sometimes it happens out of great perversity that an old man is reduced to puerile sins. Is. 65:20: *For the child shall die a hundred years old, and the sinner being a hundred years old shall be accursed.* And there is a twofold reason why this happens. For an old man is moved to this for one reason, a youth for another. For a youth is incited to these sins from the instinct of passion, but the old man does so by choice, and this for two reasons. No one wants to be without delights, and so much the more so does he want them as the greater the troubles he feels. Now, an old man suffers many inconveniences and defects of nature. And so when he does not have spiritual delights, he seeks bodily ones. The second reason is that sometimes a youth is restrained through shame. But old men, according to the Philosopher, are shameless since they are old and have experienced many things; youth, on the other hand, are vain and naturally shameful: thus they are restrained, but old men are not.

51. Likewise, old age disposes a man to prudence, on account of his experience over a long time. Job 12:12: *In the ancient is wisdom, and in length of days prudence.* Ecclus. 25:7–8: *O how comely is wisdom for the aged, and understanding and counsel to men of honour! Much experience is the crown of old men.* Hence he adds, **prudent.**

Yet it happens occasionally that an old man is idiotic. Ecclus. 25:4: *An old man that is a fool, and doting.* And it is from two things that an old man is a dotard. First, prudence is acquired through experience; when, therefore, he does not occupy himself with good things in his youth, he is imprudent in his age. Ecclus. 25:5: *The things that thou hast not gathered in thy youth, how shalt thou find them in thy old age?* And the other reason is that in youth men sometimes abound in pleasures, and especially excess of food; and therefore their brain is dried up. Prov. 20:1: *Wine is a luxurious thing, and drunkenness riotous: whosoever is delighted therewith shall not be wise.*

52. Then he posits those things to which old age is opposed: first, faith; second, love; third, patience.

Regarding the first he says, **sound in faith,** since without faith it is impossible to please God, as it says in Heb. 11:6. But that some are not sound in faith, especially in some new thing proposed to old men for belief, happens for two reasons. First, old men are not firm in something because of the presumption of wisdom, and so they do not believe others. Job 15:10: *There are with us also aged and ancient men.* Also, the natural vice of old men is that they are incredulous since they have experience that they have quite often been deceived. And so they speak always by saying, *perhaps,* or *almost,* which are adverbs of a manner that is moderate and doubtful. But disbelief is repugnant to the faith. Is. 21:2: *He that is unfaithful dealeth unfaithfully.*

Regarding the second he says, **in love.** And this because the fulfillment of the law is love. And he admonishes them for two reasons. First, among the old there is little friendship because love is nourished through dwelling together. But no one wants to live for a long time with sad people. Now, old men are sad, and so there is no friendship with them. Again, old men love only on account of usefulness, as youth do for delight. For an old man needs maintenance.

Regarding the third he says, **in patience,** and this he admonishes for three reasons. First, because many evils and inconveniences beset old men, and so they need patience against troubles. Another reason is that old men live with the memory of many things; hence they always speak of old things. Youth, on the other hand, live in the hope of great things. And from this old men are doubly moved to impatience: because of the good things which they had but now lack. Hence Boëthius: "The height of misery is to have been happy." Lam. 1:7: *Jerusalem hath remembered the days of her affliction, and prevarication of all her desirable things which she had from the days of old.* Again, because they live in their memory, it happens that some, who now despise the old, at one time were worse, and so they are disturbed. Job 30:1: *But now the younger in time scorn me, whose fathers I would not have set with the dogs of my flock.* The third reason is that the more an old man approaches the end of his life, that much more does he desire to live. Hence, seeing himself failing, he is the more disturbed.

53. Then when he says, **The aged women,** he teaches how old women are to

be instructed: first, he teaches how old women are to be instructed in their lives; second, in teaching. Again, first, how in dress; second, in food; third, in speech.

Regarding the first he says, **in holy attire,** that is, lacking wantonness and pomp. And this befits every woman. I Pet. 3:3: *Whose adorning let it not be the outward plaiting of the hair, or the wearing of gold, or the putting on of apparel,* etc. I Tim. 2:9: *In like manner women also in decent apparel: adorning themselves with modesty and sobriety, not with plaited hair, or gold, or pearls, or costly attire,* etc. But especially an old woman ought to observe this, since it is because of their husbands that young women adorn themselves modestly; this is understood simply about every movement of the body. Ecclus. 19:27: *The attire of the body, and the laughter of the teeth, and the gait of the man, shew what he is.* Regarding the second he says, **not false accusers.** For there are two things in the elderly. One is common to all old people, namely, that they are suspicious since they have seen many evil things which they likewise presume about others. Likewise, women especially are jealous, and both things happen to be in old women since by reason of their age they are suspicious and by reason of their sex they are jealous. Ecclus. 26:9: *With a jealous woman is a scourge of the tongue which communicateth with all.* And so he says, **not false accusers.**

Regarding food he says, **not given to much wine.** About men he had said that they ought to be sober. And he says, **not given to much,** since sometimes they drink it because of their coldness.

Regarding teaching he says, **teaching well.** Against this it says in I Cor. 14:34, *Let women keep silence in the churches: for it is not permitted them to speak, but to be subject, as also the law saith.* I Tim. 2:11–12: *Let the woman learn in silence, with all subjection. But I suffer not a woman to teach.*

I respond that public teaching which occurs among the people is forbidden to women; but private teaching, by which someone teaches a family, is conceded to them. Prov. 31:1: *The vision wherewith his mother instructed him.* Prov. 4:3–4: *For I also was my father's son, tender and as an only son in the sight of my mother: And she[1] taught me, and said,* etc.

And he says well, **That they may teach the young women to be wise,** more to the old women than the old men, since sometimes they teach old wives tales more than anything beneficial, and as they also associate more with children and family than men do.

54. Then when he says, **the young women,** he shows how to instruct the youth: first, he shows how to teach young women; second, young men, when he says [n. 58], **Young men, in like manner.** Again, the first is in three parts: first he shows how they ought to relate to those related to them; second, to themselves [n. 56]; third, to their subjects [n. 57].

55. Regarding the first he says, **to love their husbands,** for love is due to her

husband. Prov. 12:4: *A diligent woman is a crown to her husband.* Ecclus. 25:1: *With three things my spirit is pleased, which are approved before God and men,* etc., and then later, *man and wife that agree well together.*

Or it can be thus, that the old women teach young women and their husbands, etc. But the first explanation is better.

To love their children, which is natural. Is. 49:15: *Can a woman forget her infant, so as not to have pity on the son of her womb?*

And notice that he says, **to love their husbands, to love their children,** since love for husbands is more fervent, but for children is more natural.[2]

56. But regarding themselves he says three things. The first pertains to reason, namely, that they be **discreet.** Prov. 19:14: *House and riches are given by parents: but a prudent wife is properly from the Lord.* And this is necessary since their youth and sex are contrary to prudence. The next regards the concupiscible appetite, namely, when he says, **chaste.** The third regards the irascible appetite, when he says, **sober.** Ecclus. 26:19: *A holy and shamefaced woman is grace upon grace.*

57. But regarding subjects he first posits the care of them; second, the manner of this care; third, he gives the reason why.

About the first he says, **having a care of the house.** Prov. 14:1: *A wise woman buildeth her house: but the foolish will pull down with her hands that also which is built.*

In the care of it a woman is to observe two things, for they are for the most part of hot tempers. Ecclus. 25:23: *And there is no anger above the anger of a woman. It will be more agreeable to abide with a lion and a dragon, than to dwell with a wicked woman.* And so he says, **gentle,** as if to say: Let them rule with gentleness. The other is that when a woman has power, she struggles against her husband. Ecclus. 25:30: *A woman, if she have superiority, is contrary to her husband.* Wherefore he says, **obedient to their husbands.** Hence it is said in Gen. 3:16: *And thou shalt be under thy husband's power, and he shall have dominion over thee.* And this **that the word of God be not blasphemed,** that is, that you may not give the occasion for blaspheming.

And all these things are noted in Tob. 10:13, where it is said that Raguel and Sara admonished their daughter to honor her father- and mother-in-law, to love her husband, to rule the house, and to show herself blameless.

58. Consequently he shows what to teach young men, namely, **that they be sober,** which he repeats because drunkenness is the beginning of vices. I Pet. 5:8: *Be sober,* etc.

Lecture Two

7 [n. 59] In all things shew thyself an example of good works, in doctrine, in integrity, in gravity,

8 [n. 62] The sound word that can not be blamed: that he, who is on the contrary part, may be afraid, having no evil to say of us.

9 [n. 63] Exhort servants to be obedient to their masters, in all things pleasing, not gainsaying:

10 [n. 65] Not defrauding, but in all things shewing good fidelity, that they may adorn the doctrine of God our Saviour in all things.

59. Above the Apostle taught Titus about what things he should instruct free subjects. And since not only words are profitable but also examples as well, he teaches him to show himself an example: first, generally; second, specifically, when he says [n. 61], **in doctrine**; third, he gives the reason for this when he says [n. 62], **that he, who is on the contrary part.**

60. He says therefore: Since you are young in age, **In all things shew thyself an example of good works.** For a prelate ought to be as it were an example for his disciples. I Cor. 11:1: *Be ye followers of me, as I also am of Christ.* Jn. 13:15: *For I have given you an example, that as I have done to you, so you do also.*

61. Then when he says, **in doctrine,** he posits the specific things in which he ought to show himself an example. First, he shows what should be his action, namely, teaching; hence he says, **in doctrine.** For this is proper to a prelate. Jer. 3:15: *And I will give you pastors according to My own heart, and they shall feed you with knowledge and doctrine.* And this is most befitting to him who has other bishops under him, as is said above 1:5, *Thou shouldest set in order the things that are wanting, and shouldest establish presbyters in every city.* And so by teaching others he should give them the example of teaching. I Tim. 4:16: *Take heed to thyself and to doctrine: be earnest in them. For in doing this thou shalt both save thyself and them that hear thee.*

Likewise, he admonishes him regarding his way of living. First, he ought to turn aside from evil. Is. 1:16: *Wash yourselves, be clean, take away the evil of your devices from My eyes: cease to do perversely.* And so he says, **in integrity,** through incorruptibility. For just as a body destroys integrity through the corruption of its members, so also the soul through the corruption of sin. Now, in a prelate there is integrity of the mind through prudence, of the affections through charity, and of the body through chastity. I Thess. 5:23: *And may the God of peace Himself sanctify you in all things; that your whole spirit, and soul, and body, may be preserved blameless in the coming of our Lord Jesus Christ.* Second, that he be grave with respect to those goods which come with charity. Now, being grave has two things: one is that it descends, and according to this it is censured. Ps. 4:3:

O ye sons of men, how long will you be grave³ of heart? The other is that it is stable and firm, and so they are called grave who are not easily moved from the good. It is thus here when he says, **in gravity,** and this is commendable. Ps. 34:18: *I will praise thee in a grave⁴ people.*

Then he shows of what kind his doctrine and words ought to be. And he says that his words ought to be **sound,** that is, not corrupt with falsity. II. Tim. 1:13: *Holding the form of sound words, which thou hast heard of me in faith, and in the love which is in Christ Jesus.* Prov. 17:7: *Eloquent words do not become a fool, nor lying lips a prince.* Likewise, he shows the manner of his words when he says, **that can not be blamed,** that is, that it be brought out in due season and with all decency and challenges unto correction. Ecclus. 20:22: *A parable coming out of a fool's mouth shall be rejected: for he doth not speak it in due season.*

62. The end of doctrine is **that he, who is on the contrary part, may be afraid,** etc., as if to say: If all men, namely, prelates and their subjects, behave well, then our adversaries cannot harm us. I Pet. 2:15: *For so is the will of God, that by doing well you may put to silence the ignorance of foolish men.* I Tim. 5:14: *I will therefore that the younger should...give no occasion to the adversary to speak evil.*

63. Then when he says, **Exhort servants,** he teaches how to instruct slaves: first, he does this; second, he assigns the reason when he says in verse eleven [n. 67], **For the grace of God.** Regarding the first he does three things: first, he leads slaves unto subjection; second, he determines the manner of this when he says [n. 65], **but in all things;** third, he shows the necessity of this doctrine when he says [n. 66], **that they may adorn the doctrine.**

64. He says therefore: **Exhort servants to be obedient to their masters.** I Pet. 2:18: *Servants, be subject to your masters with all fear, not only to the good and gentle, but also to the froward.* Col. 3:22: *Servants, obey in all things your masters according to the flesh, not serving to the eye, as pleasing men, but in simplicity of heart, fearing God.* And Eph. 6:5 says the same thing.

And why does the Apostle exhort this so frequently? I respond that not without cause. For heresies began among the Jews that the servants of God ought not obey men, and from this it was derived among the Christian people that, having been made sons of God through Christ, they should not be the slaves of men. But Christ through faith did not come to take away the order of justice; rather, through faith in Christ justice is kept. Now, justice makes some subject to others, but such service regards the body. For now through Christ we are freed from slavery regarding the soul but from neither slavery nor corruption of the body. However, in the future, we shall also be freed from both bodily slavery and bodily corruption. I Cor. 15:24: *Afterwards the end, when He shall have delivered up the kingdom to God and the Father, when He shall have brought to nought all principality, and power, and virtue.*

65. But that he says **in all things** can be referred first to what he said just before, **be obedient to their masters,** so that it may be understood to refer to all things to which the right of lordly power extends. Or it can refer to what follows, **pleasing.**

For there ought to be subjection, first so that they can serve without offense, murmuring, or tardiness. Col. 1:10: *That you may walk worthy of God, in all things pleasing.* I Cor. 10:33: *I also in all things please all men.*

On the contrary, Gal. 1:10: *If I yet pleased men, I should not be the servant of Christ.*

I respond that to please a man for his sake is blameworthy, but for God's sake is praiseworthy.

Second, that they may be without resistance. And so he says, **not gainsaying.** Ecclus. 4:30: *In nowise speak against the truth.*

Third, without fraud; hence he says, **Not defrauding.** Here he removes one thing and builds up another. He removes fraud, for the goods of masters are committed to slaves. Mt. 25:14: *For even as a man going into a far country, called his servants, and delivered to them his goods,* etc. He built up goodness in all things; hence he says, **but in all things shewing good fidelity.**

66. But for what end are these things to come about? Indeed, not for earthly favor but for the glory of God. And so he says, **that they may adorn the doctrine of God our Saviour in all things.** The Gloss: "The glory of a doctor is the honest life of his disciple, just as the health of a sick man is the praise of a physician." A doctor is a caretaker of souls. If, therefore, we show good works, the doctrine of Christ is praised. Is. 52:5: *My name is continually blasphemed all the day long.* Mt. 5:16: *So let your light shine before men, that they may see your good works, and glorify your Father Who is in heaven.*

Lecture Three

11 [n. 67] **For the grace of God our Saviour hath appeared to all men;**

12 [n. 69] **Instructing us, that, denying ungodliness and worldly desires, we should live soberly, and justly, and godly in this world,**

13 [n. 72] **Looking for the blessed hope and coming of the glory of the great God and our Saviour Jesus Christ,**

14 [n. 73] **Who gave Himself for us, that He might redeem us from all iniquity, and might cleanse to Himself a people acceptable, a pursuer of good works.**

15 [n. 76] **These things speak, and exhort and rebuke with all authority. Let no man despise thee.**

67. Above the Apostle instructed Titus how to teach slaves and freemen, and he concluded with a reason, namely, that the doctrine of Christ be glorified [n. 63]; here, assigning a full reason for the foregoing, he explains what he meant by a good conduct of life. First, he gives the grace and doctrine of Christ; second, he leads him to the preaching of grace when he says [n. 76], **These things speak.** Again, first he proposes the appearance of grace; second, its instruction, when he says [n. 69], **Instructing us;** third, its operation, when he says [n. 73], **Who gave Himself.**

68. But it must be known that grace signifies mercy, since grace is about what is given gratis, and what is given by grace is given mercifully.

Now, mercy was always in God, yet at one time it was hidden as far as men were concerned. Ps. 35:6: *O Lord, Thy mercy is in heaven.* For before Christ all men, howsoever much they were just, were under damnation, but when Christ the Son of God became incarnate, **grace...hath appeared.** I Tim. 3:16: *And evidently great is the mystery of godliness, which was manifested in the flesh.* Ps. 79:2: *Thou that sittest upon the cherubims, shine forth.*

But however powerful someone is, so much more is his grace desired. Hence the grace of God is to be desired, and so he says, **the grace of God.** And this is for salvation, so he says, **our Saviour.** Is. 51:8: *My salvation shall be for ever.* Now, this grace is not proposed to only the one people of the Jews, as at one time, but **to all men.** Is. 40:5: *And the glory of the Lord shall be revealed, and all flesh together shall see that the mouth of the Lord hath spoken.* Is. 52:10: *All the ends of the earth shall see the salvation of our God.* I Tim. 2:4: *Who will have all men to be saved, and to come to the knowledge of the truth.*

And it can be said that at the birth of Christ this grace appeared in two ways. In one way, since He was given to us through the greatest grace of God. Hence, His conception, although it was an operation of the whole Trinity, yet is specially attributed to the Holy Spirit, Who is the principle of graces. And this grace appeared to all men, and especially to the man Christ. Jn. 1:14: *Full of grace and truth.*

In the other way, from this grace the instruction of the human race has been achieved, since before Christ the world was in ignorance and heresy. Is. 9:2: *The people that walked in darkness, have seen a great light: to them that dwelt in the region of the shadow of death, light is risen.* Hence he says, **Instructing us,** as a man instructs his son.

69. About two things He taught us, since two things are necessary for man: a good work and an upright intention: first, he shows how Christ taught us about the first; second, about the second, when he says [n. 72], **Looking for the blessed hope.**

70. He says therefore: **that, denying ungodliness and worldly desires.** It is to be noted that he says, **ungodliness and worldly desires,** since all sins either consist in those things which are directly contrary to God and which are called sins of ungodliness, or impiety. For properly speaking, it is piety according to which we love our parents and fatherland. But since God is our principal Father, piety pertains to the worship of God. Job 28:28: *Behold piety,*[5] *that is wisdom,* according to another translation, whereas ours has it: *Behold the fear of the Lord, that is wisdom.* And so sins against God are said to be impieties. Rom. 1:18: *For the wrath of God is revealed from heaven against all ungodliness,* and there it speaks of the impiety of idolatry.

Or they consist in the abuse of temporal things, and these are secular desires. And an age[6] is a space measuring the period of things. Therefore, by secular things are understood all sins committed against one's neighbor or against themselves through an abuse of them.

71. Then when he says, **we should live soberly,** he shows what good we should do. And he says, **soberly,** regarding oneself; **justly,** regarding one's neighbor; **godly,** regarding God.

Soberly,[7] regarding oneself, as it were with measure. For *bria* is a measure, and this is the case if a man uses exterior things and his own passions with the measure of reason. For this reason sobriety is taken for whatever measured use of exterior things and extrinsic passions. Wis. 8:7: *She teacheth sobriety,*[8] *and prudence, and justice, and fortitude, which are such things as men can have nothing more profitable in life.*

Justly, regarding one's neighbor. Ps. 10:8: *For the Lord is just, and hath loved justice.*

Godly, regarding God. I Tim. 4:7: *Exercise thyself unto godliness.*

72. Then when he says, **Looking for the blessed hope,** he instructs him about the end, which consists in two things: the glory of the soul in death and the glory of the body at the coming of Christ. Jn. 5:28: *For the hour cometh, wherein all that are in the graves shall hear the voice of the Son of God.*

Regarding the first he says, **Looking for the blessed hope,** against those who place the end of man in acts of virtue in this life. But this is not true, for even if we lived soberly, godly, and justly, still we are expectant. Job 7:1 and 14:6: *The life of man upon earth is a warfare, and his days are like the days of a hireling.* Is. 30:18: *Blessed are all they that wait for Him.* And so he says, **Looking for the blessed hope.** This can be understood in two ways: either that it is hope about beatitude or that expectation makes them blessed.

Regarding the second he says, **and coming of the glory of the great God and our Saviour Jesus Christ,** through Whom our bodies shall rise. For he who loves his friend awaits him with desire. II Tim. 4:8: *And not only to me, but to them also that love His coming.* Lk. 12:36: *And you yourselves like to men who wait for their lord.*

And he says, **coming of the glory,** since His first coming was one of humility. Phil. 2:8: *He humbled Himself,* etc. Mt. 11:29: *Learn of Me, because I am meek, and humble of heart.* But that coming will be one of glory since His divinity will be known to all. Lk. 21:27: *And then they shall see the Son of man coming in a cloud, with great power and majesty.*

And he says, **of the great God,** against Arius, who said that the Son is not equal to the Father. And well did he say that He is great, for it says in Rom. 9:5, *Who is over all things, God blessed for ever.* I Jn. 5:20: *That we may know the true God, and may be in His true Son.*

He is also our **.** I Tim. 2:3–4: *For this is good and acceptable in the sight of God our Saviour, Who will have all men to be saved.* He came for this, and His name signifies this. Mt. 1:21: *He shall save His people from their sins.*

And he adds, **Christ,** that is, He Who is anointed, in which is understood the union of the divinity to the humanity. Others are said to be united, not so that they have the essence of the divinity united to themselves, but so that they participate in something of it. But the divinity is united to Christ. Ps. 44:8: *God, Thy God, hath anointed Thee,* etc.

73. Then when he says, **Who gave Himself,** he shows the operation of grace: first, he shows the benefit of the grace of His passion; second, the fruit of the passion, when he says [n. 75], **that He might redeem us.**

74. He says therefore: I say that He is our Saviour, and how? Because He **gave Himself for us.** Eph. 5:2: *And walk in love, as Christ also hath loved us, and hath delivered Himself for us, an oblation and a sacrifice to God for an odour of sweetness.*

75. The fruit is said to be liberation and sanctification.

Liberation, when he says, **that He might redeem us from all iniquity.** Jn. 8:34: *Amen, amen I say unto you: that whosoever committeth sin, is the servant of sin.* For the first man was driven by his sin into slavery to sin, from which slavery he was inclined to another sin. But Christ made satisfaction through His passion, and so we are redeemed from slavery. Is. 43:1: *Fear not, for I have redeemed thee,* etc. And not only from original sin, but from all sins which a man adds by his own will.

Sanctification in the good is posited when he says, **that He...might cleanse to Himself a people,** that is, that He might sanctify a people, so that we might be His people, consecrated to Him. Those who were once not His people are now His people, as it says in Os. 1:10 and Rom. 9:26. **Acceptable,** namely, to God through an upright faith and intention. Prov. 14:35: *A wise servant is acceptable to the king.* But besides this, there must also be good works, and so he says, **a pursuer of good works.** Rom. 13:3: *Do that which is good: and thou shalt have praise from the same.* Gal. 6:9: *And in doing good, let us not fail.*

76. Then when he says, **These things speak,** etc., he leads him to the preaching of grace, and regarding this he does two things: first, he exhorts him to preach; second, he instructs him in the manner of preaching when he says, **with all authority.**

He says therefore: **speak** of things regarding what is to be believed; **exhort** regarding what is to be done. I Thess. 2:3: *For our exhortation was not of error, nor of uncleanness, nor in deceit.* **Rebuke** those who do evil. I Tim. 5:20: *Them that sin reprove before all.*

And this **with all authority,** since he speaks as an instrument or minister of God. And so he is to speak with the confidence of divine authority.

Yet, considering his own infirmity, sometimes in his exhortation he must speak with requests. Prov. 18:23: *The poor will speak with supplications.* Sometimes, considering the authority committed to him, he must speak with commands. II Cor. 13:3: *Do you seek a proof of Christ that speaketh in me?* Or, with meekness to the good and with authority to the obstinate.

He has to be admonished to rebuke with authority because naturally he was a mild man. I Tim. 4:12: *Let no man despise thy youth.*

Chapter Three

Lecture One

1 [n. 77] **Admonish them to be subject to princes and powers, to obey at a word, to be ready to every good work.**

2 [n. 80] **To blaspheme**[1] **no man, not to be litigious, but modest:**[2] **shewing all mildness towards all men.**

3 [n. 83] **For we ourselves also were some time unwise, incredulous, erring, slaves to divers desires and pleasures, living in malice and envy, hateful, and hating one another.**

4 [n. 87] **But when the goodness and humanity**[3] **of God our Saviour appeared:**

5 [n. 89] **Not by the works of justice, which we have done, but according to His mercy, He saved us, by the laver of regeneration, and renovation of the Holy Ghost;**

6 [n. 93] **Whom He hath poured forth upon us abundantly, through Jesus Christ our Saviour:**

7 [n. 94] **That, being justified by His grace, we may be heirs, according to hope of life everlasting.**

8 [n. 96] **It is a faithful saying: and these things I will have thee affirm constantly: that they, who believe in God, may be careful to excel in good works. These things are good and profitable unto men.**

77. Above the Apostle gave particular admonitions pertaining to the individual states [n. 49]; here he gives general ones for all. First, he gives them; second, the reason for them, when he says [n. 83], **For we ourselves also;** third, he leads Titus to the preaching of both when he says [n. 97], **and these things.** He does two things regarding the first: first, he tells everyone in what way they should

relate to their superiors; second, how they should relate to their peers, when he says [n. 80], **To blaspheme no man.** Again, the first is in two parts: first, he shows that they owe superiors the reverence of subjection; second, obedience to their commands, when he says [n. 79], **to obey at a word.**

78. He says therefore: I have spoken about what you should admonish the foregoing men, but **Admonish them,** that is, everyone, **to be subject to princes,** that is, kings and suchlike, **and powers,** that is, other officials, **to obey at a word.** I Pet. 2:13–14: *Be ye subject therefore to every human creature for God's sake: whether it be to the king as excelling; or to governors as sent by him.*

And this warning is necessary, first to take away an error among the Jews, who say that it is not necessary to obey the mandates of men; second, so that they may make no unrest in the Church; third, since they were bound to the obedience of their command. Heb. 13:17: *Obey your prelates, and be subject to them,* etc.

79. And he said, **to obey at a word,** that is, of the governor. I Kg. 15:22: *For obedience is better than sacrifices.* II Thess. 3:14: *And if any man obey not our word by this epistle, note that man.*

And not only is promptness necessary, but discretion as well. Hence he says, **to every good work,** otherwise it would not be obedience; for then is God more to be obeyed for He is greater. Acts 4:19: *If it be just in the sight of God, to hear you rather than God, judge ye.* Wherefore soldiers are not bound to obey in an unjust war.

80. Then when he says, **To blaspheme no man,** he shows how they ought to relate to their peers: first, regarding the avoidance of evil; second, doing good, when he says [n. 82], **but modest.**

81. He warns them especially about words, since in the primitive Church few sinned in deeds. But someone sins in words first against the person of another if he brings reproaches against him. Hence he says, **To blaspheme no man.**

On the contrary, blasphemy is a crime against God, and therefore there is no blasphemy against one's neighbor.

I respond that inasmuch as love of neighbor is referred to the love of God and the honor of a neighbor to the honor of God, thus the reproach of him is against God. In this way blasphemy is taken here, for any evil speech, secret or manifest. II Pet. 2:10: *They fear not to bring in sects, blaspheming.*

Second, a man sins against his neighbor on account of exterior things. And so he says, **not to be litigious.** Here it must be known that there are three kinds of men. One kind is virtuous and the other two are vicious. For certain men are grieved in no way by all the things they hear, and these are toadies. Others resist every word, and these are litigious. Against these he speaks here. And so he says in II Tim. 2:24: *But the servant of the Lord must not wrangle: but be mild towards all men.* Prov. 20:3: *It is an honour for a man to separate himself from quarrels.* But holding the middle place, such that sometimes he delights in words and sometimes is grieved, is the virtuous man. II Cor. 7:8: *For although I made you sorrowful by my epistle, I do not repent,* etc.

82. Then when he says, **but modest,** he shows how they ought to relate to their peers in doing good. And first in exterior acts, when he says, **but modest.** Now, modesty is the virtue by which someone keeps to the right manner of exterior actions, lest he offend the view of anyone. Phil. 4:5: *Let your modesty be known to all men.* Prov. 22:4: *The fruit of modesty*[4] *is the fear of the Lord, riches and glory and life.*

As much as someone is more impetuous in his interior affections, so much the more is it difficult for him to be restrained in his external actions. Now, among all the affections, such is anger. And so against this he posits mildness, which moderates the passions of anger. Hence he says, **shewing all mildness towards all men.** Mt. 11:29: *Learn of Me, because I am meek, and humble of heart.* Jas. 1:21: *With meekness receive the ingrafted word, which is able to save your souls.*

83. Then when he says, **For we ourselves also,** etc., he gives the reason for the foregoing, and mostly of the last, namely, that they should be mild. For someone could say: How shall we be meek to the infidels, how to the wicked? We cannot do this. He responds: Consider yourself, how you were. And so the best remedy against anger is the recognition of one's own weakness. Therefore, first he gives their past state; second, he shows whence they have come to the state of perfection when he says [n. 87], **But when the goodness and humanity.** Again, he first posits the defects pertaining to the intellect; second, to the affections, when he says [n. 85], **slaves to divers desires.**

84. Now, the intellect can fail in two ways: it can fail of true knowledge as through ignorance by way of negation or it may fall into a false opinion. Men perceive what is true in divine things in two ways: some only through faith and some by a certain foretaste through the light of wisdom through a certain open knowledge.

Thus, regarding the second he says, **For we ourselves also were some time unwise,** that is, deprived of that wisdom. Lk. 21:15: *For I will give you a mouth and wisdom,* etc. Regarding the first he says, **incredulous,** that is, unfaithful. Ez. 2:6: *Thou art among unbelievers and destroyers.*

But we wander, falling into a contrary opinion. Hence he says, **erring,** that is, holding what is false for what is true. Is. 19:14: *They have caused Egypt to err in all its works.*

85. Then he posits those things which pertain to the corruption of the affections: first, regarding themselves; second, regarding others, when he says [n. 86], **living in malice,** etc.

Then is the affection of man upright when it serves reason and uses licit delights according to reason. When, therefore, it does not follow reason but its own desires, then is it corrupted. Hence he says, **slaves to divers desires and**

pleasures. Pleasures refer to the sins of fleshly delight, such as lust and gluttony. Desires are certain other vices, such as ambition and avarice, and the like. Ecclus. 18:30: *Go not after thy lusts, but turn away from thy own will.* Rom. 6:12: *Let no sin therefore reign in your mortal body, so as to obey the lusts thereof.* II Tim. 3:4: *Lovers of pleasures more than of God.*

86. Then when he says, **living in malice,** he posits the sins with respect to others: first malice, which is the will to harm another, for the effect is named from the end. Therefore, he who intends to bring evil upon another is malicious. Jas. 1:21: *Wherefore casting away all uncleanness, and abundance of malice.*[5] Second he posits **envy,** which grieves over the good of another, just as malice brings harm upon him. Prov. 14:30: *Envy is the rottenness of the bones.* Third, he posits hatred. Hence he says, **hateful,** either to God, because they committed sin – Wis. 14:9: *But to God the wicked and his wickedness are hateful alike.* Rom. 1:30: *Detractors, hateful to God* – or to their neighbors, when they do that for which a neighbor should hate them.

And he adds, **hating one another,** as if to say: And we also hated others. I Jn. 3:15: *Whosoever hateth his brother is a murderer.*

87. Then when he says, **But when the goodness and humanity,** he shows the state of our salvation: first, he describes its order and procession; second, he confirms what has been said when he says [n. 96], **It is a faithful saying.** Regarding the first he does four things: first, he shows the cause of salvation; second, the reason for being saved, when he says [n. 89], **Not by the works of justice;** third, the manner of it, when he says [n. 90], **by the laver of regeneration;** fourth, its end, when he says [n. 94], **That, being justified by His grace.**

88. The cause of our salvation is the charity of God. Eph. 2:4: *But God, (Who is rich in mercy,) for His exceeding charity wherewith He loved us,* etc. He describes this charity regarding its affection and then regarding its effect.

The interior affection of charity is denoted by benignity, which is said to be a good fieriness.[6] Cant. 8:6: *The lamps thereof are fire and flames.* Therefore, benignity is interior love pouring out good things to all outside. From eternity this was in God, since His love is the cause of all things. Joel 2:13: *He is gracious and merciful,* etc.

But sometimes this was not apparent. Is. 63:15: *Where is Thy zeal, and Thy strength, the multitude of Thy bowels, and of Thy mercies? they have held back themselves from me.* But it appeared through the effect which is noted when he says, **humanity,** which can be understood in two ways. Either inasmuch as it signifies His human nature, as if he had said, **But when the goodness and humanity appeared,** when God out of His benignity was made man. Phil. 2:7: *In habit found as a man.* Ps. 64:12: *Thou shalt bless the crown of the year of Thy goodness.* Or inasmuch as it signifies virtue, which consists in the exterior assistance for the needs of others. Hence to be human is to condescend. Acts 28:1: *But the* *barbarians shewed us no small courtesy.*[7] Thus does God condescend to our defects. Ps. 102:14: *He knoweth our frame.* And this is of **our Saviour** because, as it is said in Ps. 36:39, *The salvation of the just is from the Lord.*

89. Then when he says, **Not by the works of justice,** he gives the reason for being saved: first, the presumed reason is excluded; second, the true reason is shown.

The presumed reason is that we are saved because of our merits; this he excludes when he says, **Not by the works of justice, which we have done.** Rom. 11:5: *There is a remnant saved according to the election of grace.* Deut. 9:5: *For it is not for thy justices, and the uprightness of thy heart that thou shalt go in to possess their lands,* etc.

But the true reason is solely the mercy of God; hence he says, **but according to His mercy, He saved us.** Lam. 3:22: *The mercies of the Lord that we are not consumed.* Lk. 1:50: *His mercy is from generation unto generations.*

90. The manner of securing salvation is through baptism, which he posits first; second, its effect [n. 92]; third, its cause [n. 93].

91. He says, then, **by the laver,** that is, we are saved by a spiritual ablution. Eph. 5:26: *Cleansing it by the laver of water in the word of life.* Zach. 13:1: *In that day there shall be a fountain open to the house of David, and to the inhabitants of Jerusalem: for the washing of the sinner, and of the unclean woman.*

92. Regarding its effect he adds, **of regeneration, and renovation.** For this it must be known that in the state of perdition man lacks two things which he has attained through Christ, namely, participation in the divine nature and abandonment of the old man. For he has been separated from God. Is. 59:2: *But your iniquities have divided between you and your God, and your sins have hid His face from you that He should not hear.* And he was grown old. Bar. 3:11: *Thou art grown old in a strange country.* But the first, namely, participation in the divine nature, we attain through Christ. II Pet. 1:4: *By these you may be made partakers of the divine nature.* But a new nature is not acquired except through generation. Yet this nature is so given that it is added on to our nature, which still remains. In this way participation as a son of God is generated where man is not destroyed. Jn. 3:7: *You must be born again.* And therefore it is called regeneration. Jas. 1:18: *For of His own will hath He begotten us by the word of truth.* Through Christ man also put down the old man of sin, having been renewed to the integrity of nature, and this is called renovation. Eph. 4:23: *And be renewed in the spirit of your mind.*

93. But what is the cause of this effect, that the heart is washed clean? This power is from the holy and indivisible Trinity. Mt. 28:19: *In the name of the Father, and of the Son, and of the Holy Ghost.* Hence also, when Christ was baptized, the Father appeared in the voice, the Son in the flesh, and the Holy Spirit in the form of a dove. And so he says, **of the Holy Ghost,** that is, which the Holy Spirit has done. Ps. 103:30: *Thou shalt send forth Thy spirit,* etc. Likewise is

regeneration through the Spirit. Gal. 4:6: *God hath sent the Spirit of His Son into your hearts, crying: Abba, Father.* Rom. 8:15: *For you have not received the spirit of bondage again in fear; but you have received the spirit of adoption of sons, whereby we cry: Abba (Father).*

But God the Father gives this Spirit, **Whom He hath poured forth upon us abundantly,** to signify the plenitude of grace in baptism; hence there occurs a full remission of sins. Joel 2:28: *I will pour out My spirit upon all flesh,* etc. Is. 44:3: *I will pour out My spirit upon thy seed.* And to signify the diverse gifts of grace. Jas. 1:5: *Who giveth to all men abundantly, and upbraideth not.*

This is also given **through Jesus Christ our Saviour.** Jn. 15:26: *The Paraclete cometh, Whom I will send you.* For in Christ we find two natures, and it pertains to each that Christ gives the Holy Spirit. Regarding His divine nature, since He is the Word, from Whom and from the Father together at once He proceeds as love. Now, love in us proceeds from a conception of the heart, the conception of which is a word. Regarding His human nature, Christ received His fullness, such that through Him it is derived to all. Jn. 1:14: *Full of grace and truth.* And a little later: *And of His fulness we all have received, and grace for grace.* And 3:34: *For God doth not give the Spirit by measure.* And so baptism and the other sacraments do not have efficacy except by virtue of the humanity and the passion of Christ.

94. Then when he says, **That, being justified by His grace,** the end of our salvation is given, which is participation in eternal life. Hence he says, **heirs.**

Justified is the same as regenerated, which he had said earlier. In the justification of the wicked there are two termini: the end from which, which is the remission of sin, and this is renovation; and the end to which, which is the infusion of grace, and this pertains to regeneration. He says therefore: And so the Word was made flesh, so that being justified, that is, being renovated through grace, since justification does not happen without grace, etc.

95. But could not God remit fault without the infusion of grace? It would seem so, since from the beginning He was able to constitute man to be without grace and fault.

I respond that it is one thing about the man who has offended no one, since thus he can be without grace and without fault; but it is another about the man who has already sinned, who cannot be otherwise than hated or loved. If he is loved by God, he must love; and if he loves, grace must be given to him, since without grace he does not love, and it is necessary also that through this they are made heirs. I Pet. 1:4: *Unto an inheritance incorruptible, and undefiled, and that can not fade, reserved in heaven for you,* etc.

And this **of life everlasting.** Ps. 15:6: *The lines are fallen unto me in goodly places: for my inheritance is goodly to me.* But how are they heirs? **According to hope,** for there is no longer a hope for this life. Rom. 5:2: *By whom also we have* *access through faith into this grace, wherein we stand, and glory in the hope of the glory of the sons of God.*

96. Then when he says, **It is a faithful saying,** he proves what had been said about our salvation and hope. Apoc. 22:6: *These words are most faithful and true.*

97. Then when he says, **these things I will have thee affirm,** he commands this to be preached: first, he gives his precept; second, he assigns a reason for it when he says, **These things are good and profitable unto men.**

He says, then, **these things,** namely, the benefits of God, the censuring of sinners, the teachings of faith and morals, **I will have thee affirm** to others. Job 4:4: *Thy words have confirmed them that were staggering.* Acts 15:32: *But Judas and Silas, being prophets also themselves, with many words comforted the brethren, and confirmed them.*

And the reason for this is **that they...may be careful,** etc. This can be understood to refer to prelates, as if to say: I want you to confirm the wayfarers, that is, prelates, **that they may be careful** to be at the head of those **who believe in God,** namely, the faithful in good works. I Pet. 2:12: *They may, by the good works, which they shall behold in you, glorify God.* Mt. 5:16: *So let your light shine before men, that they may see your good works, and glorify your Father Who is in heaven.*

These things are good, for they regard the goodness of God. Mt. 12:35: *A good man out of a good treasure bringeth forth good things.* **And profitable unto men.** Is. 48:17: *I am the Lord thy God that teach thee profitable things.*

Lecture Two

9 [n. 98] But avoid foolish questions, and genealogies, and contentions, and strivings about the law. For they are unprofitable and vain.

10 [n. 101] A man that is a heretic, after the first and second admonition, avoid:

11 [n. 103] Knowing that he, that is such an one, is subverted, and sinneth, being condemned by his own judgment.

12 [n. 104] When I shall send to thee Artemas or Tychicus, make haste to come unto me to Nicopolis. For there I have determined to winter.

13 Send forward Zenas, the lawyer, and Apollo, with care, that nothing be wanting to them.

14 And let your⁸ men also learn to excel in good works for necessary uses: that they be not unfruitful.

15 [n. 106] All that are with me salute thee: salute them that love us in the faith. The grace of God be with you all. Amen.

98. Above the Apostle taught Titus what sort of things to propose for the instruction of the people [n. 49]; now he shows what things to avoid in doctrine. First, he does this; second, he writes certain familiar things when he says [n. 104], **When I shall send to thee.** Again, the first is in two parts: first, he shows how to avoid useless and foreign dogmas; second, how to avoid heretics, when he says [n. 101], **A man that is a heretic.** Regarding the first he does two things: first, he shows what things are to be avoided in his own doctrine; second, he gives the reason why, when he says [n. 100], **For they are unprofitable.**

99. And it must be noted regarding the first that to him who professes the doctrine of any science it first pertains that he satisfy questions which are moved against it; second, that he treat some things in themselves; third, that he dispute with those who resist; fourth, that he teach what must be avoided regarding that science.

Now, in all the sciences no wise man responds to any question whatsoever, but only to those which pertain to his science. So the doctor of truth ought not to respond to just any question. For folly is opposed to wisdom, and this is the doctrine of wisdom. Deut. 4:6: *For this is your wisdom, and understanding in the sight of nations.* Therefore, he says, **But avoid foolish questions.** Therefore, the questions opposed to the intentions of this science are foolish. And those questions are opposed to it which are without discipline. Job 34:35: *But Job hath spoken foolishly, and his words sound not discipline.* Likewise, when something obvious is proposed as doubtful, namely, whatsoever someone ought to hold *per se* in a science.

And these are the things which look to the instruction of faith and the learning of morals. And there are certain things he ought to avoid.

Hence he says, **and genealogies.** For genealogies are placed in Scripture on account of mysteries and for the sake of an historical understanding.

In resisting assailants he ought to avoid **contentions, and strivings about the law.** For when there is a disputation for the discovery of the truth, this is laudable. But when there is contention for showing what is to be held and what to be avoided, these are to be shunned. Prov. 20:3: *It is an honour for a man to separate himself from quarrels.* II Tim. 2:14: *Contend not in words.* Those are fights about the Law which arise not from the vice of those disputing but from contrariety in Scripture or from contrary reasons.

But are such always to be avoided? It must be said that in Sacred Scripture, according to the truth, nothing is contrary. But if some things appears to be contrary, either they are not understood or they are corrupted by the fault of the scribes, which is clear especially in numbers and genealogies. And so those things which cannot be determined the Apostle wills to be shunned.

100. And this **For they are unprofitable.** And a doctor should intend two things: profit and truth. Prov. 8:7: *My mouth shall meditate truth,* etc. Is. 48:17: *I am the Lord thy God that teach thee profitable things.* Therefore, he is not to introduce useless things which do not have the solid truth. For to know singulars, such as are genealogies, is not for the perfection of the intellect, nor for the instruction of morals, nor that of faith. And they are **vain** because they do not have the solid truth.

101. Then when he says, **A man that is a heretic,** he shows who among men are to be avoided: first, he shows that heretics are; second, the reason for this, when he says [n. 103], **Knowing that he.**

102. He says, then, **A man that is a heretic.** Here it must be noted what makes one to be a heretic, and first to be grasped is the notion of this word *heretic.* For it is not said from division but from choice, as Jerome says; for in Greek *haeresis* is election. Hence a heretic is one who chooses, as it were one who pertinaciously adheres to some sect which he chooses.

Hence it must be known that every heretic is someone erring, but not vice versa, because of two things. First, on the part of the matter about which he errs, for example, if it does not regard the end of human life or that which pertains to faith or morals. For such a man thus erring is not a heretic. If he err regarding those things which do pertain to the end of human life, he is always a heretic. And I say the end of human life since among the ancients there were sects who posited diverse ends, as is clear from the Stoics or Epicureans. Or regarding the faith; and thus if someone were to say that God is not three and one, and that fornication is not a sin, he is a heretic.

Second, on the part of the choice, since the one choosing, if he be not obstinate but prepared to be corrected according to the determination of the Church, and thus it is not out of malice but ignorance, he is not a heretic.

This man, therefore, **avoid,** because of the danger. II Tim. 2:17: *And their speech spreadeth like a canker.* Let no one share in their sins, lest he seem to consent to them. II Jn. 1:10: *If any man come to you, and bring not this doctrine, receive him not into the house, nor say to him, God speed you. For he that saith unto him, God speed you, communicateth with his wicked works.* Likewise, because of punishment. Num. 16:26: *Depart from the tents of these wicked men, and touch nothing of theirs lest you be involved in their sins.*

Nevertheless, he wants him to be warned, and if he will not lay aside his error, then he is a heretic and an outcast. And he says, **after the first and second admonition.** For thus it happens in the Church with excommunications. And the reason is that the number of each thing has a beginning, a middle, and an end, and so it is taken as sufficient for all. II Cor. 13:1: *Behold, this is the third time I am coming to you.* Likewise, on account of the perfection of the ternary number.

103. The reason for avoiding him is that one who is erring must be treated from the beginning in order to be corrected. Mt. 9:12: *They that are in health need not a physician, but they that are ill.* And so a man is not to be sent away until it be seen if he can be cured; but if he cannot be healed, then he is to be sent away. Lk. 19:22: *Out of thy own mouth I judge thee, thou wicked servant.*

104. Then when he says, **When I shall send to thee,** he writes some familiar things: first, certain things regarding himself needing to be disposed; second, he ends the epistle with a greeting [n. 106].

105. He says, then, **When I shall send to thee,** etc. These two men were disciples of the Apostle. He sent others since he wanted Titus to return to himself; he does not determine the time but the place for he needed him to help preach. Yet he wanted **Artemas** to be sent first, and he shows what to do regarding him; second, he responds to an objection, when he says, **And let your men also learn.**

This Apollo, about whom it speaks in Acts 19:1, was the bishop of the Corinthians, on account of whose sins he left them and went to Titus in Crete, but, now that the Corinthians had been corrected, the Apostle recalls him.

And he calls Zenas a lawyer, although Apollo was also very learned, since in Judaism he had this dignity. The reason why he wants them to be sent first, and not Titus, is that Titus was necessary among the Cretans because of his episcopacy, but they did not have any other care. And he says, **that nothing be wanting to them,** as if to say: If you do not have something, let your subjects provide it for you.

And so he adds, **And let your men also learn,** that is, let the faithful learn to provide as the Jews do. And he says let **your men,** namely, your subjects, learn to excel over the Jews and others from Asia, who provide for their own preachers and other needy people. And he says, **for necessary uses,** that is, in cases of necessity. I Tim. 6:8: *But having food, and wherewith to be covered, with these we are content.*

The reason why they should be present is so **that they be not unfruitful.** I Cor. 9:7: *Who planteth a vineyard, and eateth not of the fruit thereof?* Therefore, the people, if they are as the vine of the Lord, ought to bear fruit, not only spiritual but also temporal, so that from this the husbandmen may be sustained; otherwise they would be unfruitful. Mt. 7:19: *Every tree that bringeth not forth good fruit, shall be cut down, and shall be cast into the fire.*

106. Then he salutes them first on the part of others; second, he asks that they greet others; third, he gives his own greeting.

Regarding the first he says, **All that are with me salute,** that is, they would like to salute, **thee.**

Second he says, **salute them that love us in the faith** of Christ, since there is no fellowship between the faithful and the infidels. II Chr. 19:2: *Thou helpest the ungodly, and thou art joined in friendship with them that hate the Lord, and therefore thou didst deserve indeed the wrath of the Lord.* Or, **them that love us in the faith,** that is, with faithful affection. Ecclus. 6:5: *Nothing can be compared to a faithful friend.*

The grace of God, which is the principle of all good things. Rom. 3:24: *Being justified freely by His grace.* And he says, **be with you all,** since he does not write to one for his profit alone but for the whole Church.

Thanks be to God.

The Commentary of St. Thomas Aquinas on
The Epistle of St. Paul to Philemon

Synoptical Outline of Philemon

I. Greeting [n. 3]
    A. Persons greeting [n. 4]
    B. Those greeted [n. 5]
    C. The good things desired for them [n. 6]
II. Epistolary Narrative [n. 7]: how a temporal master ought to relate to his temporal slaves and how the faithful servant ought to relate to his master.
    A. Thanksgiving [n. 8]
        1. Thanksgiving itself [n. 8]
        2. For what he is grateful [n. 9]
        3. The reason for which he gives thanks to God [n. 11]
    B. Petition [n. 12]
        1. The confidence for his petition [n. 13]
        2. The petition itself [n. 15]
            a. the person whom he petitions [n. 15]
            b. the petition concluding from this [n. 18]
        3. The reason for the petition [n. 23]
            a. on the part of God [n. 24]
            b. on the part of the Apostle himself [n. 25]
            c. on the part of Philemon [n. 29]
    C. Conclusion [n. 30]
        1. On the part of others [n. 30]

Prologue

If thou have a faithful servant, let him be to thee as thy own soul:
treat him as a brother. – Ecclus. 33:31

1. The wise man shows three things regarding the master and his slave: what is required on the part of the slave, what ought to be the affection of the master for his slave, and how one is to use a slave.

On the part of the servant, fidelity is required, in which is the good of the slave, since he ought to give both what he is and all he has to his master. Mt. 24:45: *Who, thinkest thou, is a faithful and wise servant.* And he says, **If thou have a faithful servant,** for fidelity is found only among few. Prov. 20:6: *Who shall find a faithful man?*

Therefore, such a slave ought to be held by his master as a friend in his affections. Hence he says, **let him be to thee as thy own soul.** For it is proper to friends that they be of one mind in their likes and dislikes. Acts 4:32: *And the multitude of believers had but one heart and one soul.* By this we are given to understand that there ought to be a certain agreement between a master and his slave, for a faithful slave becomes a friend.

The use of a slave is that he may be treated as a brother, for he is a brother, both as regards the generation of nature, for they have the same author – Job 31:13: *If I have despised to abide judgment with my manservant.* Mal. 2:10: *Have we not all one father? hath not one God created us?* – and as regards the generation of grace, which is the same: Gal. 3:27–28: *For as many of you as have been baptized in Christ, have put on Christ. There is neither Jew nor Greek: there is neither bond nor free: there is neither male nor female. For you are all one in Christ Jesus.* Mt. 23:8: *All you are brethren.*

2. These words befit the matter of this epistle. For just as above he showed how spiritual prelates ought to relate to their subjects, so here he shows how temporal masters ought to relate to their temporal slaves and how the faithful servant ought to relate to his master.

Lecture One

1 [n. 3] Paul, a prisoner of Christ Jesus, and Timothy, a brother: to Philemon, our beloved and fellow labourer;

2 And to Appia, our dearest sister, and to Archippus, our fellow soldier, and to the church which is in thy house:

3 [n. 6] Grace to you and peace from God our Father, and from the Lord Jesus Christ.

4 [n. 7] I give thanks to my God, always making a remembrance of thee in my prayers.

5 [n. 9] Hearing of thy charity and faith, which thou hast in the Lord Jesus, and toward all the saints:

6 [n. 10] That the communication of thy faith may be made evident in the acknowledgement of every good work, that is in you in Christ Jesus.

7 [n. 11] For I have had great joy and consolation in thy charity, because the bowels of the saints have been refreshed by thee, brother.

8 [n. 13] Wherefore though I have much confidence in Christ Jesus, to command thee that which is to the purpose:

9 [n. 14] For charity sake I rather beseech, since[1] thou art such a one, as Paul an old man, and now a prisoner also of Jesus Christ.

3. This epistle was occasioned by the following: among the Colossians a certain noteworthy Christian had a certain slave who, secretly fleeing to Rome, was baptized by the Apostle, on whose account he writes. And first he gives his salutation and then the narrative of the epistle [n. 7]. In the salutation he first gives the persons who are so greeting, then those greeted [n. 5], and then the good things desired [n. 6].

4. He says, then, **Paul,** which is a name to be venerated by all the faithful who are taught by him. **A prisoner.** II Tim. 2:9: *I labour even unto bands.* For then he was a prisoner in Rome. But **of Jesus Christ,** which shows the reason for his chains. Now, it is exceedingly laudable to be in chains on account of Christ, for in this is one to find his beatitude. Mt. 5:10: *Blessed are they that suffer persecution for justice' sake,* etc. I Pet. 4:15–16: *But let none of you suffer as a murderer, or a thief, or a railer, or a coveter of other men's things. But if as a Christian, let him not be ashamed, but let him glorify God in that name.* Acts 5:41: *And they indeed went from the presence of the council, rejoicing that they were accounted worthy to suffer reproach for the name of Jesus.*

And Timothy, a brother. They are brothers as regards their perfect faith. Phil. 2:20: *For I have no man so of the same mind, who with sincere affection is* *solicitous for you.* And he adds Timothy to himself so as to secure his request more easily, since it impossible that the prayers of many not be heard.

5. Then he gives the persons greeted. And first he gives the principal person greeted, and then those attached. Again, he first gives the man and his wife, who have rule over the house, to whom the slave was bound. **To Philemon, our beloved and fellow labourer; and to Appia, our dearest sister. Beloved,** he says because of his good works. Jn. 13:34: *A new commandment I give unto you: That you love one another.* **Fellow labourer,** for he tended to the needs of the saints. Prov. 18:19: *A brother that is helped by his brother, is like a strong city.*

Then he adds another person when he says, **and to Archippus, our fellow soldier,** who was so powerful in Colossae that all Christians were under his shadow. And so he brings in the whole Church there, whose bishop was Archippus, writing in Col. 4:17: *And say to Archippus: Take heed to the ministry which thou hast received,* etc. And he says, **and to Archippus, our fellow soldier,** since all prelates are as spiritual soldiers of the Church. II Cor. 10:4: *For the weapons of our warfare are not carnal,* etc. And he adds, **and to the church.** These he brings in to move Philemon to listen to him.

6. The good things desired are explained as is his custom.

7. Then when he says, **I give thanks,** the narration of the epistle is given. And first he makes a thanksgiving; second, a petition, when he says [n. 13], **Wherefore**; third, his conclusion, when he says in verse twenty-three [n. 30], **Yea, brother.** Again, first the thanksgiving is given; second, the matter for giving thanks, when he says [n. 9], **Hearing of thy charity and faith**; third, the cause on account of which he gives thanks to God, when he says [n. 11], **For I have had great joy.**

8. He says, then, **I give thanks to my God.** Col. 3:15: *And be ye thankful.* Phil. 4:6: *With thanksgiving.* It is as if he said: I so give thanks for past benefits that I yet pray for future ones. And so he says, **always making a remembrance of thee,** etc. Phil. 1:7: *For that I have you in my heart; and that in my bands, and in the defence and confirmation of the gospel, you all are partakers of my joy.* Is. 49:15: *Can a woman forget her infant,* etc.

9. While positing the matter for thanksgiving and prayer, he shows what he prays for on his behalf by petition.

The matter of this was necessary and good for Philemon, namely charity and faith, for without charity none of the rest are of any value, and by it all things are possessed. I Cor. 13:1: *If I speak with the tongues of men,* etc. Likewise, no one is able to love God without faith, since he does not know God truly. But he makes no mention about hope since it is the middle of the three and is understood by the others.

But in Whom do you have faith and charity? **In the Lord Jesus.** I Cor. 16:22: *If any man love not our Lord Jesus Christ, let him be anathema.* And this is necessary, since from Christ more sweetly loved, love for His members is derived, for no one loves the Head who does not love the members. I Jn. 4:20: *He that loveth not his brother, whom he seeth, how can he love God, Whom he seeth not?* **And toward all the saints;** faith depends upon doctrine according as it is manifested by Christ, since *No man hath seen God at any time,* as it says in Jn. 1:18. Again 14:1: *You believe in God, believe also in Me.* And so we have faith through Christ.

But how this pertains to the saints can be understood in two ways. In one way, from the faith which they have in Christ proceeds honor bestowed upon the saints. In another way, faith consists principally in the divinity, according as it is preached by Christ, but not only by Christ but also by His saints. Mt. 28:19: *Going therefore, teach ye all nations,* etc. Therefore, we must believe not only what was said by Christ but also what was said by His saints. Heb. 2:3: *Which having begun to be declared by the Lord, was confirmed unto us by them that heard Him.*

10. **That the communication of thy faith.** This is joined in two ways. In one way, so that the communication is the sign, so that the sense is: **That the communication,** etc., that is, so great is thy charity that **the communication of thy faith may be made evident.** In the other way: **I give thanks to my God, always making a remembrance of thee,** so that he shows here what he asks for him when he prays. And **the communication of faith** may be taken in two ways. In one way, he communicated in faith with all the saints, not having some new faith like the heretics. I Cor. 1:10: *That you all speak the same thing,* etc. In the other way, the communication by which you communicate good things to the saints proceeds from faith. I Tim. 6:17: *Charge the rich of this world not to be highminded, nor to trust in the uncertainty of riches, but in the living God, (Who giveth us abundantly all things to enjoy),* etc.

May be made evident, that is, that the good latent in the heart may be made evident through good works. **In the acknowledgement of every good work,** namely, that is wrought by you. And this **in Christ Jesus,** that is, for Christ Jesus. Jas. 2:18: *Shew me thy faith without works; and I will shew thee, by works, my faith.*

Or again, there are many works in the world which are good to men but not good to God since they are not done aright. Prov. 14:12: *There is a way which seemeth just to a man: but the ends thereof lead to death.* Eccles. 8:10: *I saw the wicked buried: who also when they were yet living were in the holy place, and were praised in the city as men of just works.* But this is manifested by right faith when it attains its reward from God, Who does not remunerate except right things. And therefore he says, **in the acknowledgement,** that is, so that it may be evident that you know every good, or that every good be known in you, which is the fruition of the divinity. Ex. 33:19: *I will shew thee all good.* Wis. 7:11: *Now all good things came to me together with her.*

11. Now the reason for which he gives thanks is joy. And therefore he says, **For I have had great joy.** III Jn. 1:4: *I have no greater grace than this, to hear that my children walk in truth.* For this joy relieved his concerns, wherefore he adds, **and consolation in thy charity.** Ps. 93:19: *According to the multitude of my sorrows in my heart, Thy comforts have given joy to my soul.* He assigns the reason for this saying, **because the bowels of the saints have been refreshed by thee, brother.** Col. 3:12: *Put ye on therefore, as the elect of God, holy, and beloved, the bowels of mercy, benignity,* etc. III Jn. 1:5: *Dearly beloved, thou dost faithfully whatever thou dost for the brethren, and that for strangers,* etc.

12. Then when he says, **Wherefore,** etc., his petition is given: first, his confidence in asking; second, the petition itself, when he says in verse ten [n. 15], **I beseech thee for my son;** third, the reason for it, when he says in verse fifteen [n. 23], **For perhaps he therefore departed.**

13. He says, then, **Wherefore,** that is, since you so abound in charity, **I have much confidence in Christ Jesus,** as if to say: not from myself but from the authority of Jesus Christ, in the faith of Whom I have begotten you. And so I can command you as a father, but only **that which is to the purpose,** either yours or the common one; to put it another way, a prelate has no power to command anything for himself, except what is for the profit of the one commanded, or for the Church's, or for the good practices of the Christian religion. Yet, **For charity sake I rather beseech.** Prov. 18:23: *The poor will speak with supplications.*

14. And why? Assuredly, **since thou art such a one,** etc. There are two reasons for which one ought to be entreated. First, old age. I Tim. 5:1: *An ancient man rebuke not, but entreat him as a father,* etc. Second, the honesty of virtue, for where we offend not, we are equals. Ecclus. 32:1: *Have they made thee ruler? be not lifted up: be among them as one of them.*

He says therefore, **since thou art such a one, as Paul an old man,** as if to say: If you were a child, I would command you to do this, but you are an old man.

Again, if you were superficial, but instead you are of such a life that is similar to mine. Not that he is such and so great simply speaking, but in some way, which he says from his humility. Rom. 12:10: *With honour preventing one another.* Origen: Paul lived for a long time in faith. For he was converted as an adolescent, and now he speaks as an old man. Origen: A useful teacher is rarely found in the Church unless he be old. Take the examples of Peter and Paul.

Lecture Two

10 [n. 15] I beseech thee for my son, whom I have begotten in my bands, Onesimus,

11 [n. 17] Who hath been heretofore unprofitable to thee, but now is profitable both to me and thee,

12 [n. 18] Whom I have sent back to thee. And do thou receive him as my own bowels.

13 [n. 20] Whom I would have retained with me, that in thy stead he might have ministered to me in the bands of the gospel:

14 [n. 22] But without thy counsel I would do nothing: that thy good deed might not be as it were of necessity, but voluntary.

15 [n. 23] For perhaps he therefore departed for a season from thee, that thou mightest receive him again for ever:

16 Not now as a servant, but instead of a servant, a most dear brother, especially to me: but how much more to thee both in the flesh and in the Lord?

17 [n. 25] If therefore thou count me a partner, receive him as myself.

18 [n. 27] And if he hath wronged thee in any thing or is in thy debt, put that to my account.

19 I Paul have written it with my own hand: I will repay it: not to say to thee, that thou owest me thy own self also.

20 [n. 28] Yea, brother. May I enjoy thee in the Lord. Refresh my bowels in the Lord.

21 [n. 29] Trusting in thy obedience, I have written to thee: knowing that thou wilt also do more than I say.

22 But withal prepare me also a lodging. For I hope that through your prayers I shall be given unto you.

23 [n. 30] There salute thee Epaphras, my fellow prisoner in Christ Jesus;

24 Mark, Aristarchus, Demas, and Luke my fellow labourers.

25 The grace of our Lord Jesus Christ be with your spirit. Amen.

15. The Apostle's confidence in the goodness of Philemon having been posited [n. 12], he here places his petition. First, he shows the person for whom he makes his petition; second, from this he concludes with his petition, when he says [n. 18], **And do thou receive him.** Regarding the first he does two things: first, by describing the person he shows him as acceptable to himself by a spiritual generation; second, by a change of ways [n. 17].

16. He says therefore: Truly I am to be listened to graciously, for my petition contains honesty and piety for my son Onesimus, whom my present solicitude regards. And the one who acquires a son in time of loss loves him the more, as does an old man the sons begotten in his old age. Gen. 37:3: *Now Israel loved Joseph above all his sons, because he had him in his old age.* And he begot this one while in chains.

17. Second is the change of ways. For if he had persevered in sin, he would not have been worthy of pardon.

And note that he says less and signifies more. For Cicero teaches that a man ought to humble his own deed as much as possible. Thus the Apostle speaks lightly about the sin of this one, saying he was **unprofitable,** that is, injurious in taking away your possessions, **but now,** turned from evil to the state of virtue, **is profitable** for the service of God and men. II Tim. 2:21: *If any man therefore shall cleanse himself from these, he shall be a vessel unto honour.* Prov. 25:4: *Take away the rust from silver, and there shall come forth a most pure vessel.*

18. Then when he says, **And do thou receive him,** he gives his petition. And first he posits the petition; second, he responds to a question, when he says [n. 20], **Whom I would have retained.**

19. He says then, **And do thou receive him as my own bowels.** And this because I have seen him converted, as a sign of which **I have sent** him **back to thee.**

But against this it says in Deut. 23:15, *Thou shalt not deliver to his master the servant that is fled to thee,* etc. I respond that this is true when his master seeks his death; and so he says, **And do thou receive him,** etc. Phil. 1:7: *For that I have you in my heart; and that in my bands, and in the defence and confirmation of the gospel,* etc.

20. And he responds to a question, since someone could ask: If he is profitable to you, why do you not keep him unto death? And so he says what the reason is for sending him back. First, he shows the reason for keeping him; second, why he held back from doing so, when he says [n. 22], **But without thy counsel.**

21. He speaks then to Philemon, who although he was great, was yet accustomed to minister to the Apostle. Mt. 20:26: *Whosoever will be the greater among you, let him be your minister.* Wherefore, in such confidence he proposed to keep Onesimus, to minister to himself in place of Philemon. Whence he says, **Whom I would have retained with me, that in thy stead,** etc. This was most necessary when he was in chains for the sake of Christ. For someone is to be provided for when he suffers for his lord.

22. The reason why he held back is that he did not want to use another's property while the owner was ignorant of it. Hence he says, **But without thy counsel,** etc., as if to say: If I had kept him, you would be pleased as one unable to resist, and this would have been a certain coercion. But I did not want this; rather, I

wanted it to happen willingly. Ex. 25:2: *Of every man that offereth of his own accord, you shall take them,* namely, the firstfruits. II Cor. 9:7: *Not with sadness, or of necessity: "for God loveth a cheerful giver."*

23. Then when he says, **For perhaps he therefore departed,** he gives a reason why he ought to receive him kindly: first, on the part of God; second, on the part of the Apostle himself, when he says [n. 25], **If therefore thou count me a partner;** third, on the part of Philemon, when he says [n. 29], **Trusting in thy obedience.**

24. On the part of God, for often the providence of God permits that which seems evil to happen so that some good may follow from it, as is clear from Joseph who was sold so that he could free Egypt and his family. Gen. 45:5: *God sent me before you into Egypt for your preservation.* And he says **perhaps,** since, as it says in Rom. 11:33, *Incomprehensible are His judgments.* And he says, **instead of a servant,** that is, in the place of a servant. Mt. 23:8: *All you are brethren.* And not only to you but also **to me,** in comparison to God, although he be a son in the ministry.

But how much more to thee both in the flesh and in the Lord? This can be explained in two ways. In one way, it may refer to the first origin of divine creation, and thus he is a brother. Deut. 32:6: *Is He not thy father, that hath possessed thee, and made thee, and created thee?* Mal. 2:10: *Have we not all one father? hath not one God created us?* Likewise, in God through faith. Or, it was more for the good of Philemon, since he was his relative according to the flesh, for according to that, he was his servant. Now, everything that belonged to him according to the flesh was his own. Hence, for a twofold reason is a man moved by charity, namely, from love according to the origin of the flesh and from spiritual love.

25. On the part of the Apostle, first he mentions his own friendship, under which pretext he wants him to be received; second, he is the bail for him regarding the loss, when he says [n. 27], **And if he hath wronged thee;** third, he shows the duty of receiving him, when he says [n. 28], **Yea, brother.**

26. He says then, **If therefore thou count me a partner, receive him.** I Jn. 1:7: *But if we walk in the light, as He also is in the light, we have fellowship one with another.* And he says, **as myself,** for he is attached to me. Mt. 10:40: *He that receiveth you, receiveth Me.*

27. Second, he obliges himself to make satisfaction for the loss. He says therefore, **If he hath wronged thee,** by laying down your service, **put that to my account,** as if to say: I shall make satisfaction. Gal. 6:2: *Bear ye one another's burdens.*

And more: since he first promised that he would pay, he next shows himself to be a debtor for this, not of necessity but willingly. He says therefore, **I Paul,** as if to say: So that you may be certain about restitution, I **have written it with my**

own hand. And this is not necessity, since **thou owest me thy own self,** whom I have freed from eternal death. Tob. 9:2: *If I should give myself to be thy servant I should not make a worthy return for thy care.*

28. He continues, saying, **Yea, brother. May I enjoy thee,** as if to say: If you want me to have a companion, receive him, and so I shall enjoy you, brother; that is, if you will have done this, you shall fill my will with joy. For to enjoy[2] is to use the fruit,[3] and just as use is to the useful, so enjoyment is to fruit. Now a fruit imports sweetness. Cant. 2:3: *His fruit was sweet to my palate.* It likewise imports an end, since the last thing of the tree is its fruit. And therefore it is properly to have something as sweet and final. And hence it is that Augustine says, "We enjoy those things which are known, in which the will delights because of their sweetness." Again, to enjoy is to adhere to something for its own sake. Therefore, sometimes to enjoy and to use are taken indiscriminately, inasmuch they import delight without the contrary. Ecclus. 8:10: *Enjoy[4] great men without blame.*

He says therefore: Thus may I enjoy, since in nothing are you contrary to me. And if you satisfy me in this, there will be nothing in my heart about you that grieves me, and thus you shall delight me.

But if enjoyment is taken as something final, then man is not to be enjoyed, but only God. Against this is what is said in Wis. 2:6, *Let us enjoy the good things that are present, and let us speedily use the creatures as in youth,* etc. Hence he adds, **in the Lord,** that is, may I enjoy you in the delight of God, rejoicing because of the divine good in you, namely, charity, since its act is love, and its effect, enjoyment. Thus he adds, **Refresh my bowels in the Lord.** For a man is spiritually refreshed when he satisfies the desires of his soul. This is as if he said: Fulfill the intimate desires of my heart, not in evil, but **in the Lord,** and so the fulfillment of this desire is good.

29. Then when he says, **Trusting in thy obedience,** the reason is taken from the part of Philemon, and he commends his obedience. First, he shows how he trusts his obedience; second, he enjoins upon him something similar.

He says then, **Trusting in thy obedience,** etc. II Cor. 7:16: *I rejoice that in all things I have confidence in you.* I Kg. 15:22: *For obedience is better than sacrifices.* But he writes more carefully, since a man hears someone more graciously when he hopes he will see him again than if he despairs of it. And so he says, **But withal prepare me also a lodging.** For he was accustomed to stay in his house when in Colossae.

Chrysostom: "It is a pleasing word, that a poor man would command a rich one to prepare hospitality through an epistle from beyond so vast a stretch of land. For what could be prepared for him who was content with bread and vile dust? It must be said, then, that he says this not for the sake of preparing hospitality but to insinuate his familiarity and love. And he provokes him the more to obedience through this." Therefore, the Apostle did not say this for the purpose of exterior preparation, but for his devotion. **For I hope that through your prayers I shall be given unto you.**

But on the contrary, he was never returned to them but died in Rome. Therefore, his hope failed.

I respond that the hope of the just is twofold. Chiefly it is for one's own good, and in this it never fails for oneself. The other is secondary, the approval of others, and in this it sometimes fails since the merits of others are opposed, just as when the just are sometimes not heard in their hopes for others.[5]

But was he deceived in his confidence?

It must be said that to know future things belongs to God alone and not to human knowledge, except prophetic knowledge. And none of the prophets knew everything about his own future except Christ, Who did not have the Holy Spirit to a limited measure. Thus Isaac the great prophet was deceived in Jacob. Hence, it is not a marvel if the Apostle did not know either.

30. Then he ends the epistle in a greeting: first, on the part of others; second, on his own behalf.

He says, then, **There salute thee,** etc. Something is said about all these in Col. 4:12–17.

But there is a question about this, that he says, **Demas.** How can this be, since it is said in II Tim. 4:9, *For Demas hath left me, loving this world?* How, then, does he use his name? It must be said that he already returned to him.

But this does not seem so, for this epistle preceded II Timothy, since it is said here, **I hope,** etc., and there he announces his own death, saying in II Tim. 4:6, *The time of my dissolution is at hand.* And therefore it must be said that Paul was in Rome almost nine years, and this epistle was written in the beginning. II Timothy was written at the end of his life, and Demas, wearied from long imprisonment, forsook him. And the epistles of Paul are not ordered chronologically, since the epistles to the Corinthians were before that to the Romans, and that one was before II Timothy but is placed before them on account of the greater dignity of its matter.

The greeting is the same as II Timothy. Thanks be to God. Amen.

Parallel Places Where St. Thomas Discussed the Same Topic in a Different Context

I Timothy

12–16. *Summa Theol.,* I-II, q. 99, a. 1 ad 2; q. 100, a. 10; II-II, q. 23, a. 4 ad 3; q. 24, a. 2 ad 3; q. 44, a. 1; q. 124, a. 1 ad 4; q. 184, aa. 1 and 3; III *Contra Gentes,* ch. 116 and 117; *De perfectione vitae spritualis,* ch. XII and XIII; *Contra retrahentes homines ab ingressu religionis,* ch. VI; *De Veritate,* q. 17, a. 1, sed c. 5; a. 2, arg. 8; *De Malo,* q. 7, a. 1, c.; *De Caritate,* a. 3, c.; a. 7, ad 17; *De correctione fraterna,* a. 1, arg. 19 and ad 18; *De Spe,* a. 3, sed c. 3; *De virtutibus cardinalibus,* a. 3, arg. 3; *Quodl.,* V, q. 10, a. 1, c.; III *Sent.,* dist. XXVII, q. 2, a. 2, arg. 2; a. 4, qla. 2 ad 2; qla. 3; dist. XXXVI, a. 2; a. 6 ad 1; q. 37, a. 2, qla. 1 ad 2; a. 3.

21. *Summa Theol.,* I-II, q. 100, aa. 2 and 3; q. 101, a. 2; q. 102, a. 2; q. 104, a. 2; q. 100, a. 12.

23. *Summa Theol.,* I-II, q. 95, a. 1; q. 96, a. 5; X *Ethic.,* lect. 14 and 15; II *Cor.,* n. 112.

25. III *Contra Gentes,* ch. 129; *Summa Theol.,* I-II, q. 95, a. 2; II-II, q. 57, a. 2; q. 58, a. 10.

35. *Summa Theol.,* I-II, q. 19, a. 6; q. 76, aa. 3 and 4; II *Sent.,* dist. XXII, q. 2, a. 2; *De Malo,* q. 3, aa. 8 and 13; *Quodl.,* VIII, q. 6, a. 5.

40. *Summa Theol.,* III, q. 1, a. 3; III *Sent.,* dist. I, q. 1, a. 3; IV *Contra Gentes,* ch. 54; *Compendium Theol.,* ch. 185, 200, 201; *De Veritate,* q. 29, a. 4, arg. 3.

46. *De Divinis Nominibus,* ch. V, lect. 1; ch. VI, lect. 1; *Summa Theol.,* I, q. 31, a. 3 ad 2; q. 39, a. 4; *De Malo,* q. 9, a. 2, arg. 6.

56. *Ad Romanos,* n. 955; *Ad Philippenses,* n. 157.

62. *Summa Theol.,* I, q. 19, a. 6 ad 1; q. 23, a. 4; *De Veritate,* q. 6, a. 2, arg. 2; q. 23, aa. 2 and 3; I *Sent.,* dist. XLVII, aa. 1 and 4.

64. *Ad Galatas,* n. 169; *Summa Theol.,* I-II, q. 91, a. 5 ad 2; q. 98, a. 2, arg. 4; *Quodl.,* VI, q. 5, a. 1; *Quodl.,* VIII, q. 9, a. 2, sed c.; *De Veritate,* q. 29, a. 4 ad 9.

68. *Summa Theol.,* I, q. 117, a. 1; II-II, q. 181, a. 2.

75. I *Ad Cor.,* n. 589; *Summa Theol.,* II-II, q. 149, a. 4.

76. *Summa Theol.,* II-II, q. 169, tit.; *Quodl.* X, q. 6, a. 3.

80. I *Ad Cor.,* n. 879.

83. *Summa Theol.,* II-II, q. 163, a. 4; *De Veritate,* q. 18, a. 6; *De Malo,* q. 7, a. 7, arg. 1.

84. *Summa Theol.,* I-II, q. 85, a. 3.

87. *Ad Philipp.,* nn. 6 and 173; *Summa Theol.,* Suppl., q. 37, a. 2.

89–90. *Summa Theol.,* II-II, q. 185, a. 1; *Quodl.* II, q. 6, a. 1; *Quodl.* III, q. 4, a. 1; *Quodl.* V, q. 11, a. 2; *Quodl.* XII, q. 9, a. 3; *De perfectione vitae spirit.,* ch. XIX; *Contra impugnantes Dei cultum,* ch. IV at the end.

94. *Summa Theol.,* Suppl., q. 66, aa. 1 and 4; *Quodl.* VIII, q. 8, a. 2; IV *Sent.,* dist. XLII, q. 3, aa. 2 and 4; *Ad Titum,* ch. I, lect. 2, n. 14.

133. *Summa Theol.,* I, q. 57, a. 5; q. 64, a. 1 ad 4; q. 104, a. 4 ad 2; II *Sent.,* dist. XI, q. 2, a. 4; *Ad Ephesios,* n. 162.

141. III *Contra Gentes,* ch. 127.

147. *Summa Theol.,* I-II, q. 102, a. 6; q. 103, a. 4 ad 3; *De Malo,* q. 15, a. 1, arg. 1.

148. *Summa Theol.,* I-II, q. 102, a. 5, arg. 4.

154. *Summa Theol.,* II-II, q. 101, a. 1.

159. *Summa Theol.,* I-II, q. 99, a. 6; II-II, q. 122, a. 5 ad 4.

160. *Summa Theol.,* II-II, q. 146, a. 1.

161. *Summa Theol.,* II-II, q. 30, a. 4, arg. 2; q. 154, a. 2, arg. 5; Suppl., q. 99, a. 5, arg. 4.

162. *Summa Theol.,* II-II, q. 157, a. 4, arg. 3.

163. *Summa Theol.,* I-II, q. 114, aa. 4 and 6.

178. *Summa Theol.,* II-II, q. 33, a. 4; IV *Sent.,* dist. XIX, q. 2, a. 2, qla. 3; *De Veritate,* q. 3, a. 1 ad 18.

192. *Ad Galatas,* n. 220; *Ad Hebraeos,* n. 526.

195. *Summa Theol.,* Suppl., q. 63, a. 1.

212. *Summa Theol.,* II-II, q. 103, tit.; *Quodl.* II, q. 6, a. 1.

215–217. *Summa Theol.,* II-II, q. 100, aa. 2 and 3; *Quodl.* II, q. 6, a. 2; *Quodl.* XII, q. 18, a. 3.

219. *Summa Theol.,* II-II, q. 67, a. 2, arg. 2; a. 3.

222. *Summa Theol.,* II-II, q. 33, a. 7; IV *Sent.,* dist. XIX, q. 2, a. 3, qla. 1 and 2; *De correctione fraterna,* a. 2, arg. 1; *Quodl.* I, q. 8, a. 2; *Quodl.* XI, q. 10, a. 1.

233. *Summa Theol.,* II-II, q. 10, a. 10; q. 104, aa. 5 and 6; II *Sent.,* dist. XLIV, q. 2, a. 2; *Quodl.* II, q. 5, a. 1.

246. *Quodl.* X, q. 6, a. 3; *Contra impugnantes Dei cultum,* ch. V and VII.

251. II *Ad Cor.,* n. 47; *Summa Theol.,* I-II, q. 72, a. 3; q. 77, a. 5, arg. 1; q. 84, a. 1; II-II, q. 24, a. 10 ad 2; q. 119, a. 2 ad 1; q. 155, a. 2 ad 3; *De Malo,* q. 3, a. 3, arg. 4; q. 8, a. 1; q. 13, a. 1, arg. 5.

266. *Summa Theol.,* I, q. 26, a. 1; in *Boët. De Trinitate,* q. 3, a. 4, arg. 5.

268–270. *Ad Ephes.,* n. 176; *Ad Philip.,* n. 127; *Summa Theol.,* I, q. 12, aa. 1, 3, 4, and 7; q. 56, a. 3 ad 1 and 2; q. 57, a. 5 ad 2; q. 62, a. 9; q. 86, a. 2 ad 1; I-II, q. 4, a. 3; I *Sent.,* dist. III, q. 1, a. 1; dist. XXII, a. 1; III *Sent.,* dist. XIV, a. 2, qla. 2; dist. XXVII, q. 3, a. 2; III *Contra Gentes,* ch. 55 and 56; *De Veritate,* q. 2, a. 2 ad 5 and 6; q. 8, aa. 1–5; q. 10, a. 11; q. 18, a. 1; q. 20, a. 4; *De Potentia,* q. 7, aa. 1 and 2; *Quodl.* I, q. 1, a. 1; *De Divinis Nominibus,* ch. 1, lect. 1; ch. VIII, lect. 3.

II Timothy

25. *De Veritate,* q. 11, a. 1, sed c. 1.

27. *Ad Romanos,* n. 368; *Summa Theol.,* II-II, q. 1, a. 5; q. 18, a. 4.

37. *Quodl.,* I, q. 7, a. 2; *Contra impugnantes Dei cultum,* ch. IV.

41–43. *Summa Theol.,* II-II, q. 40, a. 3; q. 77, a. 4 ad 3; q. 187, a. 2; *Contra impugnantes Dei cultum,* ch. IX; *Quodl.,* VII, q. 7, a. 2, sed c. 3.

57. *Summa theol.,* I, q. 21, a. 3 ad 2; q. 25, a. 3 ad 3; q. 100, a. 8 ad 2; III, q. 46, a. 2 ad 3; *De Veritate,* q. 3, a. 15, arg. 12; *De Divinis nominibus,* ch. VIII, lect. 3.

60. *Summa Theol.,* II-II, q. 38, aa. 1 and 2.

61. *Summa Theol.,* II-II, q. 10, a. 7.

67. *Compendium Theol.,* ch. 162; IV *Contra Gentes,* ch. 79.

72. *Summa Theol.,* I, q. 23, a. 5 ad 3; *De Veritate,* q. 6, a. 2 ad 9.

74. *Summa Theol.,* II-II, q. 183, a. 2.

91. *De Potentia,* q. 5, a. 6, arg. 5.

92. *Quaest. disput. de Caritate,* a. 7, arg. 13; *Summa Theol.,* II-II, q. 25, a. 4; *Contra impugnantes Dei cultum,* ch. XX.

106–107. *Contra impugnantes Dei cultum,* ch. XI, XXIII, and XXV.

124–128. *Principium de commendatione et partitione Sacrae Scripturae; Breve principium de commendatione S. Scripturae.*

151. *Summa Theol.,* I-II, q. 114, a. 3; *Suppl.,* q. 96, aa. 1 and 11.

Titus

12. *Ad Philippenses,* n. 6; *De perfectione vitae christianae,* ch. XXI.

14. I *Ad Timot.,* n. 94.

24. *Quodl.,* IV, q. 9, a. 3, sed c.; *in Boët. De Trinitate,* q. 2, a. 1, sed c.; *Summa Theol.,* II-II, q. 10, a. 7 ad 3.

30. I *Ad Cor.,* n. 592.

32. *In Boët. De Trinitate,* q. 2, a. 3, sed c..

40. *Summa Theol.,* I-II, q. 102, a. 6 ad 1.
41. *Summa Theol.,* I-II, q. 103, aa. 3 and 4.
43–44. *Summa Theol.,* II-II, q. 10, a. 4; q. 23, a. 7 ad 1; II *Sent.,* dist. XLI, q. 1, a. 2; IV *Sent.,* dist. XXXIX, a. 2 ad 5; *De Malo,* q. 2, a. 5 ad 7; *Ad Romanos,* ch. XIV, lect. 3.
44. *De Veritate,* q. 17, a. 1, arg. 2; *Summa Theol.,* I, q. 73, a. 13, arg. 2.
50. *Summa Theol.,* II-II, q. 142, a. 2; q. 149, a. 4.
53. I *Ad Cor.,* n. 879; *Summa Theol.,* II-II, q. 177, a. 2.
58. *De Malo,* q. 14, a. 4 ad 2.
64. *Summa Theol.,* II-II, q. 10, a. 10; q. 12, a. 2; q. 104, aa. 1 and 6; Suppl., q, 52 *passim;* II *Sent.,* q. 2, a. 2; *Ad Romanos,* ch. XIII, lect. 1.
88. *Summa Theol.,* III, q. 1, a. 2; q. 69, aa. 1 and 4; q. 79, a. 5 ad 1; I *Sent.,* dist. I, q. 1, a. 2; IV *Sent.,* dist. IV, q. 2.
93. *Summa Theol.,* III, q. 62, a. 4; q. 64, aa. 2 and 5; IV *Sent.,* dist. I, q. 1, a. 4, qla. 3.
94. *Summa Theol.,* I-II, q. 113, a. 2; IV *Sent.,* dist. XVII, q. 1, a. 3, qla. 1; *De Veritate,* q. 28, a. 2.
102. *Summa Theol.,* II-II, q. 11, aa. 1, 2, and 3; IV *Sent.,* dist. XIII, q. 2, a. 1; *Quodl.* X, q. 7, a. 1; *Quaest. disput. de correctione fraterna,* a. 2, arg. 23.

Philemon

28. *Summa Theol.,* I-II, q. 11, a. 3, arg. 1; I *Sent.,* dist. I, q. 1, aa. 2 and 3, arg. 4.

Endnotes

Introduction

1   Torrell, Jean-Pierre, O.P. *Saint Thomas Aquinas*. Vol. 1: The Person and His Work. Trans. Robert Royal. The Catholic University of America Press: Washington, 1996, p. 255.

2   *Ibid*, p. 29.

The Commentary of St. Thomas Aquinas on
The First Epistle of St. Paul to Timothy

Prologue

1   Douay lacks this second clause.

Chapter One

1   Douay – *quarrels*

2   Douay adds here *for menstealers.*

3   Douay reads *because I did it ignorantly in unbelief.*

4   This error found a proponent in Michael Molinos, the Quietist, who said that grave sins need not be confessed by the perfect since they happen in them by the violence of demons. This was duly condemned by Innocent XI, DS 2242–2253.

5   Douay – *reproaches*

6   Douay – *chief*

7   Douay – *kindness*

Chapter Two

1   *Oratio*

2   *Oris ratio.*

3   *De Veritate,* q. 23, a. 3: "In God the notion of the will is found properly…and thus the will is properly said about God. And this is the will of gracious purpose, which is distinguished through antecedent and consequent, as has been said.

     "But since the will in us has a certain consequent passion of the mind, thus, just as other names of passions are metaphorically said about God, so also the name of will. And the name of anger is said about God because in Him is found the effect which is usual for the angry man among us, namely, punishment. Hence punishment, by which God punishes, is called the anger of God. In a similar manner of speaking, those things which are usually signs of a will among us are called the will of God; and for this reason it is called the will of a sign, since the sign which usually belongs to the will is called the will.

     "But since the will can be designated both according as it proposes things to be done and according as it takes measures for the work, in both ways some signs are attributed to the will.

"According as it proposes things to be done regarding the avoidance of evil, the sign of it is a prohibition. Regarding the achievement of a good, there is a two-fold sign of the will. With respect to a necessary good, without which the will cannot attain its end, the sign of the will is a precept; with respect to a useful good, by which in an easier and more convenient manner the end is acquired, the sign of the will is a counsel.

"But according as the will makes an attempt in the work, a two-fold sign is attributed to it. One is express, which is operation, for what one does indicates expressly that he wills it. The other is an interpretative sign, namely, permission; for he who does not prohibit what he can prevent seems by interpretation to consent to it. And the name of permission signifies this."

4   Douay – *A testimony in due times.*
5   Douay lacks this phrase. It is interpolated from I Cor. 14:34.

Chapter Three

1   This clause is lacking in the Douay.
2   Douay – *and shall be well treated*
3   Latin – *sacramentum*
4   *Sacramentum...sacrum secretum.*

Chapter Four

1   Douay – *he*
2   Douay lacks this phrase.
3   Douay – *the hands of the priesthood.*

Chapter Five

1   Douay – *any man...his...her...he*
2   *Dividua* means separated; *vidua* means widow, which St. Thomas says is from *a viro idua, idua* being the common Etruscan root.
3   Douay – *Admonishing her...to take care of the family.*
4   Douay omits *for praying.*
5   Douay – *deliciousness*
6   Douay – *delicacies*
7   Douay – *virgin*
8   Douay lacks this last clause.

Chapter Six

1   Douay – *quarrels*
2   Douay – *the desire of money*
3   Most manuscripts read thus, but some read as follows: "Next he breaks out in praise of God, saying **to Whom be honour.** And he posits two things. The first pertains to the showing of reverence, saying **honour,** which is a showing of reverence. Mal. 1:6: *If then I be a father, where is My honour,* etc. The second pertains to the refulgence

of His goodness, when he says, **glory,** which is clear knowledge with praise, gleaming in the knowledge of men and angels. The third pertains to governance, when he says, **empire everlasting.**" Of course, **glory** is lacking in the Pauline text.

The Commentary of St. Thomas Aquinas on
The Second Epistle of St. Paul to Timothy

Prologue

1   Douay – *and sleep departed from my eyes.*

Chapter One

1   Douay – *to God*
2   Douay – *but of power*
3   Douay – *but labour with the gospel*
4   Douay – *the times of the world.*
5   Douay – *Reverence not thy neighbour*
6   Douay – *He is able to keep that which I have committed unto Him, against that day.*
7   Douay – *Hold the form*
8   In Latin mercy is *misericordia* and misery is *miseria.*

Chapter Two

1   Douay – *riches*
2   Latin – *procul a fano*
3   Douay – *Phigellus*
4   Douay lacks this word.
5   Douay lacks this word.
6   Douay – *And avoid foolish and unlearned questions*
7   Douay – *apt to teach*
8   Douay – *shall be well treated...*
9   Perhaps this is a reference to Is. 26:17–18: *From Thy face, O Lord, we have conceived.* Douay – *In thy presence, O Lord. We have conceived.*

Chapter Three

1   Douay – *unmerciful*
2   Douay – *stubborn*
3   A reference to St. Augustine's *On the City of God,* Bk. 14, ch. 28.

Chapter Four

1   Douay – *labour in all things*
2   Douay – *shall be well treated*
3   Douay – *ready to be sacrificed*
4   Douay – *fiurstfruits*

5   This refers to the metaphor found in Sts. Jerome and John Chrysostom, that a serpent uses all its cunning to protect its head. Cf. *Catena Aurea*, Mt. 10:16–18.

6   Douay – *done*

The Commentary of St. Thomas Aquinas on
The Epistle of St. Paul to Titus

Prologue

1   In Latin a thief is *fur*, and an oven is *furnus*.

Chapter One

1   Douay – *times*

2   Douay – *Behold the fear of the Lord*

3   Douay – *ordain priests*

4   Douay – *riot*

5   Douay – *babbler*

6   Douay – *preventeth*

7   Epimenides was an ancient Cretan religious teacher and prophet whose life was placed variously at 500 or 600 B.C., depending on the source.

Chapter Two

1   Douay – *he*

2   The two words for *to love* are *amare* and *diligere*, respectively. They are both translated *to love* in English, but do have a small difference in meaning. *Amare* is the most general word for love, yet sometimes also refers to its more natural characteristics, as opposed to *diligere*, which is a love based upon choice and implicitly consequent to an act of the intelligence.

3   Douay – *dull*

4   Douay – *strong*

5   Douay – *Behold the fear of the Lord*

6   Latin – *saeculum*, whence we get the English word *secular.*

7   Latin – *sobrie*

8   Douay – *temperance*

9   Douay – *To speak evil of*

10   Douay – *gentle*

11   Douay – *kindness*

12   Douay – *humility*

13   Douay – *naughtiness*

14   Latin – *bona igneitas*

15   Latin – *humanitatem*

16   Douay – *our*

The Commentary of St. Thomas Aquinas on
The Epistle of St. Paul to Philemon

Prologue

1   Douay – *whereas*
2   Latin – *frui*
3   Latin – *uti fructu*
4   Douay – *Serve*

Index of Authors

Index of Subjects